Tribal History of North-East India

Essays in Honour of Professor Lal Dena

About the Editor

A Doctorate in History from Jawaharlal Nehru University, New Delhi, H. Sudhir, currently with the Department of History, Manipur University, has to his credit five major publications: *Violence against Women in Northeast India (2005); Dimensions of Social Issues in India's Northeast (2007); Urbanization in Northeast India (2009); Social History of Manipur (2012); Dimensions of Conflict in Northeast India (2013)*. Author of several articles on Gender, Conflict and Social History, H. Sudhir has interest in Contemporary History of North-East India.

Tribal History of North-East India
Essays in Honour of Professor Lal Dena

Edited by
H. Sudhir

CONCEPT PUBLISHING COMPANY PVT. LTD.
NEW DELHI-110059

ISBN-13 : 978-93-5125-099-9

First Published 2014

Published and Printed by

Concept Since 1974

Concept Publishing Company Pvt. Ltd.
A/15-16, Commercial Block, Mohan Garden
New Delhi-110059 (India)
T: 25351460, 25351794, *F*: 091-11-25357109
E: publishing@conceptpub.com, W: www.conceptpub.com
Editorial Office: H-13, Bali Nagar, New Delhi-110 015, India.

Cataloging in Publication Data--*Courtesy:* D.K. Agencies (P) Ltd. <docinfo@dkagencies.com>

Tribal history of North-East India : essays in honour of Professor Lal Dena / edited by H. Sudhir.

p. cm.
Includes bibliographical references and index.
ISBN 9789351250999

1. Manipur (India)--Scheduled tribes--History. 2. India, Northeastern.--Scheduled tribes--History. 3. Kuki (Indic people)--India, Northeastern--History. 4. Kuki (Indic people)--India, Northeastern--Social life and customs. 5. India, Northeastern--Social life and customs. 6. Manipur (India)--Social life and customs. 7. Rural women--India, Northeastern--Social conditions. I. Dena, Lal, 1943- II. Sudhir, H.

DDC 305.80095417 23

PROFESSOR LAL DENA : ACADEMIC PROFILE

Name	:	Prof. Lal Dena
Post Held	:	Professor
Address	:	Department of History Manipur University, Imphal Manipur 795003 (India)
Date of Birth	:	1st December, 1943
Name of Tribe and Nationality	:	Hmar (Indian)
Educational Qualifications	:	B.A. (Distinction), Guwahati University, 1966 M.A., Guwahati University, 1970 MPhil, JNU, New Delhi, 1974 PhD, JNU, New Delhi, 1984
Teaching Experiences	:	Assistant Teacher, Pherzawl High School, 1959-60 Head Master, Indo-Burma Pioneer Middle English School, Sielmat, 1960-63 Assistant Teacher, Adimjati High School, Imphal, 1963-70 Department of History, Manipur University, Imphal, since 1973 to date

Publications Authored/Edited/Co-Joined (Books)

1. *Christian Missions and Colonialism: A Study of Missionary Movements in Manipur and Lushai Hills,* 1891-1947, Vendrame Institute, Shillong, 1988.

2. *History of Modern Manipur*, 1826-1949 (ed.), Orbit Publishers, Delhi, 1991.
3. *Hmar Folk Tales*, Scholar Publishing House, New Delhi, 1995.
4. *Zawlkhawpui Chanchin, Churachandpur*, 2004.
5. *In Search of Identity: Hmars of the North-East India*, Akansha Publishing House, New Delhi, 2008.
6. *British Policy towards Manipur* (1762-1947), Nongeen Publications, Imphal, 2008.
7. *Dialogue on Tipaimukh Dam* (ed.), Akansha Publishing House, New Delhi, 2011.
8. *Bawmzo: A Study of the Kuki Tribe of Chittagong Hill Tract* (ed.), Akansha Publishing House, New Delhi, 2013.

Articles Authored/Edited

(The list below does not include articles written in English, Hmar and Mizo published in regional and local journals/magazines/daily papers and radio talks both in English and Hmar).

Articles Published in Foreign Journals/Magazines/Books:

1. Manipur Identity Crisis, *India Abroad*, New York, 4th July, 1980.
2. The Welsh Connection, *Evangelical Magazine of Wales*, Bryntirion Wales, October-November, Vol. 24, No. 5, 1985.
3. Lessons from History In my view: A Comparison of Indian National Movement and Korean National Movement, *Korean Herald* (An English Daily National Paper), Seoul, South Korea, 1997.
4. Dr. Peter Fraser, 1864-1919: The Liberator, *Historical Society of the Presbyterian Church of Wales Journal*, 1999, Wales, U.K.
5. The Unresolved Issues of the Hmars (in Mizoram), *Indigenous World, 1999-2001, International Work Group for Indigenous Affairs*, Copenhagen, 2000.

Other Published Articles in some Journals/Books (This list does not include articles written in English for daily papers, radio talks in English and articles in Mizo and Hmar):

1. Manipur under the Paramountcy of the British Crown: Some Anomalies of Colonial Rule, 1891-1919, *Bengal Past and Present, Vol. XVIII,* No. 189, January-June 1979.
2. Manipur Identity Crisis, *Northern India Patrika,* Allahabad, 21 June, 1980; *Deccan Chronicle,* Secundarabad, 26 June, 1980; *The Mail,* Madras, 23 June, 1980.
3. The Cross and the Flag: A Study of Christian Missions and Colonialism with Special reference to Africa and Asia, *Manipur University Research Journal of Humanities and Social Sciences, Vol. II,* No. 1, 1985.
4. Violence and the Churchmen, *Kristiya Drishthanta (A Christian Viewpoint),* Tracy Publication, New Delhi, 1987.
5. The Hmars through the Ages, *Manipur, Past and Present, Vol. III,* Mittal Publication, Delhi, 1995.
6. The First Mission that sponsored William Pettigrew; *Rev. William Pettigrew; A Pioneer Missionary of Manipur,* Imphal, 1996.
7. William Pettigrew, Watkin Robert and Some of their Private Correspondences, *Rev. William Pettigrew; A Pioneer Missionary of Manipur,* Imphal, 1996.
8. Manipur: A Synoptic View of Her History, *Souvenir International Conference of Forensic Medicine and XIX Annual Conference of India Academy of Forensics Medicine,* 25-27 March, 1998.
9. Korea's March First Movement in 1919, *Manipur University Research Journal of Humanities and Social Sciences, Vol.* 5, No. 1, 2000.
10. The Constitution 73rd Amendment Act, 1992 *vis-*

a- vis the Hill Areas of Manipur, in M. Horam (ed.), *The Rising Manipur*, Manas Publication, New Delhi, 2000.

11. Nationality Problem in North-East India, *North East Voice*, Vol. I No. 3, August 1994.
12. Status of Panchayati Raj in Manipur: Post 73rd Amendment Development, Status *of Panchayati Raj in the States and Union Territories of India,* Institute of Social Sciences, New Delhi, 2000.
13. Tribalism in Manipur, in Gailangam and Gina Shangkham (eds), *Change and Continuity in the Tribal Society of Manipur*, Imphal, 1999.
14. Kuki Naga Conflict: Juxtaposed in the Colonial context, in K. Agarwal (ed.) *Dynamics of Identity and Intergroup Relations in North-East India*, Indian Institute of Advanced Study, Shimla, 1999.
15. Church and Social Justice, *Ruonglevaisuo, Vairengte,* Mizoram, 2007.
16. Anglo Manipur Relation, 1833-1891, *Manipur Today*, Vol.XXXI, No. 2, 2010.
17. How Christianity Came to Manipur, *Thukna Ropui* (Amazing Deep), New Delhi, 2010.
18. The Spread of the Gospel in South-West Manipur and Beyond, 1910-1930, *Guwahati Gospel Centenary Celebration, Guwahati,* 2011.
19. The Role of Churches in Containing Ethnic Conflict in Manipur, in C.J. Thomas & Others (eds), *Constraints in Development in Manipur,* Regency Publication, New Dehli 2001.
20. Emergence of the Tribal Middle Classes in Manipur: The Colonial and Post-Colonial Period in Gangmumei Kamei (ed.),*The Rise of Middle Classes in Manipur,* Akansha Publishing House, New Delhi, 2012.
21. Status of Mizo Women in Mizo Society, in Madhu Rajput (ed.), *Social Stratification in North East India,* Manak Publication, New Delhi, 2012.

Seminar/Conferences/Symposia Attended

(This does not include some regional and local seminars/symposia attended)

1. Indian National Army Movement in Manipur: Myth or Reality?, *Proceedings of Indian History Congress*, 35th Session, Jadavpur University, Calcutta, 1974.
2. Patterns of Leadership in a Changing Hmar Society, *National Seminar on Cultural and Biological Adaptability of Man with Special Reference to North-East India*, Dibrugarh University, Assam, 1977.
3. Colonialism and the Study of Christian Missionary in North-East India, 3rd *Session of North-East India History Association*, Imphal, 1982.
4. Archival Sources on the History of Manipur and Adjoining Areas in National, Seminar on Sources of the History of Manipur and Adjoining Areas, Imphal, 1985
5. Church as an agent of Social Change, *Seminar on Christian Involvement in the Contemporary Society*, Churachandpur, June 1990.
6. Social and Political Institutions of the Hmars, *National Seminar on Social and Political Institutions of the Hill Peoples of North-East India*, Shillong, 1990.
7. Hmar People's Movement for Self Government, *Regional Seminar on Indigenous and Tribal Peoples' Struggle for the Right of Self Determination*, Dimapur, Nagaland, 1994.
8. Toward the Devolution of Powers and Functions to be Panchayati Raj Institutions in Manipur, National *Workshop on Panchayati Raj in North East-India*, Guwahati, 1996.
9. Growth of Panchayati Raj Institutions in the Valley of Manipur: A Reassessment, Regional Tripartite

Interface Workshop on Panchayati Raj for Eastern Regions, Calcutta, 1999.

10. Evolution of Self Government in the Hill Areas of Manipur and Mizoram: A Comparative Study, *National Seminar on Self Governance Systems in Tribal Areas of North-East India and Futuristic Perspective,* India International Centre, New Delhi, 2000.
11. Manipur Lushai Hills Relations during the Nineteenth Century, *21st Annual Session, North-East India History Association,* Manipur University, Imphal, 2000.
12. Indigenous Peoples and Constructive Agreements with the State: The Case of North-East India, *International Workshop on Indigenous Peoples,* Sabah, Malaysia, December, 2001.
13. Mizo Women in a Changing Mizo Society, *National Seminar on Women Movement in the Twentieth Century,* sponsored by the Maulana Abul Kalam Azad Institute of Asian Studies, Calcutta, March 2001.
14. Nationality Formation: The Case of Kukis, *National Seminar on Kuki Society, Past, Present and Future,* Churachandpur, Manipur 2001.
15. Roots of Alienation of North-East India: Presidential Address, *23rd Session of North East India History Association,* Agartala, Tripura, 26-28 September, 2002.
16. On the Aspects of the Medieval and Modern History of North-East India: Keynote Address, *Regional Seminar on Medieval and Modern History of North-East India* , Imphal, 23-24 October, 2003.
17. Historical Perspective of the Process of Marginalization: A Study of the Hill Peoples' Experience in Manipur, National Seminar on *Marginalized Indigenous Hill Peoples in Manipur: Problems and Options* , India International Centre, New Delhi, 2006.

18. Waiting for Justice: Discrimination against Tribal Peoples in Matters of Land Management and Self Government in the Hill Areas of Manipur, *Workshop on Atrocities of SC/SSTs,* Churachandpur, 2010.
19. Aspects of the History and Culture of North-East India: Key Note Paper, Seminar at the Assam University Diphu Campus, 2011.

Other Informations

1. Coordinator, Centre for ST/SC and Minority Coaching Class, UGC NET/JRF Examinations, Manipur University, Imphal, 1990-2006.
2. Coordinator, Centre of Manipur Studies (Tribal Section), Manipur University, Imphal, 2001-2003.
3. President, North-east India History Association, Shillong, 2002 2003.
4. Foreign Visits: U.K. (1982 and 1998); Seoul, South Korea (1997); France (1998); and Malaysia (2001).

Visiting Fellowship/Professor

- Visiting Fellow, Korea Foundation, Seoul, South Korea, 1997.
- Visiting Professor, Department of History, Dibrugarh University, Assam, 2002.
- Member of Peer Team, National Accreditation and Assessment Council (UGC), Bangalore, 2001.

Research Experiences : Produced seven M. Phil. Scholars & 15 PhD Scholars

Research Projects

1. Mizo National Movement, sponsored by the

Theological Research and Communication Institute, New Delhi, 1993.

2. Evaluation of the Sectors of Development under the Special Central Assistance, Tribal Sub-Plan with Special Reference to Tipaimukh Sub-Division, sponsored by the Ministry of Tribal Affairs, Government of India, New Delhi, 2002 2003.
3. *Selected Mizo Folk Tales:* Re-reading in the Context of Modernization and Globalization sponsored by Indian Council of Social Sciences Research, New Delhi, 2011 to 2013.

Membership

1. Life Member and President of the Manipur Historical Society, Imphal, Manipur.
2. Life Member of the North-East India Historical Association, Shillong, Meghalaya.
3. Former Member of the Programme Advisory Committee, All India Radio, Imphal, Government of India.
4. Member of the Governing Body, North-East Zone Cultural Centre, Dimapur, Nagaland.
5. Member of the North-East India Council for Social Science Research, Shillong Megalaya.
6. Former Member of the Academic Council, Manipur University, Imphal, Manipur.
7. Former Member of the Committee for Advanced Studies and Research, Manipur University, Imphal.
8. Former Member of the Board of Studies for the School of Social Studies, Manipur University, Imphal.
9. Former Member of the Advisory Board on Adult Continuing Education and Extension, Manipur University, Imphal.
10. Former Member of College Development Council, Manipur University, Imphal.

11. Former Member of the Syndicate, Manipur University, Imphal.
12. Former Member of the Advisory Committee for Gandhian Studies Centre, Manipur University, Imphal. 2000.
13. Former Member of the Advisory Committee on Social Policy, Government of Manipur, Imphal, 1995 to 97.
14. Member of the Advisory Committee on Cultural Policy, Government of Manipur, Imphal.
15. Member of the Governing Body of North-East India, Cultural Centre, Dimapur.
16. Member of Advisory Body for Qualitative Improvement in the Curriculum and Syllabi for Class I to VIII, (SCERT) Government of Manipur, Imphal.
17. Former President, North-East India History Association (NEIHA), Tripura Session, 2002-2003.
18. Member of Linguistic Experts (English, Manipuri, Hindi, Hmar and other Kuki Chin Languages) for Aerodrome Committee, 2006.
19. Member of Board of Studies, School of Social Sciences, NEHU, Shillong.
20. Peer Member of National Accreditation and Assessment Council, Bangalore (Affiliated to UGC: Delhi).

Award: Writer's Award given by Mizo Writer Association, Mizoram. 2007.

INTRODUCTION

Recognizing the lasting share that Professor Lal Dena has made in the arena of historical researches and tribal studies in the North-East region and also honouring him, we, his younger colleagues have sincerely landed together to this rendezvous of producing this present volume titled *Tribal History of North-East India: Essays in Honour of Professor Lal Dena.* A product of a collaboratively joint initiative, this work, in harmony of the contributions that Professor Dena (as we affectionately call him) has made in the frontiers of the Chin-Kuki-Mizo studies of North-East India and neighbourhoods, has at best resonated to the same tune but with a central motive of essentially unearthing those aspects which are inseparably glued together in the readings of the Chin Kuki Mizo groups.

II

Let us now listen to what all the authors of the chapters have said in their chapters in this anthology. The people collectively identified as Kuki in the present day India and Bangladesh; *Chin* in Myanmar (previously Burma) themselves dissected into Chin, Kuki, Mizo, and Zomi (including some of them who embraced the 'Naga') though their genealogical histories and cultures suggested that they stemmed from the same family. This is argued by Joseph Suantak. Based on the recent genetic investigations related to worldwide human migration, the author says that they seem to be one among the pre-Dravidians in India or say the Paleo Mongoloids. It is believed that the names of rivers in India and China which end with *'ti'* and *'di'* must have been adopted from the CKZ's *tui* or *twi* for river or water. Citing Nick Thom, the CKZ language evolved in about 10,000 BC and is next to the Bodo-Garo which is marked to have already developed in about 12000 BCE as the mother language of all ST 13 languages and dialects. Quite strange, tradition further maintained that they were trapped in a cave as it was sealed by a boulder or large flat stone during a 'total darkness' throughout this planet Earth. They retold this critical phenomenon as *Thimzing, Thimzin,* or *Mujinlhun.* Thus it takes one to suggest if this 'total darkness' or *Thimzin* be the ashes, gases and clouds of the ancient volcano called 'Toba Volcano' or 'YTT 74,000 kya'. In the name of development a number of legal provisions are sanctioned without the collective knowledge and consent of the natives. And surprisingly, the term 'Scheduled Tribe' or 'Tribal' must have been imposed upon this people to evade the word 'invaded' which is incorporated in the basic elements of the 'indigenous peoples' but excluded in the 'tribal' under the principles of the ILO [International Labour Organization]. Another plight: any altruistic social and political leader and think tank will not fail to pronounce repetitively the phrase *Gam leh Nam* [Land and Ethnic], a slogan of nationalism. But, when it comes to *Gam,* it is entirely overshadowed by a psychopathical 'Nam' ism which instantaneously brings about sectarianism and communal tension among them.

D.L. Haokip attempts to locate *Sinlung* or *Khul* in the light of the available sources. He exposes that the Chin Kuki Mizo is one community under different nomenclatures. This is because that the tales and oral traditions collected from the various regions are one but retold in slightly different manners. The tales no doubt expose historical antiquities yet significance. The name *Sinlung* is a compound word which signifies the phrase 'to close with stone'. The word *Khul* indicates bowel. The word *Khulsin* stands for burying of the corpse. It denotes the closure of the graveyard with stone. No doubt, their tales fall within the parameters of the Hollow Earth Theorists' hypothesis. The forest fire, darkness and flood, communication of men and animals mentioned in the tales hint natural calamities that toll the life of many at different points of times and places and also peaceful co-existence. The recently discovered name of a cave, *Senlung (Sinlung)* located on the trans border of Manipur and the Chin Hills again reposes the importance of *bowel or cave* theory attached to their belief system. Geographical location, vocabulary or etymology of the ethnic groups, and ecological setting are the premises to locate *Senlung* caves. Their origin is much attached to the temporal and religious affairs. Their heirship, particularly chieftainship works effectively where there is undisputed genealogical tree. Thus, importance of genealogical tree had emerged in the society. The legacy and value of their origin can be seen even in the contemporary chieftainship and socio-religious affairs. Their entire social structure and church organization are based on clans and sub-clans. This is simply the legacy of the past tradition that lives in their collective memory. They believed and considered the mountains, rivers, cliffs, caves as the abodes of either malevolent or benevolent spirits. The caves were considered as important places where spirits took abode. Thus, oral traditions: folk tales, songs, lore and their genealogical trees have something to do with the theories of their origin.

Kamminlun S. Vaiphei says that the Zo family in their course of history was fragmented and disintegrated giving birth to many tribes and clannish groups. Oral traditions or legends as maintained by the elders of the Zo ethnic group hinted that the Zo people hailed from the first three brothers i.e., *Chongthulsongthu, Songja* and *Zahonglzahawng* (the progenitor of the Suantak people) who first dwelt in a cave or in a rock having a cavity popularly known by the people as *Khul or Sinlung or Chhinlung*. Tradition says that it would be somewhere in China but the exact location is still untraceable. Inter-tribal wars, conflicts between the tribes, lack of arable land in the place they adopted as their home caused the Zo people to lose their racial harmony. As they grew in size, quarrels erupted between groups; relatives were separated and driven to different regions. As a result, the Zo ethnic group gradually developed differences in their social, political, cultural and religious system. Zo people have a tradition of naming their clans after the heads of the clans. Dr. Vumkhohau, a scholar, a historian and a diplomat in

Myanmar (Burma) asserted Zo as progenitor of all races, and clans of this particular group of Tibeto-Burman are descendants from Zo. One among these tribes is the Suantak (recognized as the Vaiphei Tribe under the Constitution of India Scheduled Tribe Order 1950 which was amended as the Scheduled Castes and Scheduled Tribes Act in 1956) which later was divided into many sub-clans such as the Baite-Suantak mostly found among the Thado speaking group and they used Thado dialect for communication); Dopmul Suantak (they are found among the Zou people and they speak Zou dialect); Sizang-Suantak (found in the Siyin Valley, Burma and speak the Sizang dialect); Sailo-Suantak (found in Mizoram and they speak the Mizo language); and the Vaiphei-Suantak (speaking the Vaiphei dialect found in Manipur, Meghalaya and North Cachar Hills in Assam).The Suantaks which fall under the Mongoloid stock of races have deep lineal roots in the Chin Hills as *Twantak/Siyin/Shizang* and is one of the Chin-Kuki-Mizo tribes living mainly in Manipur, Mizoram, Meghalaya, North Cachar Hills in Assam, Kabaw Valley and the Chin State of Myanmar (Burma). Their language *Vaiphei, is* an ethno-linguistic term, i.e., a term that stands both for the tribe and for the language belongs to the Kuki-Chin subgroups of the Tibeto Burman language family. The origin of the name *Vaiphei* itself is still debated but the general understanding is that it is a name used to denote the people (the Suantak) who once lived in the village "PHAIZA" in the Chin Hills later known as *Khua Vaiphei* due to its breadth-wise horizontal expansion. There is a common belief among the Zo ethnic groups/communities that their ancestors emigrated from a place called *Sinlung* or *Chhinlung* or *Khul* or *Khurn* somewhere in South China where they moved down to Chindwin Valley and the Chin Hills in Burma. The Suantaks believed that it is from the Chin hills that they adopted the nomenclature *Vaiphei* as their identity. According to the genealogy as maintained by the Suantaks (*Vaiphei* speaking) in Manipur, there is a claim that they are the descendants of *Neilut* and *Vanglua* clan who are the second and fourth sons of Suantak. The Zo ethnic group does not have proper written records about their origin. There are different versions and theories regarding this. The result is that there are many discrepancies on the genealogical tree.

Sonthang Haokip makes an attempt to highlight who the Kukis were and its composition. The chapter is based on the historical records, documents and official accounts, etc. Since the remote past, these groups of people were clubbed together under the nomenclature Kuki and were known by the people as Kuki based on their common origin, affinity in language and dialect, customs and practices, etc. The British ethnographers, administrators, scholars and historians identify and understand these groups of people as Kuki and less by any other names. But the unity and fraternity of the Kuki Nation began to witness a fragmenting splits with the onset of India's Independence and thereafter. The chapter also discusses some suggestions so as to bring back the once splinter Kuki family under the same old roof once again.

The entire gamut of analysis carried out by Ruolkhumzo moves around the primeval religious beliefs and practices of the Hmars, one of the Hill tribes of North-East India. In the traditional Hmar religion, as discussed, Sakhuo is the God of compassion, the Creator and the Merciful Sustainer. Besides worshipping a number of gods and goddesses like *Vanhrit, Vanvomnu*, etc., their religious system prevails on the vitality of worshipping demons or evil spirits *(ramhuoi)* considering that they are the causes of their misfortunes for which sacrifices and devotions are performed. Their belief shows that all the animate or unanimated objects were actuated by spirits. Ruolkhumzo analyses the indispensability of priesthood as an institution of performing a number of various medicinal and religious sacrifices. Sacrifices to appease spirits, receive blessings from God, secure a good harvest are performed. The Hmars traditionally believed in the existence of soul and life after death. As shown, the places of death comprised three different abodes: *mithikhuo* (for the common people); *pielral* (for those who qualify for the title *Thangsuo. Thangsuos* are those persons who have killed different varieties of animals and performed certain public feasts during their lifetime); *vanram* (all the good spirits would enjoy endless happiness in *vanram).*

Ginneihching Simte and Danny Chara narrate the religious beliefs and practices among the Simtes of Manipur. They believed in spirits and demons. The spirits and demons were to be pleased for social harmony. This chapter brings out the forms of good and evil spirits which were dreaded and feared by the Simtes. The Simtes were concerned to please the evil spirits and demons lest they did no harm. Their daily lives revolved around pleasing and offering sacrifices to the spirits and demons. They performed various forms of sacrifices, rites and rituals. The Simtes believed in the existence of one Supreme Being called *'Pathian'*, the Ceator of all. In all the religious walks of life in the Simte community, the priest played an important role and His authority was next to that of the village chief. Nowadays, the old institutions and beliefs have all been forgotten. It has been replaced by the doctrines of Christianity.

Hoipi Haokip explores women's phase into the political arena from the pre-colonial to the post-colonial period. Historical accounts of the Kuki-Chin-Zo people are often depleted about the political involvement of women, argues Hoipi Haokip. She feels that the sources on the Kuki-Chin-Zo people are still a foggy. There has been a lack of women's participation in the Kuki-Chin-Zo society in Manipur. This lack of accounts has often been hinted to the customary ideology of women as subordinate position. Their sphere of influence has always been under the dominance of men. The traditional customary practice of the Kuki-Chin-Zo has always disfavoured the role and position of men. All the power structure within the ambit of the Kuki-Chin-Zo history has been one of male oriented. While men controlled political and cultural institutions, the economic sphere has been under the influence of women though she did not have the sole right to dispose it. Inheritance rights were under men's control. Men have always tried to keep women in an inferior position despite women playing a larger share in producing. Women have never been more than a symbolic representation to enhance men's pride. Women have gained only what the mean have deemed it to share and willing to grant. In such a scenario women have always occupied a back seat, yet on closer introspection it is the women who through their tact and skills as able manipulators able to wield much more than what the men are willing to acknowledge in the running of the village administration through their diplomacy.

Arfina Haokip's whole idea revolves around her attempt not simply analyzing the numerous proverbs associated with the Thadou-Kuki women but rather contexuality of those meanings. To a people who do not have the tradition of written records as a source of historical records, as Arfina concedes, folklore are regarded as the main sources of historical construction. These folklores passed on throughout generations are referred as historical documents. Folklore is the outcome of human mind with creative feelings. Similarly, it has been the traditional leaning of the Thadou-Kuki society to preserve folklores in the oral form. To them uttering a proverb was a form of correction and statement of certain facets of life. As one of the criteria of folklore, proverbs serve as an instrument of instruction to the individuals or to the community. Based on the common idioms and maxims that had conventionally been identified with women, how women are being identified is analyzed herein. The portrayal of such maxims has underlined the fact that women have always been identified with prejudice. Characterization of women in the common proverbial adages is controversial and far from appealing, argues Arfina Haokip. These proverbs have shown explicitly that women are one whose worth is left to the desire of the community. Proverbs have been used to enforce the irrelevance and unworthiness of women keeping them under male subjugation. It also gives insights to the fact that the attitude of men towards women is uncomplimentary. Though, a few proverbs extol women's virtue, more of the proverbs in existence mark negativity of women. Proverbs are meant through which men not only control the women psychologically but also undermine their values and attributes. The concept runs among the women that they are what because of such proverbs which have been adhered since generations.

Performance of marriage by marriage payment or bride

price or marriage price that is an important part in the Chikim (Chin-Kuki-Mizo) marriage should neither be understood as a sale price nor a commercial transaction, argues Priyadarshni M. Gangte. Marriage payment is made in terms of *mithun* when barter system was practised at one point of time. A *mithun* used to cost forty rupees as fixed by the British administration in the eighteenth century when currency system was first introduced in the settlements of the Chikim in north-east India. Marriage payment consisted of two parts: principal and subsidiary. The former is meant solely for the bride's father or brother, whereas the latter is for the relatives. Subsidiary price is integral as well as optional. In fact, the entire marriage payment is purposely made in most of the tribes of Chikims for two reasons: (i) to maintain good relation with maternal uncle; and (ii) probably poor financial condition. In case of acute property and inability on the part of bridegroom's side to pay it, marriage may actually take place without any payment but with a symbolic sacrificial performance. A Chikim woman is termed differently according to her married status.

In this article, S. Lhinghoijem tries to introduce the Biate people as one of the oldest tribes among the Chin-Kuki-Mizo. It tries to deal about the Biate marriage system mainly of the Biates of Jaintia hills in Meghalaya and. It also tries to reflect the rituals and ceremonies perform while seeking the bride's hand which is usually preceded with a pot of *zu* made out of rice. This *zu* is replaced now with a pot of tea after their conversion into Christianity. It also discusses about the bride price or the marriage payment reflecting its uniqueness and differences from other Chin-Kuki-Mizo groups of the North-East India. It also talks about divorce as well as the role of the clan council of the village. It discusses the norms and customary penalties which are followed by the Biate people.

The centrality of Salam Irene's chapter is how Christianity changed Kuki-Chin-Mizo society. In its background, the Kukis- Chin-Mizo believed in the existence of Supreme Being and existence both benevolent and malevolent spirits whom they propitiated through the offering of sacrifices, says Salam Irene. Some members of the 'Zo' in Manipur believed that they are descendants of one of the lost tribes of Israel, and some have in recent decades migrated and become citizens of Israel. The Kukis society is a service oriented society. Christianity is a very community oriented religion much in harmony with tribal outlook and mentality in general. As she analyses, Christianity lifted the Kukis from the old world to the new especially through the medium of education. She dwells on the impact of Christianity in the field of health.

Tingneichong Gangte's chapter talks about the changing scenario in the role and status of women in the Kuki society. In spite of their tremendous roles, as the Kuki society is patriarchal, women have no right, i.e., inheritance of property. Based on her study, Gangte shows changes taking place in the society like sharing of parental property among daughters and sons and how the Kuki women began to view their world with new eyes. The author feels that education has changed the man-woman relation and also emancipation. To her, the Kuki society has become more liberal and tolerant than it was before.

Paul B. Chonzik's article dwells on transformation in Chin-Kuki-Mizo ethnic nationality. A good number of scholarly studies had been done on ethnic nationality formation and transformation of different places. Different views and approaches are available as to how ethnic nationalities were and are being formed and transformed. These provided theoretical background on which critical studies and observations could be made on the various ethnic nationalities which had hitherto been relatively neglected. While space would not permit discussing all the theories and the approaches to ethnic nationality formation and transformation, the prominent ones which are relevant for understanding the nationality formation of nationality in North-East India are discussed briefly. For instance, we are made to understand from these studies that there are two broad ways in which nationalities are formed or transformed namely division and coalescence. Division can take place following certain processes as also division. While an ethnic nationality may be formed by the coming together of groups having close ethnic ties, some can be formed by the coalescence of groups not connected with kinship ties. Division can also take place following the division of one ethnic group into distinct ethnic groups following certain processes. The *Chin-Kuki-Mizo* nationality had undergone division and coalescence in the different phases of their formation. The process of division had resulted in the emergence of several ethnic nationalities from the original group. The forces of division percolated down to sub-nationalities resulting in the further breaking up of the nationality. However, both conscious attempts and unconscious developments operated to bring the divided nationalities to re-unite. Both centrifugal and centripetal forces appear to be operating within the nationality. The present study is an attempt to contextualize empirical data within global theoretical framework, and then tries to indentify factors contributing to the processes Chin-Kuki-Mizo nationality had undergone.

Aheibam Koireng Singh argues that the tribes belonging to the Chin-Kuki-Mizo have close socio-cultural affinity in terms of their culture, tradition, language, custom and traditional administrative system. They are one and the same people who were collectively called Kuki in India and Chin in Myanmar. They are one of the native ethnic communities in Manipur having its glorious past and rich cultural heritage. Like the term 'Naga', the term 'Kuki' was also given by the outsiders. The term Kuki was first heard of in Manipur between 1830 and 1840 though tribes of the same race had long been subjects of Manipur. In the colonial past, the Kukis in opposition to sending them as Labour Corps in France during World War I have found gallantly against the British colonial rule. It had negative consequences in the sense that it shattered the Kuki society into pieces, disintegrating and fragmenting to the extent that they never come together as they did before and during the war. With the advent of Indian Independence and implementation of Constitution of India, the tribes who were identified as belonging to the Chin-Kuki have started disowning the term Kuki and Chin. The tribes in the Kuki-Chin group present a picture of diversity in unity.

Despite their socio-cultural affinities, they were not able to come under the fold of a unified common nomenclature. In the last decade of the twentieth century, Kukis have faced various hardships and atrocities in the process of evicting them from their habitual residence for the realization of aspired homeland of the Nagas led by the faction of its rebel groups. It had miniaturised the Kuki identity further as some tribes belonging to the Chin-Kuki-Mizo group, either out of fear or at their own volition had denounced the Kuki identity. Also in 1997-1998, there were instances of violent ethnic clashes between the Thadous and the Paites in Churachandpur district (Manipur) both of which are kindred tribes of Kuki. The clash was finally concluded with an agreement to mutually respect the Zomi and Kuki nomenclature and leave it to the choice of the individuals or groups concerned. In fact, despite their close socio-cultural affinity, an acceptable nomenclature that encompasses all the tribes belonging to the Chin-Kuki- Mizo group is still eluding them. Furthermore, it is argued that fragmentation is being heightened because of inherent idiosyncrasies on the basis of the hierarchical order of genealogy and other endogenous factors as well in addition to the activities of the armed outfits.

Sanasam Amal Singh contends that all the ethnic groups have had a long tradition of associational life. The society and polity was structured by functional associations in the precolonial period. The system has been continuing till today. The Kukis of Manipur have been the major tribe spreading over a wide range of hill areas surrounding the valley of Imphal during the hey day of the Maharaja of Manipur and subsequently during the British period. The Kuki society has its own old age socio-economic, political and religious institution. In all the three spheres, the role of Kuki-Inpi, a civil body of the Kuki society took an important part. The Kuki Inpi is the apex organ representing the Kuki people. It is not for profit social organization that represents all the tribes of the erstwhile Kukis. The term Inpi has always held a sense of reverence in the Kuki society. It literally means the House the grand mansion. In the North Eastern States where Kukis are settled there are Kuki-Inpi in Assam, Nagaland and Manipur respectively. In this background the chapter focused particularly the Kuki-Inpi of Manipur (KIM) and emphasized as institutional civil body. It is an exploratory study. First, it spells out the different views of different scholars regarding how Kuki- Inpi emerges in Manipur. Second, it highlights the important role of Kuki-Inpi in village administration; and thirdly the role of Kuki-Inpi to bring peaceful solution between the Naga and Kuki ethnic conflict.

The joint chapter by S. Mangi Singh and Ningombam Akbar Singh explores the miserable life of the victims of the ethnic clashes which have largely enveloped Manipur in the 1990s. In the midst of the catastrophic consequences, many innocent people lost lives; villages torched; properties destroyed; livelihood shattered. There was a huge displacement with hunger, disease, sickness, and miseries with a loss of future hope. Though all were hard hit in the conflicts, the vulnerable social groups (children and women) due to their social status were severely hit. The situation turned out to be a far flung wildfire in the State administration that was away from 'regularity' and 'efficiency'.

Apart from supplying an analytical description of the growth of adult education, Lalnithar Joute tries to understand the contemporary state of her field of study in Mizoram. The study explores different programmes and achievements. Mizoram, which is now the second highest literacy rate in India as per 2011 Census, had no organized educational institution till 1893. With the coming of the Christian missionaries in 1894, progress had been made in the field. These missionaries transformed the language to writing and took the initiative in spreading education in Mizoram through adult education. Eradication of illiteracy was started by the Christian missionaries through social education presently known as adult education that is the key component and the guiding principle of human resource development. As a whole, its goal is to create human security and a learning society. Subsequently, the fabric of social life in Mizo society has undergone tremendous changes over years. Credit had been paid to the Missionaries, Central and State governments, NGOs, etc., through adult education programmes which were effectively introduced even in remote areas of the State before and after Independence.

III

It is much to the credit of my friends who instantly said 'yes' to the idea of concretizing an academic shape to honouring Professor Lal Dena. All the authors for their contributions are appreciated. It is my pleasure in editing the book although painstaking but the views expressed in the articles are entirely of the authors. Let me thank my friends for going through the earlier draft articles and their valuable comments: K.K. Das, N. Somorendro Singh. For editorial assistance, I must thank H. Sureshkumar Singh, Kamei Gaikhonlu and Sushma Sharma Gurumayum. I am grateful to Ashok Mittal and his team for publishing the book. The book is not at all intended to be a high claim but purpose of its publication will certainly be meaningful, as we sincerely feel, provided it potentially generates new ideas to those who are filled up with curiosities in their forward journey of academic pursuits.

H. Sudhir
Manipur University
Department of History

CONTENTS

ABBREVIATIONS

OUP	Oxford University Press
NBT	National Book Trust
MSA	Manipur State Archives
MU	Manipur University
MUTSU	Manipur University Tribal Students' Union

LIST OF CONTRIBUTORS

Joseph Suantak is the author of the books *The Vaipheis: Their History and Culture* (2010); *Khulmi? Chhinlung, Hurpi, Khol, Khul, Khur, Sinlung: Beyond Identity and Political Crises* 2012); *Chin+Kuki+Zo Genesis and Exodus* (2012).

D.L. Haokip, Assistant Professor, Department of History, Gauhati University.

Kamminlun S. Vaiphei, PhD Scholar, Department of History, Manipur University.

Sonthang Haokip, Assistant Professor, Department of History, Moirang College, Manipur.

Ruolkhumzo, Assistant Professor, Department of Political Science, Manipur University.

Ginneihching Simte, PhD Scholar, Department of History, Manipur University.

Danney Chara, Assistant Professor, Department of English, United College, Chandel, Manipur.

Hoipi Haokip, Assistant Professor, Department of History, Y.K. College, Wangjing, Manipur.

Arfina Haokip, PhD Scholar, Department of History, Manipur University.

Priyadarshni M. Gangte, Senior Lecturer, Damdei Christian College, Motbung, Manipur.

S. Lhinghoijem, PhD Scholar, Department of History, Manipur University.

Salam Irene, Professor, Department of History, Manipur University.

Tingneichong Gangte, Principal, Presidency College, Motbung, Manipur.

Paul B. Chonzik, Associate Professor, Department of History, Assam University, Diphu Campus, Assam.

Aheibam Koireng Singh, Assistant Professor, Centre for Manipur Studies, Manipur University.

Sanasam Amal Singh, Research Associate, Centre for Manipur Studies, Manipur University.

S. **Mangi Singh,** Professor, Department of Political Science, Manipur University.

Ningombam Akbar Singh, UGC Project Fellow, Department of Political Science, Manipur University.

Lalnithar Joute, Assistant Professor, Department of Education, Government Mamit College, Mizoram.

1

GENNING ON THE CKZ [CHIN+KUKI+ZO] OF INDO-BANGLA-MYANMAR

Joseph Suantak

People and their land

One among the *'indigenous peoples'* or *'Fourth World Nations'* found, approximately, within the geographical realm of 92° and 97° (longitude) E, and 20° (18° by Grierson) and 27° (latitude) N. grounding on 'Plate Tectonics Theory', the landmass inhabited by this people lies over the subduction or thrust zone of the Indian Plate and Eurasian Plate. More specifically, "CKZ ancestral land lies on top of the subduction zone of Indian Plate below the Myanmar Plate" (Joseph Suantak, 2012:139). It remained *terra incognita*, until the Dravidians, Indo-Aryans, Burmese, Bengalese and other smaller STB/TB (Sino-/Tibeto-Burman) ethnic groups arrived and made their settlements in the once lake-like valleys. No doubt, their inhabited clime was penetrated, entirely, first only by the European colonialists since the last quarter of the 19th c.CE.

Most of their populace desolated the valleys prior to the arrival of other ethnic groups owing to their uninhabitable environmental and geographical conditions. For instance, the *Tuikang* (now Burmanised as 'Chindwin'), and rivers and streams in the Kale-Kabaw valleys and their tributaries were collectively sobriqueted as *Tuitawbing* meaning 'bung up water' because they flooded throughout the present day northern Myanmar plains during rainy seasons. Tradition also has it that they took flight up on the nearby hills during the torrential monsoons. When they shifted on the nearby hills, says tradition, most of the nearby valleys (in Indo-Bangla-Myanmar borders) still look like large lakes.At the time of the establishment of the Meitei Kingdom in their neighbouring valley in *circa* 33 CE, they seem to have played a vital role. The *Cheitharon Kumpapa* (The court chronicle of the Kings of Manipur) mentioned two 'Kukis'. And the Tripura kingdom, during the 15th c. CE, also mentioned about the Kukis who lived independently in its neighbouring hill. And much later, during the European Colonial days, this indigenous people were collectively identified again as 'Koki', 'Kookies', 'Kookes', 'Cokoos', 'Cucis' or 'Kukis' in India and Bangladesh; and Chin in Burma (now Myanmar) since 12th c. CE. Yet, a section of them identified themselves as 'Zo' (Mizo/Zomi) and 'Zou' (or 'Yo' as in Carey and Tuck) from time unreckonable to this day. What is more, today, other groups of this people have also identified themselves as one among the Nagas. And thus it takes G. Amarjit Sharma to quip, "...culturally Kuki and politically Naga is pretty confusing. ...This shows that even the culturally diverse groups could become part of political Naga".[1] Quite similar to this case, few groups of the CKZ claimed that they are descendants of 'Manmasi' or 'Manasia' which they interpreted as if the Biblical 'Mannaseh', son of Joseph. However, the author finds this term 'Manasia' or 'Manmasi' as a mere distortion of the Sanskrit 'Manusia' or 'Manusya' for people, mankind, man, you, etc. Even the Darlong people, a family of CKZ, used this term 'Manmasi' to mean the same as in the Sanskrit 'Manusya'.

It may also be worth mentioning again that tradition maintains that at the time of eclipses, earthquakes, storms and funerals the phrase or terms *'Manmasi, Miachal, Niachal/ Nialachal*, and *Nelachal/Nilachal'* are muttered before prattling a ritual incantation. But an indepth study brings one to conclude that the term Miachal also like the term Manmasi is merely a distortion of the Sanskrit word Mecchal or Mechchal, non-Aryans, or wild tribes who eat all kinds of meat and brew hooch and, wearing their hair in chignon; and '*Nilachal*' and '*Nelachal*', a twisted form of the Sanskrit word Nilachal= greenly hills, or silver mountain. Now, in this regard, one thinks that comes out crystal clear is that, such thought or theory of making oneself believed to be Israelite blood must have been sprouted under the influence of the *Old Testament* world. Such idea was, in fact, first popularized by a handful of people from among the Lushei speaking family in the now Mizoram State since the 1930s. Whatsoever, though they have been classified by others and by themselves with varied names their cultures, vocabularies, and their genealogical root and tree quite clearly tells they were one and the same people but dissected by geographical conditions, the British 'divide and rule' geo-ethno-political administration, the competing modern Third World Nations, *viz*, India, Burma (now Myanmar), and Bangladesh; and, the current psychopathic and myopic ethno-politics of impulsive and compulsive unity (Joseph Suantak, 2012:213).

Scientific Interpretation of Origin Myt

Earlier historians on STB and TB in general and Chin/Kuki/Mizo/Zomi in particular were lost in imaginations and presumptions on the root or origin of the people who are variedly identified today as Chin, Kuki, Mizo, and Zomi in Zomia (Willem van Schendels, 2002, 2007; James C. Scott, 2009) and Koki country by Taranatha (1575-1634 AD). A number of contradicting theories were postulated during the 20th c.CE, however, based on recent scientific findings on the origin and evolution of humankind and their Out of Africa hypotheses it becomes more convincing to fairly infer that this people were none other but one among the Paleo-Mongoloids or Pre-Dravidians which the Vedic literatures and inscriptions marked them as *Kirata* and *Cin* in India; and 'unidentified indigenous people' based on recent archaeological information in regard to the climes of present day Bangladesh and Myanmar that share their borders with the North-East India.[2]

And again, quite conformed to what has been hypothesized, Prof. K. Saratchandra Singh, Department of Anthropology, Manipur University also asserted as this: *"Huddon [1909] tentatively suggested an ancient dolichocephalic-platyrrhine (Pre-Dravidian) type which is found strong among the Kuki, Khasi, Manipuri, Kachari, etc., but weaker among the Naga tribes"*.[3] In fact, "a people with strong Mongolian features...mostly live on the slopes of the Himalayas and mountains of Assam...and it does not appear that these peoples have made any appreciable progress during the thousands of years that have elapsed..."[4] Thus, it is believed that names of rivers in India and China which ends with 'ti' and 'di' must have been adopted from the CKZ's 'tui' or 'twi' for 'river' or 'water'. To Nick Thom, the CKZ language evolved in about 10,000 BCE, and is next to the Bodo-Garo, which he marked to have already developed in about 12,000 BCE, as the mother-language of all STB languages and dialects.[5] However, comparative study of terms and words of the STBs, TBs, and few of the South Africans impressed one to posit that the CKZ family and its language as the proto-STB [Sino-Tibeto-Burman] rather than a branch stemming from the STB or TB [Tibeto-Burman] as already guesstimated and popularized by Sir George Abraham Grierson (1851-1941) and others.[6] Besides, newer and most recent investigations based on genome mapping indicate that the STB/TB ethnic groups evolved within the realm of the present day North-East India and Bangladesh borders and thereafter dispersed and scattered into Tibet, China and South-East Asia (*'Chin+Kuki+Zo Genesis and Exodus,'* 2012:118-122, 158-163, 284-293). Tradition also has it that they first originated from a place called *Khawthippi* a.k.a. *Vanluilian*, and next, *Khaw-Awng*, and then they emerged from a place called *Khawsinlung* or *Chhinlung, Hurpi, Khol, Khul, Khur, Chhinlung*. Further research convinced one to infer that their first known cradle *Khawthippi* must be an indication of the hills and valleys that surrounds the present day Brahmaputra River. And, *Vanluilian* rather seem to be an indication of the Brahmaputra River. 'Van'=heaven, sky; and 'luilian'=large/wide river.

Khaw-Awng and *Khaw-sinlung* might be a place located somewhere within the realm of present day Indo-Bangla-Myanmar borders [(Joseph Suantak's *Khulmi* (2012); *Chin+Kuki+Zo Genesis and Exodus* (2012)]. Literally *Khul* signifies a grotto, karst, pit-dwelling, rock-shelter, or cave. But conversely, there are some sections who point the present day Xinlong [to pronounce 'Sinloung' or 'Shinlung'] in Sichuan Province in China as if their cradle due to the similarity with their tradition 'Sinlung' or 'Chhinlung'. However, this Chinese 'Xinlong' signifies 'New China'; and it acquired this name only after the Chinese occupation during the first-quarter of the 20th c.CE. On the other hand, the CKZ term *Sinlung* or *Chhinlung* qualifies 'stone seal', or 'rock/stone shutter'. True, tradition maintained that they were trapped in a cave as it was sealed by a boulder or large flat stone, during a 'total darkness' throughout this planet 'Earth'. They remember and retold this critical phenomenon as 'Thimzing', 'Thimzin', or 'Mujinlhun'. Based on scientific re-investigation this 'total darkness' or 'thimzin' rather seemed to have been caused by the ashes, gases and clouds of the ancient volcano called 'Toba volcano' or 'YTT 74,000 kya' (Joseph Suantak, 2012: *Chin+Kuki+Zo Genesis and Exodus*, p.134-150). During this 'Thimzin', according to tradition, no dry woods or twigs were at sight to make fire to warmth them, but dried skulls and skeletons of killed animals were burnt. Thus, such situation is indicative of the volcanic winter. In addition, the *'tuipisan'* [red river] and the *'leisanpa'* [red soil] incorporated in some of their ancient psalms might also be an indication of the Chinese 'Hong Ha'(Red River) or 'Yuan Chiang/Jiang'(Primary River) and 'Song Hong' to the Vietnamese, and the *'leisanpa'* must be an indication of the red soiled valley around the Hong Ha or Red River. This river takes its course and flows from Yunnan towards southeast direction into northern Vietnam and enters the Gulf of Tonkin. Undeniably, a number of several STB civilizations and cultures made their root around this river valley.

From what has been so far pictured there is probability that the proto-CKZ might have already evolved (genetically) and moseyed as forager, hunter, or gatherer around the clime of present day Indo-China-Bangla-Myanmar borders since *circa* 80-74,000 BP.

EtymoTymon of Chin, Kuki, and Zo

Contrasting views have been rendered in galore in respect of these terms or names. Of the many theories, the most popular among the CKZ historians, researchers, and scholars are the term/name 'Chin' originated from: (a) the Chinese dynastic name 'Chin', (b) the Burmese word 'Chin' for 'basket', and, (c) the Vedic literatures 'Cin'. Next, the term/word or name 'Kuki' originated from (a) Bengali word 'Kukil', or (b) from Afghanistan or Semitic word 'Kuchi'; and the other name/ term 'Zo' originated from: (a) the Chinese dynastic name Zhou/Chou, (b) the Tibetan Dzo, and (c) probably the name of the progenitor of the CKZ people. However, according to the author of this write-up, the term *Chin* must have been used, verbally, to signify this people since the arrival of the Burmese in the present day Myanmar in *c.* 2500-2000 BCE as they were frequently seen carrying bamboo basket on their backs. And, the term *Kuki* must be derived from the Sanskrit word 'Kukila' or 'Kukil', meaning 'hill' or 'mountain', verbally in use since the arrival of the Indo-Aryans in *c.* 3000-1500 BCE.

Regarding the term 'Zo', the author is quite convinced to surmised that it has its root in Africa, 'the cradle of humankind'. According to one source: '*...its origin go to the beginning of time as one of the ancient gods. The true name is quite secret, and its legend will be forever sealed. Zo supposedly means Spiritual Leader, with an African origin*' [trueghosttales. com]. In fact, no other STB culture preserved this term as popularly as the CKZ did and hence, from another angle, it authenticated that this people [CKZ] are the 'Paleo-Di' or 'Paleo-Mongoloid' from whom the STB and TB cultures stemmed out.

Plight of a Rejected Nation

'No script', 'no archaeological forum', 'no ancient cartography', etc sounds quite good and advantageous for the rapidly growing astute valley peoples who by now dominated this people, almost entirely, politically and geographically either in India, Burma or Bangladesh. Even today a number of researchers, scholars, and authors of India and South and South-East Asian history taxed this people as if immigrants, nomads, escapees, etc., as they have no written records of their cultural and geographical histories. And it is also quite absurd that why this indigenous people are not compared to the natives in the Americas and other continents.

1. Archaeology

Strictly speaking, even though they have no monument of their past, there are a number of megaliths, caves, rock-shelters, footprints of *Galngam* [a giant] on rocks, stone tools, unearthed instruments, trinkets and utensils, etc., which are living evidences of their ownership of the land where they are found spreading to this day. Of the many historical remains, the *Songbuh* rock-shelter, the *Phoikon Haosapi* cave, and the lower and upper *Senlung* caves located in present day Chandel district, Manipur are worth mentioning. Sadly, remains of humans found inside *Phoikon Haosapi* were said to have been carried away some years back by a group of archaeologists from Manipur valley. Yet, mention may be made that CKZ tradition preserved impressive tales related to these caves which no other human society in this global village ever knew or maintained.

In fact, a number of archaeological survey and excavation are already done in and around the ancestral homeland of the CKZ but without bearing them in mind.

2. Whiteman's 'Divide and Rule'

Since the British's colonial days they resisted external forces yet with no result to their favour to this day: even under the current neo-colonialists [India, Burma and Bangladesh]. Their unceasing culture of raiding the nearby valley peoples for slaves and domestic helps, and moreover, to drive them a distant away from the valleys that lies close to the foothills of their ancestral land enraged the British. In fact, until the White colonialists showed up and subjected the valleys under their protection several groups of warriors of the CKZ regularly disturbed the peoples settling close to their land. As they were disunited into several independent chieftain provinces, village-states it gave easy access to the intruding white colonialists to deeply pierce their 'divide and rule' apparatus, which still lingers under the Third World Nations—India, Burma [Myanmar], and Bangladesh. No doubt, the people and their land was segmented and stashed into the pockets of the newly independent nation-states of the post-British regime and are left like a bird with broken wings.

3. Imaginary Maps

To add their plight, "*...the more civilized yet rising kingdoms that filled the vacant lowlands depicted, in their geopolitical annals, the territory of Khul people...as their own discovered lands*" [Khulmi, 2012:188]. Had the primitive CKZ knew its importance and invented writings or at least, the art of cartography, their neighbouring valley peoples in the present India, Myanmar and Bangladesh might have preserved a different ancient map. Likewise the British Colonial cartographers too left us a number of imaginary and dubious maps which become advantageous for the valley peoples. Ridiculous maps, drawn during the 19th c.CE, by G.U. Pope and Sir Henry Yule are good examples. In this regard James S. Aber exactly states as this: "*No — never! Field measurements are subject to errors... Aerial photographs and satellite images portray only certain portions of the light spectrum, as filtered through the atmosphere and* *detection instruments... All maps are made according to certain basic assumptions... any map is the product of human endeavour, and as such may be subject to unwitting errors, misrepresentation, bias, or outright fraud."*[7] More to the point, "the head of India map, Jammu & Kashmir region is drawn variedly in Pakistan, China and India. And whereas, Indian cartographers included the entire region of what is now called Arunachal Pradesh; the Chinese claimed and included half of Arunachal Pradesh into their domain"(Khulmi, 2012:203).

In fact, ancient or old maps which were roughly drawn by the European cartographers encouraged the valley peoples and other neighbouring ethnic groups to label the CKZ as refugees, escapees, or landless tribe. Even the erstwhile geo-political movement 'Greater Mizoram', spearheaded by Laldenga (Mizo National Front) was opposed tooth and nail by some neighbouring states of the post WW-II grounding on those old and dubious maps. Today, even nearly a decade after the SoO (Suspension of Operations) and, nearly a year after the Cease Fire Agreement the geo-political demands made by the KNO (Kuki National Organization) and UPF (United People Front) in India, and the CNF (Chin National Front) in Myanmar are yet to be translated into practical; but how long shall it take these two Neo-colonialists to say 'amen' ?

4. Tribalisation

Already experienced under the White colonialists, the Third World Nations continued dehumanization and marginalization of this native of Indo-Bangla-Myanmar into an almost voiceless-landless tribal group. Under the Constitution of India they are classified as 'Scheduled Tribe' with no clear-cut definition. However, the Articles related to the Scheduled Tribes tacitly points out that they are landless nomads, economically in a deplorable condition. And the constitutional privileges laid down for the tribes rather seem to be a bait of deluding — to disintegrate them into plethora of hostile tribal groups. Worse than in India, in Bangladesh and Myanmar, to disclose the ground reality, they are deprived from any geo-political privileges, opportunities, freedom and rights. In the context of India, the report of the first Commissioner for Scheduled Castes and Scheduled Tribes, L.M. Shrikant gave three features, which according to him are applicable to all the Scheduled Tribes of India, which are: (a) Primitive way of living, (b) Habitation in remote and less easily accessible areas, and (c) Nomadic habits and love for drink and dance (James Massey, 2006:49). On the other hand, under the basic principles of the International Labour Organization the elements of tribal peoples does not include "invaded", which is incorporated in the elements of indigenous peoples. Thus, it is now quite clear that the Third World Nations categorized this people (Chin+Kuki+Zo) as "tribal" to evade the word "invaded" in order to strip them off from their natural indigenous status in this Indo-Bangla-Myanmar border realm and also, to safe their faces from the accusing fingers of the UN?

5. Forcible Possession and Desertation of CKZ Ancestral Lands

In the name of development a number of legal provisions are sanctioned without the collective knowledge and consent of the natives becomes a frequent occurrence *i.e.*, inclusion of some of the foothills that belong to the CKZ within the Constitution and law related to the valley in Manipur. No doubt, the recently proposed Manipur (Village Authority in Hill Areas)'s the Second Amendment Act 2011 was a direct threat to the existing traditional Chieftainship institution and the CKZ rights over their ancestral land. Another threat, the proposed Tipaimukh Dam: a number of the indigenous CKZ, besides being left homeless/landless, will certainly be left with no forested land for their economic survival, for instance, the present state of the Khuga Dam in Churachandpur. It left many without arable land. Moreover, a number of the once beautiful and richly forested hills are already deformed into a muddy bed of a large futile lake. And today, 'Oil'! And next, let us see at what rate crimes of all types, beggars and immigrants from the overpopulated mainland India multiplied when the first train arrived through the Jiribam railway track.

6. Unreceptive Names

Another plight— internal disunity or division among themselves due to option of nomenclature[s] is illustrated quite understandably in the words of N. Lhungdum: "*These divisive elements are reigning supreme in the minds and hearts of the people, not only of the uneducated masses but rather sadly more in the minds of the intelligentsia of the society who are supposed to be the source of light of the society. We are simply squandering the treasure of our social and cultural identity. We are yet to learn the simple truth that clannish chauvinism, dialectal fanaticism and parochial loyalty to one's own clan are the surest way of prescription for social and cultural disintegration which ultimately take us backwards instead of forwards*"(as quoted by Lal Dena, 2011).

As pointed out above, any altruistic social and political leader and think-tank will not fail to pronounce repetitively the phrase "*Gam leh Nam*" (Land and Ethnic), a slogan of nationalism. Practically, 'Gam' is entirely overshadowed by a psychopathical 'Nam'-ism, which instantaneously brings about sectarianism and communal tension among them.

How hard the CKZ try to reunite, and regain their lost ancestral land or geo-political autonomy since the 1930s, particularly in the now Myanmar and India, they remained a quashed, deceived, swindled and rejected nation to this day. They are, in other words, a Colonized Fourth World Nation plus, a marginalized people under the Third World Nations. Yet, they seem to struggle on to achieve their dream and aspiration ¯ to retrieve their timeless indigenous status — at least until they are offered, or compensated with a suitable geo-political situation. Of course, it is time to rethink for their neigbouring valley peoples or other ethnic groups who, in course of human history, steadily dominated and shared their ancestral land, to find and lay down an alternative geo-political arrangement to remedy or heal the wounds they have inflicted upon this Fourth World Nation 'CKZ' ¯ 'The sooner the better,' instead of 'The later the betters' for all.

REFERENCES

1. G. Amarjit Sharma, 'Inside and Outside of Ethnic Enclosure: Khoibu as a separate Tribe', cadmanipur.org/2011/06/29.
2. See for details, Joseph Suantak, *Khulmi? Chhinlung, Hurpi, Khol, Khul, Khur, Sinlung¯Beyond Identity and Political Crises,* Akansha Publishing House, New Delhi, 2012 and *Chin+Kuki+Zo Genesis and Exodus,* Akansha Publishing House, New Delhi , 2012.
3. K. Saratchandra Singh, An Anthropology Profile of North-East India with special reference to Manipur, presented in the 98th Session of Indian Science Congress, Chennai, 3-7 January, 2011.
4. R.C. Majumdar, H.C. Raychaudhuri, and Kalikinkar Datta, *An Advanced History of India",* Macmillan, 1976, India, p. 14.
5. Joseph Suantak: *op.cit.*; Nick Thom, *Chinese and Sino-Tibetan* (2008). The author of this presentation is quite convinced that the CKZ language must be the mother-language of all Sino-Tibeto-Burman languages and dialects.
6. *Ibid.*
7. James S. Aber , *"Brief History of Maps and Cartography",* academic.emporia.com, 2008.

2

THE TALES TELLING THE LOCATION OF SINLUNG-KHUL

ORIGIN OF THE CHIN KUKI MIZO ZOUMI

D.L. Haokip

The origin of the Chin-Kuki-Mizo ethnic groups is an area that scholars, academicians, students had touched in their works. Yet, the location of *Sinlung/Khul/Chinlung* is left incomplete. Its origin is much attached to the temporal and religious affairs. This is because: chieftainship and religious affairs largely depend on genealogy.[1] Heirship, particularly, chieftainship and ritual that appease curse from their own ancestors effectively work where there is undisputed genealogical tree. The importance of genealogical tree had emerged in the society. The legacy and value of their origin can be seen even in the contemporary chieftainship and socio-religious affairs. The churches and other social organizations are deeply rooted to it. This is how the Chin-Kuki-Mizo ethnic communities laid emphasis on their origin. This may be the reason why they established a common origin. No doubt, without one's ancestral names, priest could not perform ceremonies in the past but what is the relevancy of organizing churches on the line of clans and sub-clans in the post-modern or the present society too goes again the teaching of Jesus himself and other religious leader? This is the legacy of the past traditions that lives in their collective memory testified by the folk tales and lore. Generally, the rural people of the World believed and considered the mountains, rivers, cliffs, caves and what not, as the abode of either malevolent or benevolent spirits. The caves were considered as important places where spirits took abode. As such their oral traditions, folk tales, songs, lore and their genealogical trees have something to do with the theories of their origin. Here, we curtailed the scope and meaning of origin to suit our purpose. Generally it will stand for a place.

An attempt is made to locate and identify *Sinlung/Khul* which many tribes of this ethnic group considered as their place of origin. On the basis of data(s) available we assume that the location is within the territories they inhabited from the remote past until now. This is because their oral tradition lacks names of territories or regions and rarely mentions the territories not other than the region they inhabited. Thus, our interpretation would be on the basis of the premises available to us to avoid misinterpretation on the subject matter and keeping more rooms for academicians and scholars for further deliberation and interpretation. In the absence of authentic chronicles, we have to entirely depend on oral traditions: both temporal and socio-religious affairs and the accounts compiled or written down by outsiders besides validating with the topography or natural setting available in the regions mentioned in the tales. Shakespeare, Lewin, Shaw and McCulloch and other native writers or ethnographers collected from the people who inhabit the great mass of hills which separates the plains of Bengal and Burma. Shakespeare observes that the tales they collected from the Lushai, Kuki and Chin are closely connected. *"These tales come from many other tribes besides the Lushai, but are closely connected, and the same tale in slight different forms, is found in places very far apart"*.[2] He has compiled the tales of the *Aimol, Anal, Koms, Lamkang, Hmar, Purum, Thadou* tribes of the Manipur and the *Bunjogi* clan of the south Lushai Hills, *Kumi* clan of the Chittagong Hill tracts. His compilation includes the name of legendary personalities, folk stories, myths and traditions relating to their origin, culture, manners, etc. The term repopulation sounds like a theory but in practice it signifies their occupation of the land they inhabited.

The tales describe the origin of these ethnic groups and other aspects of their society. For space and time we will now come to our discussion. We would like to raise a few questions. Where is the cave mentioned in all these tales? What is the name of these caves? Was it a single cave or different caves? To give an accurate answer is by no means easy. But here an attempt is made to give the name of cave and its location. Let us now come to the debate on the meaning and location of the cave.

The word *Sinlung/ Chinlung/ Khul* should be considered as one name of the same place. For the word *Sinlung* and *Chinlung* is identified by many writers as a cave or hole closed with stone. In the second word, H is a silent letter. *Sin or Cin* in the local word stood for 'to close'[3] and *Lung* for 'stone'. The same idea is found from those who claim *Khul*, which they believed to have found in the subterranean region. Thus, these words are different ways of addressing one place. The name *Khul, Sinlung* or *Chhinlung* appeared to be a cave or hole or the place of their origin in the works of Shakespeare, Shaw and native writers K. Zawla Ginjatung, Lian, Z. Sakhong Singkhawkhai, etc. In fact, McCulloch did not mention the name *Shongthu* but addressed the hero as 'their king's brother'.[4] Yet, the chronicles of Tiddim and many clans of the Kukis of Manipur mentioned the name *Shongthu. Lewin* did not mention the name of cave when he wrote the tales from the Bunjogi, an allied tribe of the *Lushai.* Interestingly, Lian Sakhong quotes all the earlier works. In his work, one can observe that the name *Chinlung* stood for cave or hole.[5] Recently, J Guite had argued that cavern, hole or Sinlung should not be identified with the place of their origin but it is the place they passed through in the course of their migration.[6] We do agree with him for the ethnic group under study had shown a much civilized state especially the oral tradition passed on among the Kuki that narrates their progenitor's origin. The Kuki Research Forum's discovery of the name *Senlung* identified with the spirits of the Haosapu/Sohlumol

(Songko) cave would surely linked to the oral traditions with archaeological studies. No doubt, the hilly region of Manipur has been included in the pre-history map with the publication of the findings of O.K. Singh from the Khangkhui cave.[7] Stone age and claim for the paleolithic period come into light from the reports of renowned Anthropologist, N.J.K. Singh claiming (Songbuh) stone hut cave at Khomunnom near Sajiktampak in the Chandel district to be the abode of Paleolithic Men, the oldest known human culture and civilization based on the type of tools and artifacts discovered. He gives a tentative date between 2,00,000- 50,000 BCE.

Interestingly, one can see that the whole story of *Shongthu* and his men is found in adventure, hunting, migration or separation of village. This also reminds us the journey from the plain to hilly tracts where plenty of wild animals are found. The eyewitness report of the Kuki Research Forum convincingly tallies the ecological setting of the *Selung* cave environments with the kind of topography or spot mentioned in the tales of the descendants of the *Shongthu*.[8] K Zawla identified the name *Chienlung/Chinlung* with the name of Chinese emperors while all the other writers are united as far as the name of *Chinlung/Khul* is concerned. They identified with a cave/hole that is closed with a stone as is shown in the tales. To elaborate, the word *'Sin'* or *'Chin'* also signifies 'to care or to memorize and 'lung' that of human heart. Thus, the word *sinlung* in other words, stood for that of memorizing their tales particularly those tales that the priest had to take down. They have to keep in their memories and should not disclose unless they transmit to the newly appointed priest of the village who will succeed his position when he retires or is too old to perform ceremonies. It must be noted that transmission of such religious oral tales needs screening which is not a subject that we will bring into light here.[9] Undoubtedly, the literal meaning of *Sinlung/Chinlung* would mean a cave or hole that is closed with a stone or the secret and sacred tradition. The name *Khul* sounds differently but the three words are considered as one entity and place for the tales talk about some sort of cavern, or hole closed. Otherwise, the word cave in Kuki is called *Sonbuh* if human settled there and *Songkuo* would mean those cave(s) where men and animals take temporary shelter. Hole would mean *kuo*, semi-circular or circular pits found on the surface of the earth or tree for that matter. If we read in details, the existence of a city or big village inside the earth that has tunnel closed by stone came into our mind. Considering the tales, if the caves (any cave) are to be identified with these names, the cave would have large chambers where about 50-100 people would assemble. It is a challenging subject for the academicians, scholars who are taking interest into it. Further research is required to bring out the undisputed views despite of its closeness with the two terms. If underworld or subterranean region which the Kuki called *Noimang* is explored with evidences of human habitation inside the earth or hollow earth that would describe the best the so called *Khul*. In fact, this reminds us the hollow earth theorists of the world that survive until now in some parts of the world.[10] Hollow earth as a theory is also attached with the Buddhist. In the words of R. W. Bernard *"the word 'Agharta' is of Buddhist origin. It refers to the Subterranean World or Empire in whose existence all true Buddhists fervently believe. They also believe that this Subterranean World has millions of inhabitants and many cities, all under the supreme domination of the subterranean world capital, Shamballah, where dwells the Supreme Ruler of this Empire, known in the Orient as the King of the World. It is believed that he gave his orders to the Dalai Lama of Tibet, who was his terrestrial representative, his messages being transmitted through certain secret tunnels connecting the Subterranean World with Tibet".*[11] Thus, the tales they have taken down from their ancestors, no doubt resolve in the 'Hollow Earth Theory' that works even today. The Buddhist origin 'Agharta' as a subterranean world impresses us and reminds us the relation between the Chakma Kuki and Buddhist from the time of Asoka. [12] The Buddhist historians claim that *Samghas* were established in the Kuki country from the time of Asoka. The Chakmas, no doubt, are an allied community of the Lushais. The rapid conversion of the Kuki into Buddhism resulted to a large number of monks from the Kuki community. To quote "their number went on increasing so that during the time of four Senas, more than half of the monks of Magadha were from the Koki (Kuki) community". In the light of the above passage, we are certain that the influence of the Buddhist to the community under study cannot be ruled out. Without elaborating the subterranean region or hollow earth theory we can say that the kinds of tales or beliefs that they have taken down from their ancestors are fulfilling all the parameters set in the Hollow earth theory which was and is still widely accepted till date. Surprisingly, the tales of the *Kumi* clan inhabiting the Chittagong Hill tract bore the creation of man by the God from mud. They believed that God made man and animals. The *Khongsai* tales are silent about *Khul* but advocate *'Vanthang'* origin from above. Yet, the idea of heaven maids getting married with the Lushai king, Hlandokpa[13] and other tales relating to the God, Sun and Moon come under this category.

Coming to the debate on the location, we would like to look back the earlier works on this subject matter. K. Zawla, a Mizo historian claims the Great Wall of China[14] (225 BC) to be the place and origin of these people. He asserts on the assumption that the communities under study is a group of the Mongolians who migrated from the western China lying between the sources of the Yangtze and the Hoang-Ho Rivers.[15] Nevertheless, Paramesh Choudhury who carried out a research in China claims that Shi Huang Ti is the emperor of the Chin who migrated probably from India in ancient time and took with him the legacy of India's irrigation system.[16] In his version, Chin is very inclusive nomenclature. One reason we can believe him is that the Chinese used to treat them as an alien or foreigner (the Chin) for being semi barbarous living on the frontier. To quote him "*She Huag-ti, the great emperor of the Chin dynasty, who founded the empire built the Great Wall, burnt the Confucian books and the lietrati. His capital was at His-an Fu (called in those days Ch'ang–an) and his tom is a hill, less than a mile to the south-east of the Lin-tung known as the Li shan. Su ma-chien, the Herodotus, of China, says that ' ...more than*

70,000 labourers gathered from all parts of the empire, was employed in excavating the bowels of the earth at this spot, down to the 'three fold depth', and in the heart of the cavern thus formed palatial edifices were constructed ...the artificer made the enginery know all that has been done, and the secret of the treasure will be noised abroad. When the great ceremony was over, the central gate of the avenue of the approach having already been closed, the lower gate was shut, and the artificer came out and no more. Trees and hedges were planted over the spot to give it appearance of ordinary mountains".[17] On the basis of the Chinese Herodotus account, we can also discuss the location of *Senlung/Sinlung* by considering the underworld palace constructed at the spot where She Huang-Ti, the Chin's emperor was buried. The terms cavern, gate and to close or shut remind us the tales. But these tombs with human habitations need an experimental research. If we put the compound word Sin+lung and *Khul* in reverse, we derive the world *'Khulsinlung'*. This will describe the tombs or graveyards covered with stones. The word *Khulsin* in Kuki is much close to tombs or a buried place. Now let us relate to the tombs of Shi Hung-Ti, the emperor of the Chin, which appear to be cities inside the earth or bowel. This needs a close observation. In this context, if the word *Sinlung* and *Khul* mean fragmented word of the word, *Khul sin*, it can be said that the bowel found at the place where their chief was buried can be related to the meaning of the words. The Chins were minority and such hiding palatial would protect them at best. Here, the term *Khul* can be fitted. In the absence of corroborated accounts, further research is required and conjecture would invoke nothing. Many local writers subscribe it today. John Pulamte claims that all the Mizo, Hmar and other R groups are convinced of their originality from China and G groups claim two places[18] Chimnuaigeltui about six kilometres east of the *Tiddim* town of the present Myanmar and the upstream of the Manipur river which Shaw had suggested on the basis of the word *Gun* identified with the Imphal river in the oral tradition.[19] Ginjathang claims Tibet.[20] Nevertheless, the name *Chogthu* (similar with the term *Chongthu* tribe of Manipur and Mizoram) and *Chongyas* (that of *Chongja*) mentioned in the tales of many Kuki clans had figured out in Tibet. [21] One comes across some similar vocabulary as well in Tibet. *'Chang'* is called paddy among the Kuki of Manipur and it is a name of beer made of rice in Tibet. The *'Bon'* as a traditional religious system of the Tibet and the compound word *Indoi* better known as *Doibom* that some of the Kuki clans of Manipur, Myanmar, and other north-east States had in their traditional religious system should be cross checked before arriving a conclusion. The basis of Sakabpa's claim for Tibet once again resurfaces in the subject we discuss here. Holkhomang Haokip comes up to the extent that the Kuki chieftainship had its genesis in Tibet.[22] Lian Sakhong and Gangte suggest the Chindwind valley, on the basis of derivation of the term Chinlung from Chindwind that stands for cave or hole of the Chin people.[23] The *Bunjogi* clan of the south Lushai Hill gives the location of a cave. "*The cave whence man first came out is in the Lushai country closed to Vanhuilen's village, of the Burdaiya tribe and can be seen to this day, but none could enter.* [24] The recently discovered name *Senlung* (name of spirits) identifies with a cave located near *Kholmunlen* village on the trans-border of the Manipur Chin Hills and it opens up another location for discussion. The Kuki Research forum cave expedition 2012 had explored from the chief of Aigijang the ties with the spirits of *Haosapu/Sohlumol* cave. According to him, the name of the chief spirit who took abode there is *Senlung*. This perhaps is located at the centre of the region inhabited by the ethnic groups under study. The etymology of the Kuki of Manipur is much attached to the valley: Burma plain and Manipur plain. Johnstone claims that the Chassad had originally lived in Manipur but afterwards took up their abode on the border of the Kabaw valley but often this territory was claimed by the Burmese.[25] The etymology of the ethnic particularly those who live in Manipur corroborate it.[26] Within the parameters of tales particularly collected from the ethnic groups from the Manipur, we can say that the location of *Khul/Sinlung/Chinlung* is on the trans-border of the erstwhile Manipur Chin Hills (now Indo-Myanmar border).

Coming to the important events mentioned in the tales: forest fire, darkness, flood and earthquake mentioned in the tales, we are not out of historical event when we analyze them. The events mentioned remind us the history geological sciences. The Lushai tales mention the forest fire as the cause of their migration to their present habitation site.[27] In fact this reminds us the recent Llaima lolcano eruption 2008.[28] Interestingly, after two volcano eruptions in Chile in 2008, earthquake of an 8.8 magnitude struck central Chile on 27 February, 2010 that tolls much life. Perhaps, when forest fire or volcanic eruption had occurred; it tolls the life of many and even destroyed town and the smoke causing darkness for several days in the region where it occurred.[29] The darkness lasted for seven days. But due to lack of research on the subject matter in the region, it will be difficult for us to draw a hasty conclusion here. The historic events need a thorough study. But, the events like the human beings turn into wild animals and *vice versa* as they narrated could be that of human imagination and parts of the tales and in due course of time mixed up with all the contents.[30] Shaw had drawn the rough chronology of these events. He held that fire from the earth preceded darkness accompanied by the flood that causes the people to migrate towards the hill. Darkness again figures in a slightly manner but most of them attributed Awk who is believed to swallow the sun.[31] This reminds us the natural events like the solar eclipse as well. The story of forest fire and darkness of course are not limited to the ethnic group under study.[32] The Anal tribe and other who live in Manipur claim that the whole earth was flooded and the entire human race except a couple who took refuge on a high tree that stood near a large pond had survived.[33] They believed that the Creator had sent a man and a woman to re-populate the world as the couple who had survived already transformed into a tiger and tigress. This tale holds some truth for whenever flood occurred people moved towards the mountains or higher lands to survive. The Anal tales remind us the *Koubru* and *Thenbung* mountain tops where water is found in the form of small pond till the present days. The Anals who live in the Manipur south are much close to *Thenbung Hills* near *Sugunu* area where such pond is found on the top of the hills. The word *Tuikang*, which means white water, reminds us that probably the people lived at a place from where water can be seen. Loktak lake and Chinwind river[34] had figured out as *Tuikang* among the Kuki. The Kuki of Manipur kept in their mind archival, about the flood of Manipur Valley as *Tuitobin*.[35] The oral tradition of the *Lushai* mentions the flood and credited to the king of water demon who falls in love with a beautiful maiden, *Ngaiti*.[36] Frazer in his folklore in the *Old Testament* notes that flood bearing story is distributed all over the south eastern Asia and the Indian Archipelago and seems to extend even to Oceanic and America.[37]

The time frame would be a great problem until more research on the natural calamities is taken up in the region. But we are certain that due to natural calamities, people died and the survived race or ethnic had occupied the territories vacant which the earlier ethnographer called 'repopulating the world.' How to fix a date when none of the tales tell us the exact date? Here comes the weakness of oral history. *Songthu* and *Chawngthu* as a clan in Manipur and *Lushai* Hills is an established fact[38]. It may suit or not, we do not know, but in the absence of the contemporary written record, counting of their genealogy (chronology) and their belongings at the time of their migration for better world would give us some information. Based on the calculation modalities shown by Shaw[39], the Chassad, an important clan of the descendants of *Shongthu* dated it to be 900-950 A.D[40]. The same date is surprisingly derived by K. Zawla, a Mizo historian. So, it must not be mistaken that their ancestors who died of unnatural deaths are deleted from their genealogical tree. It will be difficult for us to push back before Iron Age for the word *Namchem* (sword) is the weapon of the *Shongthu*. This leads us to fix a later date for we do not know how many of their ancestors died of unnatural death.

The tales resolved themselves into one spirit with regard to the re-population of the earth surface. Debate on the location and name or nature of *Khul/Chinlung/Sinlung* will continue. The names Sinlung and Khul seem to be derived terms from the word *Khulsin* and *lung* is suffixed to it. With this their tales will go longer in digging out their origin. No doubt, their tales fall within the parameters of the word folklorist and also touched or connected with all the elements or fragmented pieces of the 'Hollow Earth Theorists' hypothesis which survive until the present century. The forest fire mentioned in the tales, darkness, flood and the days when men and animals could communicate hints the kind of natural calamities that tolls the life of many at different points of time and places. The recently discovered name of a cave, *Senlung (Sinlung)* locally called Haosapu or *Sohlumol songko* (cave) located on the trans-border of the Manipur and Chin Hills again resurfaces how the *cave/hole* theory is much attached to their belief system. This appeared to be the cave mentioned in the tales for no cave bearing the name *Senlung/Sinlung* for that matter is explored or traced so far.[41] There are more reasons to believe it. Firstly, it is assumed that the people migrated from this place and moved to different four corner directions. Secondly, the vocabulary or etymology of the ethnic groups under study had immensely supported. Thirdly, the name *Senlung* that is identified with a cave does not figure at the places suggested by other writers. Fifthly, we are certain that the ecological setting at the said areas or locations is still intact as good as mentioned in the tales. Tiger, snake, porcupine or hedgehogs as mentiond by the ethnographers are still available. This is because the Kuki Research Forum members had carried out a field survey. Lastly, the moment *Sinlung/Chinlung* is identified with man, the roots of the Chin-Kuki-Mizo languages is invalid. *Lung* is no doubt a stone. Take for example, *Lungthu*, a tripod or traditional tripod made of three pieces of stone. The tales that are collected from various pockets of the entire present North-East India, Myanmar, Chittagong Hill tracts no doubt clearly indicate the territories they inhabited from the remote past to the present day. Though international, national and State boundaries divided them excepting Government project areas or dams, they are still found intact in the region before the colonial period and at the time when the colonial ethnographer collected the tales that shed their tears for they are now trans-border nation with creation of all sorts of boundaries.

REFERENCES

1. By genealogy we mean the list of ancestors who died of *thipha* (natural death).
2. J. Shakespeare and T.C. Hodson, 'Folktales of the Lushais and their Neighbours', Taylor and Francis Ltd. publication on behalf of Folklore Enterprise Ltd. URL: http://www.jstor.org/stable/1254435. Accessed: 01/03/2012 06:32, p. 390.
3. J. Pulamte, Development of Education in Churachandpur District, Unpublished PhD thesis, MU, 2002, p. 59.
4. W.McCulloch, *An Account of the Manipuris and the Hill Tribes,* Calcutta, 1859, p. 55.
5. Lian H. Sakhong, *In search of Chin Identity,* Thailand, 2003, p. 2.
6. J. Guite, 'Memories of Origin and Migration', JNES, ISSN 2277-6869 (online), pp. 2-3.
7. Gangmumei Kabui, *History of Manipur,* Vol. l, Delhi, 1991, p. 49.
8. For detail see *The Kuki Research Forum Cave expedition report,* 2012.
9. For detail see D. Letkhojam Haokip, *Thempu Ho Thu,* Churachandpur, 2000. The writer of this paper had interacted with the traditional priests and the villages chiefs who are the temporal and religious heads. The book heavily deals on the various ceremonies and their origins that are deeply rooted *Shongthu* and his men.
10. In 2011, Horatio Valens and Paul Veneti presented a two-hour "Lazeria Map Collection" video on centuries old maps of the Arctic region and the North Pole making a case for a 100 miles wide canyon in the centre of the physical North Pole into which north flowing rivers drain into a hollow Earth. The maps were collected by Harry Hubbard. (sources: From Wikipedia, and The Free Encyclopedia).
11. R. W. Bernard, *The Hollow Earth,* Chapter II: Agharta, Subterranean World, New York, 1964,(access from Hollow Earth Website on the 3rd October, 2012.
12. Debiprasad Chattopadhyaya (ed.), *Taranatha's History of Buddhism in India,* Simla.1970, p. 330.
13. J. Shakespeare and T.C. Hodson, *op cit.,* p. 391.
14. K. Zawla, Mizo Pi Put e leh an Thlateh Chanchin, p. 2.
15. T. S. Gangte, *The Kukis of Manipur,* New Delhi, 1993, p. 17.
16. Paramesh Choudhury, *The Mystery of the Chinese Dragon,* Kolkata, 2005, pp. 125-133.

17. *Ibid.*, pp. 127-128.
18. R group and G group here signify the division of the Chin-Kuki-Mizo language. For instance, local word for land is 'Ram' among the R group and 'gam' for the G group. The entire Chin-Kuki-Mizo literature falls under these two categories.
19. John Pulamte, *op cit.*, p. 59.
20. Ginjathang, *Zomi Inkuan Laibu*, 1973, p. 7.
21. Tsepon W.D. Shakabpa, *Tibet: A Political History*, Yale University Press, 1967, pp. 103-104.
22. Vide our interview with Holkhomang occasionally, the last being during July 2012 at his residence, Haokip Veng Imphal. He is an ex-Minister of Manipur Assembly, a one term MP from the outer Manipur Parliamentary constituency.
23. Lian h. Sakhong, *op. cit.*, p. 5.
24. J. Shakespeare and TC Hodson, 'Folktales of the Lushais and their Neighbours', Review works, *Folklore*, Vol. 20, No. 4 (December 30, 1909, pp. 388-420) Taylor and Francis Ltd. publication on behalf of Folklore Enterprise Ltd. URL: http://www.jstor.org/stable/1254435 Accessed: 01/03/2012 06:32, p.390.
25. B.C.Charkravartee, *British Relation with Hill Tribes*, Calcutta, 1964 p. 54. Foreign Department: Political A. 1870, Relation Between Looshais and Munipurees, Calcutta, 1979, p. 26.
26. *Jangsel* (Plain mithun). *Jangva* (a plain bird), *Jangsa* (Plain animal), *Janglei/Jangtol* (plain), *Jangbe* (Plain peas), and plants jangbe (plain peas), Kolchang (Burmese rice), Kolbu (Maize) but when translated it means Burmese food or Indians food for Kol also stood for Mainland people. The nearest plain available to them was Koljanglei (Kabow valley) and Phaipi that of Manipur valley Phaibi, a thatch that valley people commonly used. The meaning of Kolcan be interpreted in three ways. Kol means, slope rocky places and a community in mainland India. *Kolninou, Asohtai Kolninou* mean the sun rise in the east. The term Jang indicates plains in the context of topography.
27. J. Shakespeare and T.C. Hodson, *op. cit.*, p. 391.
28. Sources: Wikepedia search on Ring fire, accessed on 1st October 2012.
29. Lhingneilam lupheng, a government college lecturer of geography at Moirang College had suggested the possible cause of *thimjin* or darkness discussed above on the 23 February, 2012.
30. J. Shakespeare, *The Lushai Kuki Clan*, p. 92
31. J. Shakespeare, *op. cit*, pp. 393-395; The legend of Khasi claim that a very big tree had grown up on a Diegiei peak and cause darkness but on cutting it down light came to the world once more.
32. Darkness story appeared in the oral tales of the Nagas like Ao,

Lhota, and Chang Nagas; Hos and Santhals of the Bengal, the Shans and Ami of Formosa.

33. J. Shakespeare and TC Hudson, *op. cit.*, pp. 391-392.
34 Lian H. Sakhong, *op. cit.*, p. 7
35. William Shaws, *Notes on the Thadou Kukis*, Guwahati, 1997, p. 28.
36. J. Shakespeare, *The Lushai Kuki Clans*, Tribal Research Institute, Aizawl, 1988, p. 94
37. Shaw, *op.cit.*, p. 28.
38. C. Chawngkunga (ed.), *Important Documents of Mizoram*, Art and Culture Department, Aizawl, 1998, p. 29.
39. Shaw calculated that the Thadou Kukis married at the age of 30. Based on the formula formulated by him for calculating genealogy, the date of Khul origin cannot be later than the dates mentioned here.
40. D.L Haokip, Historical Traditions and Customary Laws of the Chassad, Unpublished PhD Thesis, MU, 2006, p.24.
41. During the 22- 24 February 2012, the Kuki Research Forum Manipur found and identified a cave called Senlung/Sinlung (matter of pronunciation) located near Kholmunlen village on the trans-border of the erstwhile Chin Hills and Manipur. For details see The Cave Expedition reports of the Kuki Research Forum, 2012.

3

SUANTAK TRIBE

SOME ASPECTS OF AN ETHNOGRAPHIC STUDY

Kamminlun S. Vaiphei

Introduction

Increasing assertion of tribal identity today is a part of the overall process of social change and modernization of the tribes. The massive induction of administrative resources into the hitherto isolated areas is the main factor for this new phenomenon. Consequently, small and distinct local groups combine to form bigger groups and adopt a common appellation, through the creation of some socio-political organization, which may be viewed as an adoptive mechanism to the changed social, cultural and political circumstances. The process of modernization has also intensified the search for an identity on the part of the tribal communities. The *Zo*, an ethnic group of people, is one among such tribes who are becoming conscious of the need to be a viable human resource. No doubt in identity movement for wider social base, there are ethnic and political overtones, however, the fringe or the marginal groups when unified for political action are a source of strength in a struggle for economic and political advantages as deprived people. Large or small these groups stand out as one ethnic group carving for a distinct socio-cultural identity and displaying ethnic psyche; seeking socio-cultural and economic protection, reservation and so forth. It must also be noted that the rising tide of ethnic self-consciousness is partly due to the prospect of increased social and political gains as against the entrenched class.

Most of the tribal of the North-Eastern States have no early history or written records nor any script of their own and their origin and history are lost in the midst of antiquity. The only records or sources from which their history can be studied or known are folklores, folk songs, folk tales and legends. The *Zo* ethnic group is one glaring example in this field and constant research is the need of the hour to once again establish what is lost in the past.The *Zo* family in their course of history fragmented and disintegrated giving birth to many tribes and clannish groups. Oral traditions or legends as maintained by the elders of the *Zo* ethnic group states that *Zo* people are hailed from the first-three brothers, i.e., *Chongthu/ Songthu, Songja and Zahong/Zahawng* (the progenitor of the Suantak people), who first dwelt in a cave or in a rock having a cavity popularly known by the people as *'Khul' or 'Sinlung' or 'Chhinlung* which tradition says to be somewhere in China but the exact location is still untraceable by research scholars and anthropologists.

The *Zo* ethnic group has freedom and sovereignty in their land. Their territory stretches from the Chindwin river in the east, the Naga Hills in the north, North Cachar Hills in the west and the Chittagong Hills Tract in the south.[1]

The *Zo* ethnic groups are found in three countries, i.e., India, Myanmar and Bangladesh and also in some other countries of the world. Prior to 1937 the *Zo* ethnic groups live as one in the Indian sub-continent. However, when Myanmar is separated from India Sub-Continent in 1937, the Chin Hills and Upper Chindwin of the *Zo* people went to Myanmar. After India's independence in 1947, Bangladesh was separated from the Indian Sub-Continent. Then, Chittagong Hill Tracts went to East Pakistan now Bangladesh in 1971. Thus, *Zo* ethnic group were scattered into three independent countries or three different administrative units and the consequence is the difficulties in the gigantic work for common platform or amalgamation.[2]

Inter-tribal wars, conflict between the tribes and lack of arable land in the country they adopted as their home caused *Zo* people to lose their racial harmony. As they grew in size, quarrels erupted between groups and even relatives were separated and driven to different regions. As a result of these kinds of forces the *Zo* ethnic group gradually developed differences in their social, political, cultural and religious system.

Zo people have a tradition of naming their clans after the head of each clan.[3] The oral genealogy of *Zo* claims that a man named *Zo* was the progenitor of all the *Zo* people. The generic name *Zo* has no relation with the geographical climatic term "ZO" and it might have been derived from the real ancestor known by the name *Zho or Zo,* who was supposed to have established or set up a Zho-Dynastic rule in China from 1027-256 B.C. The argument or the hypothesis is that in ancient time the name of the ruling dynasty became the identity for its subjects.[4] In support of this idea, Dr. Vumkhohau, a scholar, a historian and a diplomat in Myanmar (Burma) asserted that *Zo* as progenitor and thus all races, clans of this particular group of Tibeto-Burman directly descended from *Zo*. One among these tribes is the Suantak (recognized as the Vaiphei tribe under the Constitution of India Scheduled Tribe Order 1950 which was amended as the Scheduled Castes and Scheduled Tribes Act in 1956); which later was divided into many sub-clans such as the Baite-Suantak (this group of people is mostly found among the Thado speaking group and they used Thado dialect for communication); Dopmul-Suantak (they are found among the Zou people and they speak Zou dialect); Sizang-Suantak (they are found in the Siyin Valley, Burma and speak the Sizang dialect); Sailo-Suantak (they are found in Mizoram and they speak the Mizo language); and the Vaiphei-Suantak (speaking the Vaiphei dialect found in Manipur, Meghalaya and North Cachar Hills in Assam).

The Vaiphei is recognized under the Constitution of India Scheduled Tribe Order 1950) was classified as the Old-Kuki by John Shakespeare.[5] However, this group of people (Vaiphei) was none other than the Suantak group of people. The Suantak like any other Zo ethnic groups (members of the Kuki-Chin-Mizo) maintained their genealogical tree and their earlier history is based on legends and oral traditions.

The Suantaks which fall under the Mongoloid stock of races have deep lineal roots in the Chin-Hills as 'Twantak/Siyin/Shizang' and is one of the Chin-Kuki-Mizo tribes living mainly in Manipur, Mizoram, Meghalaya, North Cachar Hills in Assam, Kabaw Valley and the Chin State of Myanmar (Burma). Their language 'Vaiphei' which is an ethno linguistic term, i.e., a term that stands both for the tribe and for the language belongs to the Kuki-Chin sub-groups of the Tibeto-Burman language family.[6] The origin of the name 'Vaiphei' itself is still debated but the general understanding is that it is a name used to denote the people (the Suantak) who once lived in the village "Phaiza" in Chin Hills later known as 'Khua-Vaiphei' due to its breadthwise horizontal expansion. There is a common belief among the Zo ethnic groups/communities that their ancestors emigrated from a place called Sinlung or Chhinlung or Khul or Khur, somewhere in South China where they moved down to Chindwin Valley and the Chin Hills in Burma.[7] The Suantaks believed that it is from the Chin Hills that they adopted the nomenclature 'Vaiphei' as their identity. According to the genealogy as maintained by the Suantak (Vaiphei speaking) people in Manipur, there is a claim that they are the descendants of 'Neilut' and 'Vanglua' clan who are the second and fourth sons of Suantak.[8]

Origin of the Suantak

In the words of Z. Z. Lien, "The Vaipheis are one of the most sophisticated and well cultured tribes, having deep lineal roots in the Chin Hills as 'Thuantak' or 'Suantak'.[9]

Like other tribes of Manipur, the origin of the Suantaks is shrouded in mystery. The Suantaks in general assented that they were originated from a cave called 'Khul'. The oral geneological tree maintained by the Suantaks of Manipur and Chin Hills State of Myanmar extended supporting the Khul Cave origin theory of the Suantaks. However, there is not any written text which can definitely indicate the place and time where the Khul is located and when.

It is said that, Zahawng once lived in the subterranean world. One day Nuaimangpa the king of the subterranean world conducted a *Chawn,* which means a feast. In the feast, all the youths contested in the high jump (jumping over a mithun). Zahawng who was doing *nangmet* (cutting bamboo into pieces for binding things) was called to join the high jump. However, when he jumped he hurt one pregnant woman with his sword and she died. Zahawng felt so sad and shy. He decided to leave the subterranean world. However, the *khul* (cave) was closed by a big stone and a big serpent called *gulheupi* was on the side of the stone. *Vangalpa* a colleague of Zahawng lifted the stone and Zahawng covering his head with a thick cloth called *phoipi* killed the serpent and cut it into three pieces. It was because he opened the gate of the cave for many and so he was called Zahawng (*Za* means many; *Hawng* means open or open for many). It is because of this that when his descendants (the Suantaks) killed an enemy or a tiger, they shout or chant what is called *Hanla* (songs of the brave) saying-

"Kathange Kathange, Khulsin Dongkot Kahonge"

Free Translation:

"I am famous, I am famous, I open the gate of the Khul."

Here the one who shouts *hanla* is identified with his ancestor Zahawng and says "I open the gate of the cave."

There are different versions regarding the origin of Zahawng. Some tradition says it was Sattong, descendants of Zahawng, who came out of the Khul (cave). Some Suantaks (descendants of Suantak) claim that it was Suantak who came out of the Khul (cave). Another version also says that it was Tualzamang the father of Zahawng who came out of the Khul. Thus, Tualzamang named his son as Zahawng because he opened the gate of the Khul (cave). Moreover, the descendants of Hangmi identified their progenitor Hangmi with Zahawng and the Suantaks identified their progenitor Suantak with Zahawng. However, it is commonly agreed that it was Zahawng who came out of the Khul (cave).

After they came out of the Khul, the Suantaks family lived at a place called *Khuasinlung*. A tradition says that a darkness called *Thimzing*, which lasted for seven days, and seven nights occurred during this period. Some say it was during the time of Zahawng and some say it was during the time of Suantaks. Moreover, it is sad to learn that many identified Suantak with Zahawng.

The Zo ethnic group does not have a proper written record about their origin. There are different versions and theories regarding this. The result is that there are many discrepancies on their genealogical tree. According to the people of the Chin Hills, the first man (human being) was Zo. Zo has two sons—Kipmang and Cinhil. The son of Kipmang was Nawphut and that of Nawphut was Nawsawng. Nawsawng was the father of Songthu/Chongthu. Songthu/Chongthu was the father of Sunmang and Sunmang was the father of Songkip, Songza, Zakhai and Zahawng. Songkip was the progenitor of Nongchom, Akgal, Manlun, Manchuang, Mangson, Hangvung, Matmang. Songza was the progenitor of Mate, Hehthang, Langsun and Langen. Zahawng was the progenitor of Thadous and Suantaks. According to them, Seaktak/Sehtha, the progenitor of the Thadous and Suantak were brothers. Pu. Vumkhohau in his book *A Profile of Burma Frontier Man* states that Pu. Zahawng had three sons — Tohin, Seaktak and Suantak was the youngest one among them.

However, the versions of Thadous and the Suantaks in Manipur reveals that Songthu/Chongthu is the progenitor of the Titou (Doungels), Tohin (Thadous), Touthang (Lamhaus) and Zahawng is the progenitor of the Suantaks and the people of the Thanglun clan, i.e., the Gangtes.[10] Suantak was the main progenitor of the Siyin (Sizang Suantak), Sailo (Mizoram) and the Suantaks who are recognized now as the Vaiphei under the Constitution of India. An early settlement on the eastern side of the Siyin Valley was named after him and still bears the name.[11]

Separation among Suantak Descendants

The Zo ethnic groups believed that their foremost fathers settled in Ciimnuai, Saizang from where they spread to other places in the Chin Hills. Local tradition has it that the ancestors of some of the people forming the principal tribes ascended the Chin land from Kale-Kabaw and the Myittha river valleys. One group went there by the foothill Burmese village, Yazagyo, and they are the clans now inhabiting the north-east region of Tedim. Another group went up Mount Kennedy from the Kale Valley. Then they descended the western slope of Kennedy peak and settled in Zangpitam above Thuklai village in Siyin Valley and later they continued their move to Sokte areas. Their descendants spread along various routes from Ciimnuai and are believed to be the ancestors of the present tribes of Suantak, Sokte, Kamhau, Thado. The remainders moved from the Myittha River valley into the Central Chin country and were the ancestors of the Zanniats, Zahaus, Tashons of Falam and various tribes of Haka.[12]

Lehman confirmed the north to southward movement of the Mongolian population (Mon-Khmer, Tibeto-Burman, Tai-Chinese). He wrote, *"Historical, linguistics, archaeology, and racial relationships definitely indicate that the south-east Asian peoples, especially the ancestors of the various hill and plain peoples did indeed come from the north, but they did not come as the social and cultural units we know today and cannot be identified with any particular groups of today. History showed, however, that both the hill and plain peoples have moved about the general region of south-west China and south-east Asia over considerable distance for many centuries, until the recent past."*[13]

Sir George Scott wrote, *"Tibeto-Burman migrating from the eastern Tibet into Burma came from the Tien Shan, that range of mountains which divides Chinese from Turkestan into northern and southern sections.*[14] It is difficult to ascertain the exact dates of the Zo people's entry in the Shan states due to lack of historical records. The local names of the present Shan states, the borderless of Yunnan-Burma and Thailand, such as Sinlum, Kutkai, Lampang, Monglem, etc., indicated that they could have been given by the Zo's. For example, Sinlum could have been given by the Zomi (Zo's) after the name of their ancestral place, Sinlung/Chhinlung, when they settled in the Shan states.[15]

It was said after a prosperous settlement in the Shan states for centuries, the Zomi (Zo's) migrated from Shan states to the Chindwin plain and Kabaw Valley due to severe famine.[16] Suantak and his ancestors are said to have already lived with other Zo race of Tibeto-Chinese origin in 'Khol-Khen' (which was said to be on the present site of Kalewa town of Kale-Kabaw valley in Myanmar). While living at Khol-Khen, fear gripped them as the Shans were advancing fast in expanding their kingdom. As such, they shifted their village and settled down at 'Khol-Jang' which later became the city of Kalemyo.[17]

Regarding their movement in northern plains of Burma, B. Lalthangliana writes, "*Because of the penetration of the Shans, again Zo people left the Kabaw valley in different directions for the Chin Hills.*" He also further asserts that, "*Though it might not be exact, it is most probable that all the Zo descendants might have left the Kabaw valley by 1200 A.D.*"[18] Hence, the migration of Suantak family into the rugged yet forested hills of Chin Hills must have started in about 1250 A.D. And it is most probable that they were shanghaied to flee by the infiltration of the invading Shans.[19]

From Khol-Jang (Kalemy), Suantak descendants rest for some days in a mountain peak Thangvum that has been re-named as Kennedy Peak today. Moving towards the southern direction, Suantak set up his own village with his family named Khawasak[20] also known as Suantak-Jang by many. Vaiphei tradition has it that the Suantak lived peacefully in Khawsak without any fear of strong invader or an enemy for many years.

In the late sixteenth century, Seipui (Lusei clans/village) and Tedim (Thado and Guite clans) fought wars and the Seipui villagers captured Chhuahlawma, son of Ralna[21], son of Boklua (Sizanga), son of Ngengu (Nenu), son of Suantak. Chhuahlawma was adopted by the captors and was given a wife. His first son was named Zahmuaka by his wife. Zahmuaka had six sons. They were Zadenga, Paliana, Thangluaha, Thangura, Rivunga and Rokhuma. Thangura was the grand-father of Sailoa, whose descendants ruled Lusei and other Zo clans who occupied the Lusei or the Mizo Hills.[22] The descendants of Thangura, the Sailos, became the most powerful chief in the Lushei Hills.[23]

From Khawsak the Suantak family moved to Saizang village which was already crowded with people belonging to various clan and tribes of the Chin-Kuki-Mizo-Zomi group. For how long the Suantak people made their home in Saizang village cannot be reckoned. All the information one could offer is that, Suantak people multiplied greatly here. However, due to scarcity of drinking water and arable land that resulted from explosion of population, Suantak family once again left Saizang for good with a number of their congeners for Chim-nuai in around 1300 A.D.[24] from Chim-nuai, the Suantak clans moved southward and settled down on the banks of Ngatan stream. But due to unknown reason, the descendants of Suantak from his first wife, i.e., the Neilut groups settled on the eastern bank whereas that of the descendants of the second wife, i.e., Ngengu groups settled on the eastern bank. Nevertheless, the Suantak clans keep in touch in family and social affairs. During their stay on the banks of the Ngatan stream, the Suantak population increased considerably which necessitated them to look for a new settlement. Opinions were drawn to which direction they should proceed. However, the elders among the Ngengu sections opted to occupy again Khawsak village, which was the first settlement set up by their progenitor Suantak. On the contrary, the Neilut sections opted to search a new and better place, which could accommodate them all. Eventually, both the parties could not come into terms and other clans of the Neilut and Ngengu were given freedom to choose either to move with the Neilut or the Ngengu. As a result, they Suantak descendants scout into two groups towards opposite directions to make an epoch in the chronicle of the Suantak tribe.

A large number of Vanglok (Vanglua in Vaiphei) descendants moved with the Neilut group, few number of Vanglok descendants resettled with other Sijang members under the leadership of Ngengu in their ancestral home-land Khawsak. And in the meantime, Neilut and his band of younger clans moved towards the far north-west of Chin Hills by crossing the Ngun-Tui (Manipur river) to open a new chapter in the history of the contagious tribes of Indo-Myanmar.[25]

As there was, in Vaiphei vocabulary, a 'sipi' meaning 'brine spring', located at a place below the slope of where Ngengu and his brothers' descendants settled they received the name Siang' from their neighbours. Since then they came to be known as the 'Sijangte or Sijang Suantak'. Its name has been passed down in its perverted form as 'Siyin' by the Burmese, and in the British-Burma official records with the arrival of the colonialists.[26]

Leaving behind their cousin, i.e., Ngengu sections on the other bank of the Ngatan stream, the Neilut sections crossed Ngun river (Manipur river), thereon the hill ridge, they set up a village called Phaiza, later known as Khua-Vaiphei due to its breadth-wise horizontal expansion in around 1425 A.D.[27] The place was productive and great transformation took place in their cultural and economic life. In Phaiza or Khua-Vaiphei many cognate tribes too settled and the Suantak happens to be the last to leave.

Tradition says that there was a war between the Thadous and the Vaiphei (Suantak). The Suantak were very proud and said with a haughty spirit *"Can we not combine killing the Thadous with smoking tobacco pipe"*. In the war the spirit (demons) of Lunglen took the side of the Sitlhous (Thadous) and the Suantak were defeated in the war. They surrendered to the Thadous and gave the ivory of Sipi known as *Sipite Saiha* and the Thangniang Dak (the gong of Thangniang) to the Thadous as peace negotiation gifts. After this defeat, the Suantak became very weak and could not live at Phaiza-Khuavaiphei because of inter-tribal conflict and because of the frequent attack carried out by the Pawis. Thus, the Lutnguls (Sub-clan within the Suantak) shifted to Haimual and settled there. [28] At Haimual too, the Pawis did not give them a peaceful life. Life at Chin Hills was not stable anymore in any form as well-armed Pawi warrior on the south; Sukte warrior on the north and east surrounded them.

Unable to withstand the frequent inter-tribal wars and to escape the impending dangers surrounding them, the Suantak split up into three different sections with each group marching towards different destination.

1. Majority of the Hansing, Khaute, Thangniang proceeded towards Lungthul, Lunglen, Tuithang in Lushai Hills and made their settlement at Sialkal Tlang.
2. The Hanngul group stayed back among the Kamhau and settle at Tongjang village, Tiddim. However as the Tedim people used them for Vawktual Khawnan (as slaves) this group of the Suantak clan also proceeded towards Manipur in around the latter part of the nineteenth century as in the Manipur-Kamhau War., of 1857 this Hanngul group were still with the Kamhau fighting for Kamhau.
3. Majority of the Lutngul, Leisel, Thanglet, Dak-on, Dakthang, Neihsial, Luangte, Chawnlu, Buite, Mate, Gangte, Hawinge, etc., settled at Haimual Luangpawn under the Chiefship of the Lutngul clan. From this Haimual Luangpawn village the Suantaks proceeded towards Manipur under the leadership of the following:

1. Pauneimang Lutngul
2. Zakhuathang Lutngul
3. Lutzangul Lutngul
4. Pauzakhup Lutngul
5. Sawipimang Luangte
6. Vungzangul Leisel
7. Bawla Thanglet
8. Lulzathang Neihsial
9. Pakhai Sengtong
10. Sellunthang Khaute
11. Kamthat Hangul
12. Zawmsing Buite
13. Semthat Thangniang
14. Tuanthaw Pulam (Neichal)
15. Zangngul Chawnlu
16. Pauhen Mate
17. Zawnngul Baite
18. Ngulhawl Gangte
19. Neihen Lutngul
20. Lutzamang Thanglet
21. Dakkhawmang Hangsing
22. Chawikhawhau Hawinge

It is said that while proceeding towards they were unable to cross the Tuivai due to its high current. So, *Pauzakhup Lutngul, Lutzathang Neihsial* and *Soipimang Luangte* took the courage of swimming to the other side of the river so as to make a rope bridge across the river. It is said that this group crossed the Tuivai river with much difficulty by walking passed the rope bridge. On reaching the Manipur territory, they first made their settlement known by the name Maokot, in present day Churachandpur.

Unable to establish a well-settled life best known to them they once again left Maokot and established Suangpijang village; from Suangpijang they moved to Thangching Koubru Hills; from Thangching Koubru Hills to Natakjang; from Natakjang to Mahadev Hills (Ukhrul District). It is from this Mahadev Hills that a hunting party of the then King Gambhir Singh took notice of them and which on his advice they settled at *Mongba Hanba Forest (Mahabali)* area. While settling in Mahabali area, they feel bored as the place was far from deep woods where they could practice hunting and slash and burn culture. Moreover, the Raja issued a decree –'The decree was that all the Suantak men must hold a gun in their hands' which means 'all the Suantak men must join the Manipuri army' and all the Suantak ladies must hold a broomstick which means 'they would be used as a slaves to clean up the palace'. Unable to comply with the decree, they left Mahabali and found settlement near Thoubal river. They named the place Kamuching meaning *'the hill of mourning'* as many of them perished due to unknown epidemic. To escape the death valley the Suantak people regroup at *'Bawkjang'* (which they fortified it so as to prevent themselves from enemy invasion or raid) the present day Salam Patong where their church is being planted presently. From Bawkjang they moved up the hills and on the top they established a fortress and they named the place *'Kulbung Veng'*. After finding a settled life in this Kulbung Veng the people performed the famous *"Thajing Lap"* (Autumn Dance) for the first time in Manipur under the leadership of – *Vungzangul Leisel, Lulzathang Neihsial, Soipimang Luangte, Neihen Lutngul, Semthat Thangniang, Pauhen Mate, Tuanthaw Pulam, Ngulhawl Gangte, Sellunthang Khaute.* A stone was erected and the stone still stand as where it was erected and can be seen by all. They used to perform this dance even in Chin Hills as a sign of their well settled life free from any kind of hardship and it lasted for three (three Months).[29]

Enrouting Palsang and Darlawn (Mizoram) from Maokot, the Tongkhothang section resettled at Hiang-Tuinek from the last part of 1833 to the last part of 1834. Simultaneously, in 1835 A.D. Tongkhothang raised Suangpilon (now Suang-puilawn) with 200 households and his younger brother Mangzasum raised Sialkal Tlang with 100 households in the northern hills of present Mizoram or the Lushai Hills.[30] Sialkal was raided by the Pawi warriors; hundreds of them were killed and many taken as captives. After Silkal was devoid, Tongkhothang moved out of the Lushai Hills and settled at Sungkang in Chin Hills. In this Suangkang village, they lived independently for about four years. But the Suktes penetrated the area in 1844. Subsequently, they claimed the area as within their territory and demanded them to pay tributes. As a result, some leaders of the Suangkang headed by two diplomats by the name *Kampithang* and *Papum*, rushed to Khuasak immediately. They beseeched Khuppau (Sizang Suantak) the then chief of Khuasak to shelter them. Khuppau, then, responded warmly saying, *"Here we are 80 households, and with another more 30 households from my cousins Vaipheis (Suantak); whom shall we fear anymore?"* The same day a number of Khuasak volunteers were dispatched and within the night all the villagers of the Suangkang were deported at Khuasak.[31]

The Vaiphei (Suantak) *'made a pact with the Siyins (Sizang Suantak) by the customary tradition of touching one another with buffalo tails, to help each other in time of war'*.[32] There was normalcy and stability in the lives of the Vaiphei-Suantak and the Sizang-Suantak for nearly half a century until the British campaigned the upper realm of Burma from the last quarter of the nineteenth century.

Consequent to the intrusion of the British troops, the people of Khawsak (Vaiphei and Siyins) abandon their village and took refuge in the forest.[33] Life became miserable and the British were no match with their superior firepower. The Vaiphei elders subscribed unanimously to move out of Chin Hills at the earliest available opportunity. Naturally, yielding to the decision of their elders, hordes of Vaiphei (Suantak) proceeded northwards from the Chin Hills in the month of May 1981. The same month they reached the soil of Southern Manipur, and sojourned one year at one place (now Umtal village). The following year (1892), they moved further northwards and settled at another place in a stone's throw from Mualnuam village, which was set up only a year or two earlier before they came here. After neighbouring Maulnuam for three years, they settled down on the bank of Tui-Vai River in 1895. On the bank of Tuivai, they raised three villages, which were in close vicinity. These villages were named as Thuangchm, Teikot and Mualnga. At the same time, some of them were dispatched to survey and look out for a better place other than these. Finally, in around the month of April/May 1898, they settled at a place called *Maite* which was named and deserted by a group of Hmar tribe nine years before the Vaiphei (Suantak) came here. Basing at this place, a number of Vaiphei (Suantak) villages began to flourish in the southern regions of Manipur from 1899 onwards.[34]

The Suantaks are spreading over the Chin-Hills State of Myanmar, Manipur and Mizoram in the north-eastern region of India. Mainly the Suantaks are found inhabiting Churachandpur district, Senapati district and Chandel district in Manipur.

The district wise settlements of the Suantak in Manipur are given in the Table below:

Sl. No.	*Name of the Districts*	*Name of the village*	
1.	**Churachandpur**	1. Bualjang	21. S Kawtlian
		2. Bisanmual	22. Sumtuk
		3. B Phicham	23. Saipum
		4. B Vaiphei Veng	24. S Bualkawt
		5. Compound Veng	25. Tangmual
		6. Hill Town	26. Tualnuam
		7. Headquarter Veng	27. Thingchawm
		8. Laika Mualsau	28. Thawroiluak
		9. Loklaiphai	29. Torbung
		10. Lingsiphai	30. Tuikham
		11. Liklai	31. Kangvai
		12. Leisang	32. K Kawtlian
		13. Mualkawt	33. Zikpi Tampak
		14. Mata	34. Zews Colony
		15. New Mata	35. Chawngkhawzo
		16. Neihsial veng	36. Chiangpi
		17. Ningthiching	37. C Munpi
		18. Panglian	38. Dawzang
		19. Pengjang	39. D Munhawi
		20. Phuaisanphai	40. D Munlui

Sl. No.	*Name of the Districts*	*Name of the village*
		41. D Lopum
		42. Geltamjang
		43. Kawlhen
		44. K Munpi
		45. Khawzim
		46. Khantang
		47. K Tuili
		48. Lungchuang
		49. Luangpi
		50. Mualdak
		51. Munlai
		52. N Saikawt
		53. Naupanglon
		54. Puaktam
		55. Suangpha
		56. Sailum
		57. Sainoulian
		58. Sanglel
		59. Thingkeu
		60. Tawnglawn
		61. Thencham
		62. Tallian
		63. Vantungbung
		64. B Munpi
		65. Bualtang
		66. Leizangphai
		67. Mualhoichiang
		68. Maite
		69. Mualkui
		70. Phaipheng
		71. Phailianbung
		72. Phunchongzang
		73. Phainuam
		74. Phaiba
		75. Sinjang
		76. S Tuili
		77. Tuipiphai
		78. Tuikumvallum
		79. T Phaikhawlum
		80. Thiakbung
		81. Umtal
		82. Bijang
		83. K Mualzawl
		84. Lengluang
		85. Leikawt
		86. Tuaitengphai
		87. Tualnuam
		88. Buallian
		89. Belpuan
		90. Belbing
		91. Bualmual
		92. B Tuallian
		93. Dongzang
		94. Dumdephai
		95. Gangpimual
		96. Hawnglian
		97. Hengken
		98. Khonuamphai
		99. Lailoiphai
		100. Lungil
		101. M Phaimual
		102. Mualjol
		103. Makhao
		104. Mualvom
		105. N Lengkawt
		106. Pantha
		107. Sugnu Centre
		108. S Geltui
		109. Salvaphai
		110. S Bualkawt
		111. Dumlian
		112. T Lamlai
		113. T Kawtlian
		114. Tanglian
		115. Tuiningkhal
		116. Vawkbual
		2 Senapati
		1. Changoubung
		2. North Changoubung
		3. South Changoubung
		4. Suangpekjang
		5. Leimakhong Mission Veng
		6. L Phaijang
		7. L Champhai
		8. Leilonkhawpi
		9. Misihobi
		10. Lawibuk
		11. Harauthial
		12. Kharam Vaiphei
		13. Nakhawjang
		14. S.Molnom

Sl. No.	*Name of the Districts*	*Name of the village*
		15. Geljang
		16. Happy Valley
		17. Thianzawl
		18. L.Phaijang
		19. Mualkawn
		20. Pheitaiching
		21. Canan
		22. Heirawklian
		23. K.Tangnuam
		24. K.Lairawk
		25. Sarawnphai
		26. Kamutampak
		27. Lairawk Vaiphei
		28. Langmaiching
		29. Kamuching
		30. Bewlahland
		31. Salam Patong
		32. Thanga
		33. VaipheiPakai
		34. Phailengjang
		35. Sialhau Vaiphei
		36. Haukhuangphai
		37. Elimphai
		38. Nuangpuak Centre
		39. B. Phainuam
		40. Phawibi
		41. S.Kanan
		42. Nongpokphai
		43. K. Thiamdawi
		44. L. Munlui
		45. L. Phaikawt
		46. Leilon Suangtun1.
3	**Tamenglong**	1. Lengluang,
		2. Leikot,
		3. Mualjawl,
		4. Changjal,
		5. Bijang,
		6. Tualnuam,
		7. Tuaitengmun,
		8. Suangphu
4	**Ukhrul**	1. Lamlai Chingphei
		2. Litan
		3. Lakhan
		4. Mongngeljang
		5. Meiti
		6. Lanlei

Sl. No.	Name of the Districts	Name of the village
5	**Chandel**	
		1. Chalsun Tengnoupal
		2. Maipi Mangsom
		3. B. Bongjang
		4. S. M. Lhangjol
		5. L. Bongjol
		6. Khumkhot Village
		7. Chongjang Village
		8. Maojang
		9. T. Jangnom
		10. Sibong Area
		11. H. Vanomjang
		12. Tatjang
		13. T.P.L Phalbung Area
		14. Moreh

Source: Vaiphei Peoples' Council Electoral Roll – 2011

There are more than three hundred households in both Imphal East and Imphal West Districts. In Imphal East and West Districts the Vaipheis are mainly concentrated at New Lambulane, Old Lambulane, Lamphelpat, Langol, Mantripukhri, Salamching, Zomi Villa and Cananveng.

Polity

The Suantak traditional polity was based on chieftainship. Village administration was the only traditional political institution. The chief was the head of the village and all the administrative and judiciary powers were vested in his hand. No subjects in the village can challenge the Chief's authority or act against the wishes of the chief. The chief has an arbitrary power and even can expel any subjects who acted contrary to his will from the village.

In the village administration, the chief was assisted by his council of elders. The council was constituted by the elders of the village, nominated by the chief. Usually the term of the council was one year but extendable by the chief at his will. The strength of the council was fixed by the chief and differed from village to village and the chief has every right to reshuffle and replace any member whom he found disloyal to his authority at any time. All the important decisions of the village affairs were taken by the council. However, the chief possessed veto power to dismantle the decision taken by the council and his decision in every matter was final and binding. Like today's minister, the members of the council of elders were allotted certain portfolios for the smooth and better functioning of the village administration. The main portfolios of the council are :

1. *Siamang* : Siamang is the official in-charge of the village administration. He is appointed by the chief from among the village elders who had outstanding experience and skill in the field of administration. Siamang has a significant role to play in the village. His most important duty is to maintain the functioning of the village administration smooth and transparent. He has to look after the day to day affairs of the village and update the chief about it. Siamang has the right to suggest the chief to take up any welfare programme for the benefit of the villagers.

   Another duty of Siamang is to give report to the Chief of those who committed a crime and acted contrary to the village norms. The chief, would then issue a summon letter to the wrongdoers and befitting action is taken up. If the crime is severe, heavy fine can be imposed. It is said that whatever report made by the Siamang to the Chief, the chief accepted without any complaint as truth. So, in the Suantak village, Siamang became very powerful and being only next to the chief he earned the respects of the villagers.
2. *Pachawng* : Pachawng is the official in-charge of tax collection. His main duty is to collect taxes. Tax is the main source of income for the chief. Therefore, giving taxes is necessary for every villager, but widows and the relatives of the chief are exempted from all kinds of taxes. A person who is unwilling

to give tax faces grave penalty with heavy fine. Some of the most important taxes enjoyed by the chiefs are :

(a) *Paddy Tax:* Paddy Tax is the most important tax every household should give to the chief at the end of every harvest. The amount of Paddy Tax differed from village to village. But, in general, one household gives paddy worth to three times (measured in mustard oil tin) for one field. If a person cultivates two fields or farms, he must give tax in double.

At the end of every harvest, the Pachawng informed every house of the village the date scheduled for the collection of the Paddy Tax by the chief. On this day, the chief killed a pig called 'Changseu Sa' and offered a grand feast and rice beer to all the villagers as a sign of his gratitude and love to them. Sometimes, the chief also exempted paddy tax to those who did not gather adequate paddy for the year. In big villages, the chief never engaged himself in cultivation and fully depended on the Paddy Tax. However, the chief is also sometimes generous enough to provide paddy to those villagers who are extremely poor.

(b) *Flesh Tax :* It is an important tradition of the Suantak to give Flesh Tax to the chief. Usually, the hind leg of the animal is given as the Flesh Tax. When a villager killed or trapped a wild animal (deer, wild boar, tiger, bear. etc.), he has to give the hind leg of the animal as Flesh Tax to the chief. However, in case of small animal, tax is exempted.

(c) *Honey Tax :* A certain quantity of honey from a particular beehive is also given as tax to the chief when the villagers took honey. However, there is no fix amount or quantity of honey to be paid from one beehive and it is to be decided by the chief and the person concerned.

(d) *Tax on Precious Things:* The chief also enjoyed taxes on precious things which can be sold, such as gold, diamond, cane and timber etc. If a person finds gold or diamond and the like, he must give certain amount of money to the chief as tax. The amount to be paid depends on the price of the sold items.

3. *Tunpu:* Tunpu is the official in-charge of youth affairs in the village. His duty is to look the overall affairs of the youths. He has to guide and lead the youths while performing social services such as beautification of the village surroundings, roads, ponds, etc. He also has to lead the youth in the field of games and sports.

4. *Tangsam* : Tangsam is in-charge of information and publicity. His main duty is to give information to the council members the schedule of meeting or assembly and communicate the resolution of the meeting to all the villagers. There is no fixed schedule for the council's meeting but it can be held at any time if the chief felt it necessary. The new council session usually fall in the month of January and it is in this session that the council decides which region of the land would be distributed for the year's cultivation. The villagers can only clear the areas or regions which the council confirmed would be distributed for cultivation purpose. In big villages, sites for paddy cultivation is distributed by holding a lottery draw but in the case of smaller village' people are free to choose the region they desired most for *jhum* cultivation.

   Whenever the village council held a meeting, it is the duty of the widows to prepare tea for them. The widows' in turn enjoyed certain privileges from the chief in return such as exemption from all kinds of village tax. Besides, the house of the widows are constructed free of cost by the youths of the village.

Apart from his administrative power, the chief also possessed extreme judiciary power in his hands. All the disputes and conflicts in the village are decided by the chief assisted by his council of elders and the verdict of the chief in every matter is final and binding.

It is interesting to learn how cases are decided by the chief and his council of elders. With a jar of rice-beer the chief and his council of elders can be approached for certain cases. The chief would then ask his council to conduct an enquiry and after enough enquiries is carried out the chief then summons the person with whom a case has been raised. On the day of the judgement, the chief orders his council to kill a pig called 'Salam-Sat' the cost, which is to be born by the culprit of the crime. Besides, the culprit is also made to pay heavy fines according to the weight of the crime. Sometimes, the chief can award equal punishment to both the disputed parties if he is unconvinced by the evidences produced by either of the parties.

Relating to cases of murder, the chief immediately summoned the murderer, and ordered him to kill a pig and prepare a meal called 'HIAMKHAM AN' which means a meal to cease the bloodshed. The chief then invited the family of the deceased and the case is decided according to the customary laws. According to the customary laws of the Suantak, a murderer is fined with one traditional shawl (PUANDUM), one pig and one mithun. After the meal is over, the chief made a strong appeal to both parties not to commit further bloodshed and also asked them to abide by his order. If further bloodshed is committed by any of the party further, then they are made to pay heavy fine or expel from the village.

There is also another way of giving judgment, i.e., based on swearing. The perpetrator of the crime is allowed to swear in the name of wild animals, may be tiger, lion and bear, etc., by biting the animals tooth. It is believed that if the person shielded the truth and swear, his life always ended up according to his oath. One particular way of swearing goes like this *"Lei leh Van in he hen, kei kadik lo ahi leh, Sakei in eithat hen"* which means "let the heaven and earth be a witness, if I'm found guilty of the crime, let the tiger devour me." This type of judgment is considered as the fairest way of deciding a case. Here, the punishment is to be delivered by the animals, the animals which the person spells out in his oath. So, for fear of the consequence which is placed at the disposal of the animal, the truth is always exposed to the king and his council of elders.

There is still another way to unearth the truth. In this practice, the conflicting parties are taken to a big river and make them swear in the name of heaven and earth. They are also asked to take a dive in the water. It is said that the party guilty of the dispute could not dive in the water for even one minute as they feel that the water is too hot. However, the party who is not guilty can easily dive in the water.

Another extra privilege enjoyed by the chief is that the villagers constructed his house free of cost. During the construction the chief has to kill a pig or a cow or any animal and feed the labourers everyday. However, feeding the labourers with meat is not compulsory to every chief. The house of the chief is generally located in the heart of the village. It is comparatively big and magnificent than other houses in the village.

The chief also held a supreme position in every festival and occasion. All the village festival and functions are usually inaugurated by the chief. In every occasion, a special meal is prepared for the chief. No festival and functions can be organized without the chief's knowledge. Relating to family festival or occasion like 'Bu-ai' or 'Sa-ai'; one must obtain prior permission from the chief for organizing such functions. The chief is entitled a portion of meat of every animal slaughtered in every festival.

The chief is the commander-in-chief of the village defence system. All diplomatic relations with the neighbouring villages or signing a treaty to extend help and co-operation in times of difficulties is done by the chief. At times of war or inter-village feud, the chief personally lead the village youths in raiding rival village.

Succession

The Suantak chiefs follow hereditary system of succession based on primo-geniture in which the eldest son succeeded his father. According to the custom of the Suantak, the eldest son of the chief, unless debarred by physical or mental disability, must inherit the land and property of his father. If the chief dies while his son is still young, the overall in-charge of the village administration must be taken up by the younger brother of the deceased chief till the young son attain maturity. Only when the young son became mature, he will resume the power of his father and then became the chief.

If the deceased chief has neither a son nor a brother, the chief post will be inherited by the head of the chief's clan. Adopted son has no right to inherit the properties of the deceased chief and also cannot claim the chief's post. Besides, the daughter of the chief also has no claim of the chief's properties. If the chief has more than two sons, the chief creates a new village and made the other sons the chief of the new village. Here it must be noted that, the eldest son should remain with his father and inherit his father's property. If the younger son, the chief of the newly created village died without a male issue all the land and properties and the chieftainships shall return to his father again.

If an ordinary Suantak wants to become a chief, he must obtain a permission to buy a land from the chief of his village. If the permission is granted, he can invite his relatives and friends to establish a new village and he can become a chief of that newly established village. Regarding the succession and chieftainship, he has to follow the same system adopted by the Suantak chiefs.[35]

Manipuri-Kamhau War (1857)

In the Treaty of Yandaboo, 1826 between the King of Burma and the British representatives Captain Pemberton, an imaginary line was drawn through the Zo country, and the hilly regions of present eastern and southern Manipur were given to Manipur. This area had been the home of Thado,

Hmar and Yo. During Kamhau's reign, Zo people moved to the north because of his territorial expansion. The Thado settled in the hilly regions south of Logtak (Loktak) Lake in Manipur, which belongs to Manipur according to the Yandaboo Treaty. The Kamhau regard this as their region and the Thado as their subjects. The Thado were also in conflict with the Guite, who settled to the south of them. The Guite lived in the villages of Lawmpi and Mualpi, and they were also subjects of Kamhau.[36]

We find the Soktes first called Kanhows (Kamhau) by the Manipuris at the end of the fifties, and from information locally acquired it would appear that Kanhow commenced to rule in about 1848. Guns have began to find their way into the hands of the Soktes at the end of Kantum's (father of Kamhau) reign, being acquired from Burma, Manipur and Lushai, and during Kanhow's lifetime the tribe became fully armed. After his father's death (Kantum) Kanhow who was the eldest at once adopted an aggressive policy, and although his father earned the title of "the conqueror" to Kanhow belongs the credit of consolidating the aliens into one tribe, whose name became a terror to Manipur, Lushai and Burma.[37]

The Kamhau-Manipur war began because of belief in witchcraft. Thus when the Thado accused the Guite of having witch power the Guite had to protect their dignity, and Chief Ngokhothang of the Guite attacked the Thado villages. The Manipur Maharaja Chandrakirti Singh (Ngameingam) had been disturbed by these outrages as well as other Kamhau activities in the area, and he resolved to punish the Kamhau. An expedition of 1500 men left for Tedim in January 1857, and the Maharaja placed such importance on the success of the operation, that he was carried in a palanquin and led the expedition himself.[38] In 1856 the Soktes committed a serious raid on a hill village in Manipur.[39] Kamhau-Hautinkhup chief of Tongjang in the Chin Hills annexed the southern part of the Manipur kingdom (presently Churachandpur).

The Meitei king vowed to get back the lost territories and keep looking for people who would be familiar with the geographical landscape but not of the people can do so. These Suantak groups of people apprise the Meitei king about their knowledge of the geographical landscape. Soktes and Siyins tell us that the Maharaja, who was carried in palanquin, led his army right upto Tedim, Kanhow allowing it to advance in peace. Kanhow meanwhile collected his forces at Tiddim (Tedim). Here, Yapow (Zapau) joined him with the Suktes, and the Siyin (Suantaks) under their chief also came to Tiddim to fight the common enemy.[40]

As a result the Manipuri king along with 59 Suantak warriors along under the command of *Ngultong founder-Chief of Salam Patong village,* and *Lutzakai* from the same village approached the Kamhau-Hautinkhup group. On reaching the river Tuivai the Manipuri armies along with these 59 Suantak warriors make a camp and settled at the bank of the Tuivai river for whole nine months.

While on the bank of the Tuivai river, these Suantak people came to learn about the presence of their Hanngul brethren on the side of the Kamhau-Hautinkhup army and the Hanngul group acknowledged the presence of the same. To mislead the Meitei, they felled pine trees on the top of the Lailun Hills. At night the Kamhau burned the logs to make it appear that a large army was camping on the hill. Kamhau then led the combined forces to meet the Meiteis a few miles north of the camp fires, where they surprised them by firing into their midst.[41] One can understand what one was communicating with each other. It was a herculean task for the Suantak warriors who accompany the Manipuri king to communicate in Manipuri as they were not fluent enough and also communicating in the Vaiphei dialect will cause more harm than good as their Hanngul brethren on the Kamhau-Hautinkhup side understand their language. The Suantak warriors fought the war with so much enthusiasm and courage despite knowing that they were fighting their own brothers. However, the Kamhau-Hautinkhup groups proved a better warrior using the guerrilla tactics. The Manipuri king lost the war and many soldiers perished; some of them shot; some of them drowned in the Tuivai river; some of them taken as prisoner.

The Manipuris tried to return home along the course of the Manipur river locally known as the Tuivai and the Soktes state that more were drowned in the river than were killed by the Chins (combined forces).[42]

It is also stated by the Suantak elders that, while the Manipuri forces retreated they were unable to cross the Tuivai river. Two Suantak warriors by the name Zakhothang Suantak and Pumkhojam Neihsial with their might held the rope bridge tightly (Leilawn Kidaw) and made the King and his men cross the Tuivai river. Suantak elders also stated that while on the other side of the river, the King was heavy hearted. Pumkhojam acknowledging the King's emotion approached him, firing a shot from his rifle and said, *'My King why are you so sombre, am I not here to protect you; with me besides none can harm you.'* After hearing the soothing words, it is said that the King smiles.[43]

After the defeat, a boundary line was drawn making the Tuivai river the line of control. It is said that the Meitei king named the place Churachandpur after his son's name Maharaja Churachand.

The Soktes assert that they captured forty guns, and the rewards of the Siyin-Suantak for their assistance was three Manipuris head. [44] After the 1857 war both the Kamhau and Sukte promised the king of Manipur they would no longer molest his subjects. But quarrels between the Thado, under Manipur jurisdiction and Guite under Kamhau, caused a continuous war like situation between the independent Kamhau and the British ruled Meitei. The British took more and more Manipuri affairs into their hands and they accused the Kamhau and Sukte of destruction actually caused by the Guite.[45] After this and during the rest of Kamhau's reign his people from time to time raided into Manipur but no more major escalation between the two is heard of.

The Siyin Rebellion 1888-1889

In 1886, the British annexed upper Burma and capture Thibaw, the King of Burma. He was transported to life to the Andamans, and his possessions were transferred to the British. The British then advanced to the Burmese western borders to occupy the Kale and Yaw valleys. (Kabaw fell into British hands in 1826).[46]

In 1887, after a short period in the Kale area, British administrative officer Captain Raikes sent out messengers to the Chief of Sukte, Kamhau, Sizang, Falam and Haka asking them to come down to the plains and meet him. The Sizang chiefs refused to go down by themselves but sent four warriors—Tunsuang, Hausuang, Doson and Tensang. A meeting was held on March 26, 1887 at the Kale Phongyikyang (monastery school). The topics were :

1. The British Government recognized Muang Pa Gyi as Governor (Sawbwa) of Kale state. The Sizang should in the future make no more raids within the Sawbwa's territory and no more slaves should be taken but could keep slaves already taken from the Kale area.
2. The British intended to open a trade route to Chittagong from Kale. Would the Sizang oppose it? Moreover, transport coolies (carriers) and guides would be needed which the Sizang should supply.
3. The British intended to visit the Letha range (Thangmual). Would the Sizang oppose them?

Tunsuang as the speaker of the delegation replied that they were willing to have friendly relations with the Sawbwa and had not attacked him since he was installed as Sawbwa. The route to Chittagong would have to pass through the Pawi country, and this has to be discussed with the Pawi. Tunsuang said that he opposed strongly any exploration by the British in the Sizang area. Should the British visit Letha Range (Thangmual), they should inform the Sizang prior to the visit; otherwise, as the people had never seen a white man before, the British visit could have a disastrous effect. Captain Raikes then presented the delegation 5 *gongs*, which measured 8 *tongs* (from finger tip to elbow) in circumference, five blankets, five pots (earthen ware) and 120 *hangkes* or Burmese longyis. The present were taken to the hills and divided among the Sizang Chiefs.[47]

On the return of the delegation the Sizang chiefs held a conference in which the delegation reported their impressions. *"These enemies (British) are different from other people we have ever seen. They are as white as goats. They clothed themselves from head to foot. They cover their feet with leather and we believe that they will not be able to climb the slopes of the Zo hills."* When the Sizang chief council discussed the terms of the British, they concluded that the British intention was to rule and dominate the Zo people, and that they were going to make the Zo people their slaves. Therefore, the chiefs decided to oppose and to attack them wherever they were. A few days later information was received that the British were building roads from Kale towards the Sizang country. The Sizang then sent a delegation demanding the British withdrawal. The British however ignored and the Sizang armed with all available arms, including knives, spears, bows and arrows and guns attacked the British. In the fight, Haumang (Khuasak), Sonawn (Buanman), Kimlam and Sonlam (Thangnuai) were killed and the British were driven back to Kale. Seventeen Burmese employed by the British were captured and taken prisoners.[48]

An expedition against the Chins on a modified scale was now sanctioned. It was determined to deal first of all only with the Siyins and to inflict on them such a crushing blow as not only to cripple them for the future, but also to terrify the Tashons into giving up the rebel Shwe Gyo Byu, his followers and the Shan captives. The month of November was spent in arranging for the expedition. Captain Raikes and his Assistant Mr. Hall busied themselves with obtaining intelligence regarding the Chins, their villages and the routes into their country. The plan of the campaign decided on was to march first against the Siyins (Suantak), the head village of the Siyins, and from this centre to deal with the surrounding villages of the tribe.[49]

The British then returned to road construction and reached Thuangthi (a plain hill boundary now called mile 9). The Sizang attacked and captured four guns and four mares and lost one man. The British then retreated to Kale for the second time (Kambale).[50]

On the 7th December, 1887 the Siyins (Sizang) commenced the fighting by mortally wounding, Lieutenant Palmer, R.E. who was in command of the Madras Sappers. He was shot through the stomach from an ambush closed to the stockade and died the next day and was buried at Kambale. On the 24th a sepoy of the 2nd Gurkhas was killed whilst covering the working party.[51]

On the 30th December, 1888 Sir George White arrived at Kambale (near Kalemyo) and accompanied the forces which continued steadily advancing up to the hills, the sappers assisted by coolies making a road in their track, along which were constructed rough stockade, in which the troops slept and rations were stored. On 27th January, 1889 the road making party was again confronted by Chins. The working party was sent back to the stockade and the troops, now unencumbered, attacked the enemy, who retired slowly, making a stubborn resistance, till they reach some formidable and skilfully placed stockades, where they made a stand. Sir George White joined the attacking party with a small reinforcement of the 42nd Gurkhas, and at once ordered, and took prominent part in the charge, which was brilliantly led by Lieutenant Colonel Skene, D. S. O. (afterwards killed in Manipur). General Sir George White, in the historic telegram No. 82 dated the 28th January, 1889 to the Chief Commissioner of Burma described the action as follows :

> *"Enemy yesterday attacked our working party on road above this and held our covering party, 40 British and 100 Gurkhas, from 9 till 2, when I arrived and ordered their positions to be charged. We carried all, driving them entirely away, getting off ourselves wonderfully cheaply, only one Norfolk dangerously wounded, enemy in considerable numbers using many rifles and plenty of ammunition. They fired at least 1000 rounds, standing resolutely until actually charged, even trying to outflank us. They lost probably about eight or ten, but they were carried down to Khuds at once. Most difficult enemy to see or hit I ever fought."*

The result of this action was a serious blow to the Siyins (Sizang) and they now realized that it was impossible to save their villages. On 22nd January, 1889 General Faunce proceeded to the summit of the Letha Range. No. 4 stockade was established on 31st January and No. 5 three days later. Accompanied by George White and Major Raikes, General

Faunce advanced on Koset (Khuasak) on 4th February, with a strong force. On the 13th the column left the camp at Koset (Khuasak) and moved to Tokliang where a post was built, the houses of the village furnishing material for it.[52]

The Battle of Tartan (4th May, 1889)

On 4th May, 1889 the last action of the expedition was fought and it merits full description. Some new huts had been noticed on the site of the Tartan, and to destroy these parties was sent from Fort White (Thuklai) on 4th May. The column, consisting of 65 rifles of the 2nd Battalion Norfolk Regiment and 60 rifles of the 42nd Gurkha Light Infantry, occupied the heights above New Tartan without opposition. The main body advanced with the intention of rushing the village, but encountered determined resistance from the Siyins, who were strongly posted in two stockades.

At the lower stockade, early in the action, second Lieutenant Michel felt mortally wounded. The troops at first endeavoured to turn out the defenders of the upper stockade by firing through the openings between the logs.

In this action one officer was killed and two (Captain Mayne and Surgeon Le Quesne) severely wounded and three men killed and eight wounded. Surgeon Le Quesne received the Victoria Cross for conspicuous coolness and gallantry displayed whilst dressing Lieutenant Michel's wound. On the Siyin side 29 Chins were killed and 11 wounded. As a result of the above battle the number of the Kimlai clan were greatly depleted by the British troops under Captain Westmoreland as the lives of women and children were not spared.[53]

The Suantak (Vaiphei) true to their allegiance assisted the Siyins (Sizang) in their war against the British. The list as told to Pu Vumkhohau by his uncle, Chief Pu Khuplian of Lophei on the 4th of July, 1960:[54]

1. Mang Thual, a commanding Vaiphei leader
2. Mangpi Lam
3. Kailal, The above three were the heroic leaders.
4. Thawng Khaw Lun
5. Pa Lal
6. Tawngpi Mang
7. Thang Ko Lian
8. Kai Lal
9. Pa Vel
10. Vungh Kam
11. Mangnei Khai
12. Kawltin Thang
13. Nei Thang
14. Pa Sum
15. Khawl Tiin
16. Lun Za Tawng
17. Minh Pau
18. Tong Lian
19. Thang Kap
20. Pau Tho
21. Vungh Za Pau
22. Thang Nei Khup
23. Vung Lian
24. Nei Pau
25. Pum Kam
26. Pi Mang
27. Awn Khup
28. Lul Khup
29. Pau Khaw Lun
30. Thang Bawng
31. Hau Zang
32. Thual Za Thang
33. Mat Kham

On March 6, 1888, all Sizang villages fell to the British. But the Sizang people did not surrender themselves nor their slaves as the British demanded. Instead they took to the jungle, and the fight went on.[55] Although the villages of Sizang, Kamhau, Sukte and Khuano had been burned, no one in eastern Zoram had submitted to the British. Khaikam of Khuasak moved his headquarters to Suangpi, from where he organized his resistance movement against the British. The Sizang lived for two years in the jungles, changing their hiding places whenever the British forces detected their whereabouts.[56]

By the end of 1893, the British managed to position small army detachments in all key villages. Their main object was to capture or eliminate Khaikam and Khuppau and their some 127 followers. All paths and all villages were closed to them, and they had to switch their headquarters to the jungles near Yazagyo. In May 1894, after their family members were taken hostage and threatened with death until the "rebels" surrendered, Khuppau, Khaikam, Vumlian and Suangson gave themselves up. This was the last group resisting the British rule. Khaikam was deported for life to the Andaman Islands, and all others were banished to Burma.[57]

Khaikam of Khuasak is the man who fought the British for the longest term in the whole of South-East Asia using Guerrilla tactics. He is the man who with his might and wisdom along with a sacrificial spirit fought for his country until his arrest in 1894. As a prelude to his courage and strength, he is given the title "Zogam Zeranimo" and he served in the Andaman jail for 17 years until his release in 1910.

S. Vaiphei gives a critical appreciation of the Siyin/Sizang Rebellion and at the same time adds that 'The Siyin/Sizang Rebellion is not the appropriate term, for it was not the Sizang who fought the British alone but their cousin Suantak (Vaiphei) also took part in the said Resistance under the commandership of Mangthual'. He further adds that the said resistance should be named or known as the "Suantak-British War of 1888-1889".

Conclusion

It can be asserted from the finding that the descendants of Suantak had spread among different communities of the Zo ethnic groups. However, senses of oneness and belonging to one ancestry have considerably changed their outlook in terms of various socio-political dimensions in the present days. Looking back to their past, small though they are and spread among their cognate tribes, the Suantak people having shared more or less relationship is deeply rooted in their ancestry. Nevertheless, we can also see that there has been a cordial relation with their neighbouring tribes but we also learn that due to certain economic and political reasons, peace and tranquillity is often disturbed where the stronger prevailed and the weaker seeking for safer environment. The Sailos can be considered to have almost walked away off the mainstream body, Suantak. Their history has already spoken itself that Sailo group emerged only after the prominence of Zamuaka who is the decendant of Suantak. The bloodline relationship maintained by the Suantak people is one significant point in determining their relation. This factor has been breached to the effect that they are looking forward in maintaining a stronger bond tying themselves today, when as for an instance, Unau Kut was celebrated in February 2001.[58]

The Suantak people in their most dark episode of their history during the pre-colonial period could have been their constraint relation with the Pawis. To them the Pawis were considered to that of warmonger or mercenaries. Some of the Suantak elders have held the Pawi responsible for their dispersement. Legend also says that the Pawis were strong at that time and wanted to expand their influences over others territory. Their continuing aggression led to the fall of various Suantak villages and in search of safer place move to different strong chief where they are sheltered. It also led the Suantak to migrate to the Manipur hills. The Suantak has reached the Manipur hills during the first quarter of the nineteenth century. Having settled in the land, they help the Manipuri King in his expedition against the Kamhau-Sukte in the year 1857. However, on the latter's side we also see the presence of their Suantak brethren aligned to the Kamhau side. The interesting part of this incident can be put that the Suantak brethren were on both the warring group.

The Vaiphei Suantak and the Siyin Suantak have lived together as a family since their origin. They were separated and acquired different names. The one group settled near Si (salt spring) and became to be known as Sizang (siyin) while the other group lived in Khawvaiphei and came to be known as Vaiphei. Their peaceful existence was disturbed by the rising tide of the Pawi invasion into their territory. Some Vaiphei Suantak had settled in this territory for some more time. The Chin Hills Expedition of the British forces came into direct contact with the Siyin principalities. Thus, this leads to Siyin Rebellion of 1888-1889. The Vaiphei Suantak and the Siyin Suantak had long time back made a pact to help each other in times of wars. True to their allegiance the Vaiphei Suantak under the leadership of Pu. Mangthual fought along side their Siyin relatives against the British. As a punishment for helping the Siyin, the British burnt a Vaiphei Suantak village which Carey and Tuck referred to as the last remnant of the Vaiphei village in the Chin Hills and noting them to have migrated toward north to joint the other Vaiphei group who have already left the Chin hill. Khaikam, the chief of Khuasak was the most prominent figure in this war. His heroic act is recalled till today.

Having ruled under the British administration for a long period, the introduction of Western education had considerably changed their way of life. Also Christianity have various transforming impact upon their culture and society. Introduction of modern system of administration have affected their practice of chieftainship, which was the centre of administration. Although chieftainship still prevails, however, it more or less acts as mere nominal. People can raise their head and reasoned on various matter on community issues. As already discussed the colonial and post-colonial period witness the formation of a number of social and political organizations. These organizations are meant to serve the community interest rather than a selected few. It has well served them in many ways. The Vaiphei National Organization was floated out to deal in matters of polity, the Young Vaiphei Association, a voluntary or a philanthropic organization and a student association called Zillai. All these, on their respective field had functioned for the cause of their community. Besides this Suantak Peoples' Council was also formed to unify all the Suantak under one banner. Till date, geographical boundary have divided these people and separated them, however, these hurdles are no longer a difficult task. They started to cross the boundary for better future campaigning to renew their long loss ties, relationship and their history.

REFERENCES

1. *Ahsijolneng*, Annual Magazine, Kuki Students' Organization Publication, Shillong, 2006, p. 45.
2. *Lawmgual*, Zillai Shillong Block , Silver Jubilee Souvenir, 2006, p. 43.
3. Zo Vumson, *History*, Aizawl, undated, p.6.
4. *Lawmgual, op. cit.*, p. 44.
5. J. Shakespeare, *The Lushai-Kuki Clans*, Delhi, 1994, p.76.
6. K. S. Singh, *The Scheduled Tribe People of India*, Vol. I, Delhi, 1994, p. 37.
7. Zo Vumson, *op. cit.*, p. 26.
8. S. Vaiphei, *Historical Background of the Vaiphei Tribes*, Seminar Paper, 29 October 1999, p. 3.
9. Z. Z. Lien, *The U-New People*, Churachandpur, 1981, p. 167.
10. Rev. S. Prim Vaiphei (ed.), *Customary Laws and Women in Manipur*, 1995, p. 42.
11. Vumkhohau, *A Profile of Burma Frontier Man*, Bandung—Indonesia, 1972, p. 214.
12. *Ibid*, p. 297.
13 . F.K. Lehman, *The Structure of Chin Society*, The University of Illinois Press, 1963, p. 11.
14. Sir James George Scott, *Gazetteer of Upper Burma and the Shan State*, Government Press, Rangoon, 1990, p. 12.
15. Sao Saimong Mangrai, *The Shan States and the British Annexation*, Data Paper: Number 57, Southeast Asia Program, Department of Asian Studies, Cornwell University, Ithaca, New York, 1965. *See* Appendices.
16. L. Hranglian Songate, *Hmar Chronicle (Hmar History)*, L&R Press, Churachandpur, 1977, p. 11.
17. Joseph Suantak, *The Vaiphei: Their History and Culture*, Akansha Publishing House, Delhi, 2010, p.82.
18. B. Lalthangliana, *India, Burma* leh *Bangladesh, A Mizo Chanchin*, Aizawl, 2001, p. xxx.
19. Joseph Suantak, *op. cit.*, p. 83.
20. *Ibid*, p. 83.
21. S. Thangkhangin Ngaihte, *History of the Zomi of Mizoram and the Surrounding Area: Aspects of Pre-colonial Society*, Unpublished M. Phil. Dissertation, JNU, 1979, p. 57.
22. Vumson, *op. cit.*, p. 64.
23. *Ibid*, p. 68.
24. Joseph Suantak, *op. cit.*, p. 86.
25. *Ibid.*, p. 88.
26. *Ibid.*, p. 87.

27. *Ibid.*, p. 90.
28. Rev S. Prim Vaiphei, *op. cit.*, pp. 44-45.
29. Interview with Rev. S. Prim Vaiphei, New-Lambulane, 23 July 2009.
30. Joseph Suantak, *op. cit.*, p. 108.
31. *Ibid.*, p. 111.
32. Vumkhohau, op. cit., p. 235.
33. Vumson, *op. cit.*, p. 119.
34. Joseph Suantak, *op. cit.*, p. 114.
35. Interview with Liankhothang Vaiphei, Churachandpur, 27 July 2008.
36. Vumson, *op. cit.*, p. 90.
37. Bertram S. Carey & H. N. Tuck, *The Chin Hills Gazetteer*, Vol-I, Cultural Publishing House, Delhi, p. 120.
38. Vumson, *op. cit.*, pp. 90-91.
39. Bertram S. Carey & H. N. Tuck, *op. cit.*, p. 120.
40. *Ibid.*, p. 121.
41. Vumson, *op. cit.*, p. 91.
42. Bertram S. Carey & H. N. Tuck, *op. cit.*, p. 121.
43. Inerview with Rev. S. Prim Vaiphei, New-Lambulane, 23 July 2009.
44. Bertram S. Carey & H. N. Tuck, *op. cit.*, p. 121.
45. Vumson, *op. cit.*, p. 92.
46. *Ibid.*, p. 113.
47. *Ibid.*, pp. 113-114.
48. *Ibid.*, p. 116.
49. Bertram S. Carey & H. N. Tuck, *op. cit.*, pp. 26- 27.
50. Vumson, *op. cit.*, pp. 116-117.
51. Bertram S. Carey & H. N. Tuck, *op. cit.*, p. 27.
52. *Ibid.*, pp. 28 -29.
53. Vumkhohau, *op. cit.*, pp. 168-169.
54. *Ibid.*, p. 235.
55. Vumson, *op. cit.*, p. 119.
56. *Ibid.*, p. 121.
57. *Ibid.*, pp. 132-133.
58. UNAU KUT conference was organized on 24 February 2001 at Ngathal School Campus, Churachandpur. Here in this conference they once again pledged their common ancestry from Suantak.

4

THE KUKIS
FROM MACRO TO MICRO ENTITIES

Sonthang Haokip

Historical Records

The word *Kuki* is a generic term which includes a number of tribes and clans.[1] This generic term covers a large number of people who migrated to different parts of North-East India from contiguous areas lying further east at different points of time. The term is a historical, colonial concept; it was a generic category for the tribal communities not only in Manipur but in larger parts of North-Eastern India.[2] The origin of the word *Kuki* is not known but it has been used since time immemorial. It first appeared in Bengal. There is Rawlin's writing of Cucis or Mountaineers of Tiperah. There are many conjectures and theories about the origin of the word *Kuki*. Some believed that this had been derived from Baluchistan word *Kuchis* meaning wandering people. And some say that it comes from English word *Kooky* which means peculiar or unusual people. It was perhaps used as a derogatory name given by the outsiders to an ethnic group of people living in the western Burma, North-East India and Bangladesh. They are a sub-family of the Tibeto-Burman or Indo-Chinese family.[3] Another version claims that the word *Kuki* has originated from a Chinese word. The literal meaning of *Ku* is a lake, that *Ku* is accepted to be the name of a lake in China and *Ki* means the people. Therefore, according to this view, the Kukis are believed to be the original inhabitants of the tracts around the *Ku*, a lake in China.[4] According to Dun, "The origin of the term 'Kuki' is not certainly known; but it is said to be derived from a word applied to a system of cultivation by the Bengalis. The whole of the wild tribe who dwells in the mountain district contained between Bengal and Burma, Cachar and Manipur and Arakan have received this designation".[5] The Kuki and Chin are synonymous.[6] To Grierson, Kuki is an Assamese or Bengali term applied to various hill tribes such as the Lushais, Rangkhols, Thados, etc.[7] He further states that the word Kuki is more especially used to denote the various tribes which have successively been driven from the Lushai and Chin Hills into the surrounding country to the North and West.[8] As such Kuki is the term applied in India and Chin is applied in Burma for the same nationality.[9] The Kukis are described as a nation of hunters and warriors ruled by their principal hereditary chief but divided into clans, each clan under its own chief.[10] They are known to their neighbours by different names. The British knew them by Kookies, Lushais, Pois, Sindus and Chins. The plain people called these tribes Kukis or Kuki-Chin whereas the Dimasa- Kacharis called them Thanggumsa and in Manipur the Meitei name for the Kukis is Khonjai or Khongjai.[11] As such, R.B. Pemberton also refers to them as Khongjuees.[12] The word Khonjai was perhaps a tonal corruption of Khongsai which is one of the ancestral lineages of the Kukis.[13] According to Goswami, the family lines of the Kukis are broadly placed under two ancestral lines of descent, namely Khongsai and Chongthus. Elly says that the tribe is called Kuki by the Bengalis. An attributed meaning of the term is 'hill people'[14]. In reference to the Kuki identity and their territorial domain, the Encyclopedia Britannica records: 'Kuki, a name given to a group of tribes inhabiting both sides of the mountains dividing Assam and Bengal from Burma, south of the Namtaleik river'.[15]

In the like manner Lt. Col. Shakespear also writes about the Kukis as "....closely allied clans, with well marked characteristics belonging to the Tibeto-Burman stock. On the Chittagong border, the term is loosely applied to most of the inhabitants of the interior hills beyond the Chittagong Hill Tracts, in Cachar, it generally means some family of Thado or Khawtlang clan locally distinguished as new Kuki and old Kuki.......in Chin Hills and generally on the Burma border these clans are called Chins......that these Kukis are also closely allied to the Chakmahs', and the Lushais are more closely allied to the Chiru, Kom, Khawtlang families and are also related to their eastern neighbours who are known as Chin".[16] He concluded that "there was no doubt that the Kukis, Chins and Lushais are the entire same race".[17] Vumkhohau also states "The Chin Hills Gazetteers recorded the fact that the Zo (Chins) and the so-called Kukis were one and the Suktes, Yos and the Kamhaus were one people. He further summarized the fact that all belong to one and the same people".[18] To P.S. Haokip, "The term Kuki appears to find its origin in the Chittagong Hill Tracts. The first recorded usage of the term was by the Bengalis who used it in reference to the hill tribes of the Chittagong Hill Tracts. It was subsequently picked up by the British in the course of their eastward expansion of their empire, and they applied it as a common nomenclature, for all the same family of tribes they came into contact with".[19]

The Kuki-Chin is both a linguistic group and an ethno-cultural entity. On the basis of the linguistic classification adopted by G.A. Grierson, the Kuki-Chin is a linguistic sub-family of the Tibeto-Burman group comprising of Kuki-Chin-Mizo and the Meitei (Manipuri speakers).[20] Both, by language and race, there is no doubt that the Manipuris (Meitei) are closely related with their neighbours and form a part of the Tibeto-Burman family. With regard to the racial stock of the Kukis, different views and opinions have been put forth by a number of scholars and British administrators. In spite of that, through linguistic affinities and ethnic relationships, the Kukis are identified with the Mongoloid racial stock of the Austro-Asiatic group of Tibeto-Burman linguistic family.[21]

Another authority on the Kukis, Capt. T.H. Lewin said,

"The Loosei (Lushai) commonly called the Kookie are powerful and independent people who are known to the Bengalese by the name of Kookie and the Burmeses as the Lankhe".[22] As regards to the tribal ethnic composition, William Shaw wrote: "The Kom, Khawtlangs, Thadous, Lushais, Chins, Pois, etc., are undoubtedly all connected and are Kukis, and that the language alone has many similarities and the syntax is not dissimilar. Again, there are their customs which have a common principle running through them all".[23]

During the British period before 1950, the tribes which were known by the term Kuki are Aimol, Anal, Chothe, Chiru, Gangte, Hmar, Koireng, Kom, Lamgang, Lushai, Moyon, Monsang, Paite, Thadou, Vaiphei, Zou, Purum, Simte, Sukte, Ralte, etc. In Tripura, they are still known as Hrangkhol Kuki,Darlong Kuki, Biete Kuki and so on.[24] On the original place of habitat and racial traits, the latest authorities on the Kukis, Carey and Tuck have maintained that "Without pretending to speak with authority on the subject, we may reasonably accept the theory that the Kukis of Manipur, the Lushais of Bengal and Assam and the Chins originally live in what we know as Thibet (Tibet) and are of the same stock, their form of government and method of cultivation, manners and customs, beliefs and traditions all point to one common origin".[25]

With authority on the Kukis, Robert Reid pronounced that the Kukis form mingling of clans speaking dialects of the same language who are known to us by various names such as Kookies, Lushais, Pois, Shendus, Chins, etc.[26] It is clear from the above facts that the Mizos or Lushai are none other than the people known as Kuki in India and Bangladesh and Chin in Myanmar (Burma). The name *Kookie* was given to the tribes inhabiting the Chittagong Hill Tracts. It is also written in the Encyclopaedia Britannica, that "the first dwellers in Lushai Hills were Kookies".[27] It can, therefore, be said that the Lushais are Kookies/Kukis or *viceversa.*

With regard to the constituents of the ethnic tribal groups and clan diversities of the Kukis, a correct picture is not available in the old Census Reports and other ethnographic notes as these reports basically relied on the information furnished rather than on the basis of actual field studies which needed to be carried out. While as in the Assam Census Report 1911, Major J. Shakespear, the Superintendent of Lushai Hills, put Lushai-Kuki-Chin people under fifteen ethnic communities such as:

(i)	Lushai	(ix)	Darlong
(ii)	Khawtlang	(x)	Pante
(iii)	Thado	(xi)	Routhlei
(iv)	Ralte	(xii)	Poi
(v)	Kiangte	(xiii)	Nagente
(vi)	Lakher	(xiv)	chunthu
(vii)	Paitlei	(xv)	Hmar.[28]
(viii)	Raite		

Lt. General M.W.G. Gob,[29] the Superintendent of Lushai Hills, on the other hand, groups the Lushai-Kuki-Chin people under nine ethnic communities which are mentioned in the Assam Census Report of 1911:

(i)	Lushai	(vi)	Poi
(ii)	Ralte	(vii)	Fanai
(iii)	Paite	(viii)	Lakher
(iv)	Hmar	(ix)	Sailo
(v)	Thado		

Further, Soppit classified the Kukis into four main tribes:

(i) Rangkhol; (ii) Bete; (iii) Jansen; and (iv) Tadoi.

He further identified the Langrong and the Kelma as two sub-tribes of the Rangkhols and the Lanlonga as a sub-tribe of the Jansens.[30]

Shakespeare's Lushai-Kuki Clans further claimed that the following ethnic groups or clans belonged to KUKI nomenclature:

(i)	All Lushai Clans (Rokhum, Zadong, Thangluah, Pallian, Rivung and Sailo)	(xv)	Paihte / Vuite
		(xvi)	Rangte
		(xvii)	Aimol
		(xviii)	Anal
(ii)	Chawthe (Chothe)	(xix)	Chiru
(iii)	Chawngthu	(xx)	Kolhen
(iv)	Hnamte	(xxi)	Kom
(v)	Kawlni	(xxii)	Lamgang
(vi)	Khawlhring	(xxiii)	Purum
(vii)	Khiangte	(xxiv)	Tikhup
(viii)	Ngente	(xxv)	Tukhup
(ix)	Pautu	(xxvi)	Vaiphei
(x)	Rentloi	(xxvii)	Khawthlang
(xi)	Vanchiah	(xxviii)	Khawchhak
(xii)	Zawngte	(xxix)	Thado
(xiii)	Fanai	(xxx)	Lakher/Mara (Maring).[31]
(xiv)	Ralte		

Under the Independent India, (the Modification Order Nos, S.R.O. 2477, A. dated New Delhi, the 29 October, 1956 of the Ministry of Home Affairs, Government of India) in the Scheduled Tribes lists, in the case of Manipur's Kuki-Chin groups we find the following ethnic groups as listed:

(i)	Aimol	(v)	Gangte
(ii)	Hmar	(vi)	Monsang
(iii)	Lamkang	(vii)	Ralte
(iv)	Mayon	(viii)	Shahte

(ix) Thadou
(x) Chothe
(xi) Koireng
(xii) Chiru
(xiii) Kom
(xiv) Paite
(xv) Vaiphei
(xvi) Simte
(xvii) Zou
(xviii) Any Mizo (Lushai) tribes
(xix) Purum
(xx) Koirao
(xxi) Anal[32]

According to Roy, the Kuki-Chin group consists of the tribes: Aimol, Chothe, Chiru, Kom, Purum, Gangte, Paite, Simte,Thadou, Vaiphei, Hmar, Zou, Ralte, Mizo, Sukte.[33] During the British rule, the Kuki-Chin groups in India were known as Kukis such as Lushai- Kuki, Hmar- Kuki, Paite-Kuki, Thadou- Kuki, Kom- Kuki,Anal- Kuki, Vaiphei- Kuki, etc and in Burma they were known as Chins. Even today Kuki-Chin people of Tripura identified themselves as Kuki e.g Darlong- Kuki, Biete- Kuki, Hrangkhol- Kuki.

Scenario in the Post-Independence Period and After

However, in the post-independence period the identity of the Kukis got fragmented and tribalised. The common identity of the former got dwindled which spelt a direct co-relation to their spirit of nationalism. The Kukis got themselves fragmented into groups of insignificant hundred after getting recognition of their own tribes separately. This is especially true in the case of the Kukis of Manipur.

With the passage of time the term *Kuki* began to be disowned by the tribes and clans who were once under the *Kuki* fold. The first dismemberment of the Kukis appeared in the Lushai Hills (present Mizoram). Historically speaking, the term Kuki was replaced by the term *Lushai* after the Lushai Expedition of 1871-72 in the official records which was again later changed to *Mizo* in the 1940s. In the Chin Hills of Burma too, the term *Kuki* came to be disowned subsequently. The people preferred to be called as Chin and later as *Laimi, Zomi,* and so on.

However, in the case of Manipur, different groups of the Kukis remained under the Kuki fold till India's independence (1947). In Manipur, the recognized Kuki tribes during the colonial period were: Aimol, Anal, Chothe, Chiru, Gangte, Hmar, Koireng, Kom, Lamkang, Lushai, Moyon, Monsang, Paite, Thadou, Vaiphei, Zou, Purum, Simte, Sukte, Ralte, Lushai, and others.

The new political awakening in the post-independence era proved a great setback to the unity and oneness of the Kuki family. The consciousness of their separate identity led them to ask the Government for recognition of their tribe. As a result, tribes, clans and sub-clans which have been within the Kuki fold sought and got their respective tribe/clan recognition as a separate entity which marked the beginning of the Kuki fragmentation as a great nation.

With the primary objective of fostering consciousness of common identity and making a single political unit of the Kukis, the Kuki National Assembly (KNA) was formed in 1946. However, not pleased with the Thadou dominancy and supremacy, the non-Thadou ethnic groups started searching for a more democratic organization as an alternative to the Kuki National Assembly. The fragmentation of the Kuki polity was started with the formation of Khulmi National Union (KNU), a breakaway of the Kuki National Assembly. Thus, another generic group *Khulmi* constituted by the Vaiphei, Gangte, Paite, Simte, Zou and other non-Thadou tribes from the Kuki-Chin group who claimed to have originated from *Khul* (Cave) came into existence. However, in 1951, the unification of different groups of the Kukis under the nomenclature of *Khulmi* received a fatal blow as it was not granted recognition by the Government of India. Another setback to the unity of the Kuki fraternity was the formation of another term *Komrem* which was formed by the erstwhile Kuki tribes such as, Kom, Aimol, Chiru, Koireng, Purum, Kharam, etc. Furthermore, the so-called old Kukis of present day Chandel District of Manipur merged to the Naga fold during the 1960s. Thus, there began the political disintegration of the Kuki tribes of Manipur into many splinter groups.

The dismemberment of the Kukis could also be seen in their religious sphere too. This could be seen mainly in the case of the southern district of Manipur where the Kuki ethnic groups largely concentrated. Since 1910, when the first light of the Gospel of Christ reached their land, almost all the Kuki ethnic groups were under the North East India General Mission (NEIGM). But, as time passes by, differences cropped up among the constituent churches leading to split into different denominations. The first breakaway took place in 1949 when the Paite tribe separated the Assembly under the name of Convention. But they maintained their membership in the North-East India General Mission (NEIGM). In the year 1953, during the Assembly at Saikot village, the remaining tribes such as Hmar, Thadou-Kuki, Vaiphei, Lushai and Gangte unanimously decided to break up into five different presbyteries. The Hmar tribe came under the Assembly church, the Thadou-Kukis came under Kuki Christian Association, (which came to be rechristened as Evangelical Churches Association (ECA) and the Vaiphei tribe came under Manipur Christian Organization. The Gangte tribe came under Manipur Christian Synod. The Lushai tribe merged with the Mizoram Presbyterian Church and left the NEIGM shortly after this.

Conclusion

It is said that the people identified themselves as Kuki in order to get military service in the pre-independent India and Burma. But, after India's independence, the Government of India recognized the various tribes of the Kukis and they could get their services as members of a recognized tribe in India without mentioning whether he was a Kuki or not. In the past, till the end of British rule in India, different ethnic groups did not object to being identified as Kuki when inter-tribal feuds were the practice of the time. The term 'Kuki' gave security and protection and was an expression of solidarity and identity. After independence, the Constitution of India provided special provisions for growth and development of the weaker sections of the people. These (smaller tribes) groups no longer feel the necessity of being called 'Kuki' or being under the Kuki fold. They feel that they should avail to the fullest extent possible of the privilege being accorded to them by the Constitution of India.

Some arguments put forward by those who are opposed to the 'Kuki nomenclature' was that it was a name imposed by the outsiders with no place in their vocabulary. The same is in the case of the term 'Naga' — a term given by the outsiders. But the Nagas could embrace the 'Naga nomenclature' as a means and a platform for unity of nation building. But for the Kukis, it was or is just the opposite. At this vital juncture, it would be extremely impractical to dwell on finding an alternate identity to Kuki. Instead, it would be prudent to set aside internal animosities that have crippled the Kuki community for the last half century or so and converge on the identity as Kuki for the community's benefit in the near future. Kuki is not being proposed because it sounds like a good name but because of its potential as leverage for actuating what is politically achievable for the people concerned. The term Kuki has drawn a lot of flacks in the past but it also has its plus points as an identity because of documented facts available in prominent libraries, national and international, and also in many of the official records. The world knows the people in question as Kukis, and less by any other name.

Owing to petty differences and misunderstanding in the realm of social and politics, myopic interest or absence of vision among the past leaders, the unity of the Kuki society have been severely dented but the new millennium has seen a strong wave of pan-nationalism (intellectual awakenings) with university students, research scholars, college and university teachers as the vanguard of the movement advocating the imperative need for a common platform that would re-unite and bring back all the cognate tribes having close-knit blood relationship and cultural affinity so as to assert a strong and viable political space in the present democratic dispensation which was otherwise stymied owing to the absence of the zeal for oneness or lack of farsightedness among the past leaders.

Succinctly put, the term Kuki, in spite of its drawbacks and shortcomings, is the only viable platform which has the potential to regroup the once splinter family under the same old roof once again.

REFERENCES

1. Gautam Bhadra, 'The Kuki Uprising (1917-1919)', *Man In India*, Vol. 55, (1), 1975, p. 11. See also Gangmumei Kabui, *History of Manipur—Pre-Colonial Period*, Vol. 1, National Publishing House, New Delhi, 1991, p. 23.
2. Satinder Kumar, *Encyclopedia of South Asian Tribes*, Vol. VI. Anmol Publications Pvt. Ltd., New Delhi, 2000, p.1773.
3. *Ibid.*, p. 1778.
4. B.N. Bordoloi & G.C. Sharmach Thakur, *Tribes of Assam*, Part XI, Tribal Research Institute, Assam, Guwahati, 1988, p. 44.
5. E.W. Dun, *A Bridged Gazetteer of Manipur*, 1891, p. 18.
6. G. A.Grierson, *Languages of North-Eastern India*, Vol. 11, Gyan Publishing House. New Delhi, 2006, p. 509.
7. *Ibid.*
8. *Ibid.*, p. 510.
9. H.Doungel, Sociological Study of the Customary Laws of the Kukis, Unpublished M. Phil Dissertation, NEHU, Shillong, p. 2.
10. E.T. Dalton, *Tribal History of Eastern India*, Cosmo Publication, Delhi, 1973, p. 44.
11. B.N. Bordoloi & G.C. Sharmach Thakur, *op. cit.*, p. 44.
12. A. Mackenzie, *The Report on the Eastern Frontier of British*, Cosmo Publication, Delhi, 1973, p. 6.
13. Tarun Goswami, *Kuki Life and Lore*, Halflong, Assam, 1985, p. 295.
14. E.B. Elly, *Military Report on the Chin-Lushai Country*, Firma KLM (P) Ltd., Calcutta, 1978.
15. Encyclopedia Britannica, Vol. 13, 1962, p. 511.
16. J. Shakespear, *Lushei-Kuki Clans*, Cultural Publishing House, Delhi, 1912, pp. 1-2.
17. *Ibid.*
18. Vumkhohau, *Profile of a Burma Frontier Man*, Kilatmadju Press, Bandung, Indonesia, 1963, p. 297.

19. P.S. Haokip, *Zalengam–The Kuki Nation*, Kuki National Organisation Publication, 1988, p. 61.
20. G.A. Grierson, *op. cit.*, Vol. III, Part II & III.
21. Vumson, *Zo History*, Aizawl, undated, p. 26.
22. T.H. Lewin , *Wild Races of South-Eastern India*, Mittal Publications, Delhi,1978, p. 130. See also T.S. Gangte, "Who are the Kukis? Where are they?" Souvenir of the Kuki Rebellion, 1985, p. 36.
23. William Shaw, *The Thadou Kukis*, Cultural Publishing House, Delhi,1983, p. 16.
24. Satinder Kumar, *op. cit.*, p. 1778.
25. Bertram S. Carey & H.N. Tuck , *The Chin Hills*, Vol. I, Gyan Publishing House, Delhi, 1983, p.24.
26. Sir Robert Reid, *History of Frontier Areas Bordering on Assam*, Spectrum Publications, Guwahati,1942, pp. 2-3.
27. Encyclopedia Britannica, Vol. 13, 1962, p. 511.
28. Quoted in H. Doungel, *op. cit.*, p. 24.
29. B.N.Bordoloi & G.C. Sharmach Thakur, *op. cit.*, pp. 46-47.
30. C.A. Soppit, *A Short Account of the Kuki-Lushai Tribe*, Firma KLM Pvt. Ltd., 1979, pp. 2-3.
31. J. Shakespear, *Lushei-Kuki, op. cit.*, and also T. S. Gangte's Chin-Kuki-Mizo Nationalism' presented at the General Assembly of Kuki Students' Organization, Tuibong, Churachandpur, 29 January, 2002.
32. Sheikhohao Kipgen, Political and Economic History of the Kukis of Manipur, Unpublished PhD thesis, MU, 2005, p. 7.
33. Prim Vaiphei, *The Vaiphei Tribe*, MBC, Imphal, 1975, p. 22.

5

ANCIENT RELIGIOUS BELIEFS AND PRACTICES AMONG THE HMARS IN MANIPUR

Ruolkhumzo

Introduction

The Hmars are one of the Hill tribes of North-East India. They belong to the Kuki-Chin-Mizo group of the main Tibeto-Burman race. Their original home was *Sinlung* (Sin=closed; lung=stone) which was believed to be somewhere in China. The traditional Hmar religion was known as *Sakhuo.* The word *Sakhuo* owes its origin from *Sa*-animal; *Khuo*-God. It implies that *Sakhuo* is the worship of God through animal sacrifice.[1] In fact, the term *Sakhuo* means a coherent system of beliefs and practices relative to super-natural order of being which marked the religio-cultural matrix of the people.

Concept of God

God is Pathien: the Creator, the Merciful, and the Sustainer.[2] In common parlance, Pathien is interpreted as God but it has a deeper meaning. The word Pathien has been derived from Pa=Father; Thien=Holy, which in its primary sense means Holy Father. The application of the term Pa suggests a close relationship or tie of blood between father and children and Thien is the Supreme object of worship.

The basic spells, castings or affirmations and phrases used in ritualistic ceremonies are focussed to the Almighty-Pathien. These provide the basis for the development and understanding of the early Hmar religious philosophy.

> Hei Chibai Pathien
> Inchon raza ka hnina,
> Khuongsen, khuongngo ka hnina,
> Changchung hmingin mi hung sawn rawh.

English Version

> Hail to thee Almighty God (three times)
> I beg thy providence in hundred folds,
> The red-drum and White stem I entreat,
> In thy Glorious Name I pray.

This affirmation has been quoted at length because it offers the most explicit interpretation of the omnipotence of Pathien and His attachment to the people. Here God-Pathien is hailed as the all-in-all of all, the focal point of *Sakhuo* and every prayer. The Hmar people used Pathien at the time of personal blessing, swearing valediction, taking oath, allegiance, etc., in their day to day activities.

Pathien is believed to be somewhere above and the people called upon Him as Chunga Pathien which affirmed the fact that Pathien is the most conspicuous cosmic power in the universe.[3] So far as the word Pathien is concerned, He is reverend as the Father in Heaven and all things were made through Him. He, therefore, is the God of compassion, the Bountiful Creator, and the Merciful Sustainer.[4]

Transformation of Structures

Monotheism gradually transformed into a certain unique kind of polytheism or henotheism as time passed on. In the heavenly abode of Pathien, another co-eternal goddess known as *Vanvomnu* came into prominence thereby opening a new vista of Dual worship for the people. *Vanvomnu* is regarded as the wife of Vanhrit who is equally powerful and has more assignments in the spiritual realm. The God *Vanhrit* is believed to be the care-taker of every soul after death and the chief warden of death man's abode: *mithikhuo*. Moreover, every born or unborn child is his main concern and it is even believed that he can cause death to any infant child at will.[5]

A tradition tells us that *Khuonu-Khuopa* is the God who has an absolute power over human life.[6] It is said that he determined the span of every life on earth and as such the people worshipped him for the longevity of their lives. *Khuonu-Khuopa mi huol raw sen.* (let the Khuonu-Khuopa guide and protect us) were the repeated words used in their prayers. Another important god is *Tuikhuong Lalpa*: the Lord of all rivers, who can cause floods, droughts etc.

Again, in the religious system of the Hmar people, *Ramhuoi* the demons or evil spirits are considered to be the vital objects to be worshipped and they were given the ranks of semi-gods. From time immemorial, it was a popular belief among the Hmars that Pathien in heaven had left them to the care of *Ramhuoi* or *Khohri.* He had little to do with human affairs. Therefore, most of their sacrifices and devotions are directed towards the *Ramhuois* who are supposed to be the causes of their misfortunes in the society. Traditionally, the people had recognised five to six different forms of *Ramhuois or Khohris* as an object of worship and propitiation in the society.

1. *Khuovang*

They are believed to be active at dusk and assigned the task of taking souls from men. Children were not allowed to stroll or move about after nightfall in the village.[7]

2. *Khochom*

They are believed to be one of the most formidable ones who used to torment their domesticated animals at night.

3. *Lashi*

It has been believed that *Lashi* are friendly fairies who appeared in the forms of beautiful ladies. Since early times, some young men are said to fall in love with these alluring fairies. Those who had an intimate relationship with them were often becoming famous hunters in their lifetime because *Lashis* are regarded to be the care-takers of wild life.

4. *Zasam*

These *Zasam* are believed to be another dreadful demons who used to mislead weary travellers, hunters, workers, etc. Once a person had been bewitched by *Zasam* he would perceive that he was travelling in an emerald city of gods. This type of hallucination is known as *Khomu Choi* by the people.[8]

5. *Nelhau a Rawi*

They are said to be mischievous who moved about in single file formation. They are not much harmful to mankind but noted for their mischievous and unrelentable menaces, i.e., damage to the standing crops, scattering of agricultural implements in the *jhum*-huts during sleep, etc.

6. *Phung*

The people described *Phung* as daylight spirit very black and large, frequenter of village, who had the power of inculcating madness, the power of causing fits, of making epileptics.

Animistic Worship

In the traditional Hmar society, it was a commonly accepted fact that all the animate or inanimate objects were actuated by spirits. The spirits associated with unnatural phenomena were held to be empowered to do much harm or much good to mankind. For example, *Muollukhim:* unusual mount that sprouted in two hills or mountains; *Rawlpuk:* strange cliffs;

Khursie: deep ponds or pits; *Bungthing:* an old mangroves; *Thingjungkai:* big trees extending its roots from one bank of a river to another; *Thingjik bul* or *Thinglu bul:* any tree of unusual shapes or sizes without any leaves; *Lungpuilien:* rocks which are abnormally big and so forth. Therefore, they went to such places and offer sacrifices of fowls, pigs, goats or any other animals which are deemed fit for the purpose.

Ancestral Worship

The Hmar people have been worshipping their ancestors in a common as *Rau biek* or *Pipu thlarau biek.* They used the words, *Miachal, Niachal, Nelachal* as their sacred incarnations when they performed sacrifices.[9] These three words are said to be the names of their great ancestors which are passed on generations. Every new year, before their works in the *jhum,* they prayed to the spirits of their great ancestors muttering in their mouths: *Miachal, Niachal, Nelchal* to bless them with rich harvest from the bounty of *Pathien:* God the Almighty. Again, at the end of the same year, they did as before, but this time with offerings of alms and so on.

The Role of the Priest

Thiempu or Priest was an indispensable person in the village whose religious service was required in almost all walks of life.[10] He, therefore, became the obligatory intermediary between the people and God or gods in the society. He performed all sacrifices for the sick and the dead, offered prayer for the prosperity of the crop and sanctified the village from the influence of demons and evil spirits. In the case of an epidemic in other villages, he influenced the chief to issue an order to disallow visitors to pass through the village. He received fees for all his services.[11]

To become a priest, one has to go long years of apprenticeship for one must combine in himself all the qualities of a sorcerer (person who are engaged in the art of black magic); a diviner or seer (persons who could foretell the future); a witch doctor who can cure or defend by means of magic ; prophet (person who speaks to the people on behalf of the supernatural power), etc. Generally, man of merit who was well versed to the practices of Hmar religion was appointed by the chief for this position.[12] The priest was not confined in a shrine or temple. He, however, went to work among the people as an appointee of the chief and member of the village council.

Patterns of Ritualistic Sacrifices

The priest performed a number of sacrifices inside the village. These sacrifices were of different types. While some were performed to cure individuals from sickness, others were performed for the welfare of the family or the village as a whole. He also performed sacrifices for appeasing spirits to seek blessings from God, for securing a good harvest, etc. These sacrifices which he performed may be discussed as follows:

One of the most important sacrifices performed by the priest was that of the *bawlpui.* This sacrifice was made for curing a sick person. It was the most complicated one. The animal which was sacrificed on this occasion was usually a pig. When such a sacrifice was about to be made, the priest himself went to an outskirt area of the village. The area had to be the one where the individual or the patient for whom the sacrifice was to be made had not gone before. There the priest moulded a figure of a man and a woman and place them on the altar which was made of bamboo splits. Then the priest put seven leaves, one each from seven different trees which grew on the cliffs, seven replica each of *phawlim* (shield), *chemte* (knife), *fei* (spear) and seven *theibiel* (a particular fruit), etc., along with the male and female figures on the altar.[13] Then the throat of the sacrificial pig was cut and the blood was allowed to flow over the *beiphit* (flour) which was kept on the altar. Then the female figure known as *chawmnu* was made to bite the thin (liver) of the sacrificial pig whereas the male figure known as *chawmpa* was provided with a pipe along with garland made of the pig's liver. The meat was cooked on the spot and it was forbidden to take back home. Other villagers were allowed to join and eat it with the priest. If the patient did not die during the ceremonial rites it was believed that he/she would surely recover from his/her sickness.[14]

Another important sacrifice performed by the priest was that of *arthiem inthawi*. In this sacrifice, the priest had to cut off the head of a fowl. After chanting the sacrificial hymn known as *dawihla,* the priest allowed the blood of the fowl to flow down the backside of the neck of the patient. The priest, to heal illness like rheumatic problems, performed this sacrifice.

There was another sacrifice known as *ui-ha-awr* performed by the priest. He performed the sacrifice for persons prone to constant illness. In this sacrifice, he killed a dog. As soon as the meat was prepared, a tooth of the dog was removed and he tied it around the neck of the person for whom the sacrifice was performed.[15]

The priest also performed a sacrifice khown as *hringaitan* for persons suffering with symptoms of *ngawr* (tuberculosis). This sacrifice was also a complicated one. While performing this sacrifice he put on a long rope and a turban.[16] Then he surrounded the house of the patient with a long rope of *pawi* plant and planted branches of *khawnghma* tree around the house which was supposed to have magical powers. In front of the house, he planted a branch of yet another tree known as *inkhieng* tree which was also supposed to have magical powers. Once these arrangements were made, the priest cut the neck of a dog. He then smeared all the branches of the magical trees with the blood. As he passed from one branch to another he recited sacred hymns.[17] Not enough with this, he mixed the blood of the dog with fresh turmeric juice and made the patient drink it. Later, the patient's family arranged a small feast with the meat. It was a must that the dinner party should exhaust the meat or throw the left over because it was forbidden to eat the sacrificial meat the next day.

The priest also performed sacrifices on behalf of the

families in the village. These sacrifices were performed mainly to seek blessings from their forefathers and *Pathien*, their God. The priest performed these sacrifices usually inside the house of the family. In this sacrifice he killed a fowl with a sharp knife.[18] Then he went around the house chanting *dawihla*, a song which was supposed to have magical powers. After this he put the blood of the sacrificial animal along with cereal flour on green leaves (usually plantain leaves).[19] Then he took the head of the family to a place where the latter stood with him facing the sacrificial altar. Then he invoked blessings from God and forefathers of the family concerned for the well-being of the family. The blood of the animal killed was collected in a basin or plate. The priest then sprinkled the blood over the cereal flour and rice. In this the priest performed sacrifices for the welfare of the family.

It was also the priest who performed for securing good fortune for the village. He had to perform this rite twice a year. For this purpose an altar of stones was constructed approximately five to six feet high. After constructing the altar the priest, with the help of village elders, slew the animal. Then the priest sprinkled the blood of the sacrificial animal together with cereal flour over the carcass and recited the following hymns three times :[20]

> Hei Chibai, Chunga Pthien;
> Tiena ka pu lei, Chin leilung Himaloi.

English Version:

> Hail to thee, God of above;
> The ancient home of my grand-father, and land of Kachin, Himalaya.

Then he moved around the altar and invoked blessings from God for the well-being of the village community.[21] On this particular day, no noise was allowed. The people even forbade the cocks to crow.[22] They observed silence inside the village throughout the day. The youths went into every house and swept every corner of the houses with bunches of leaves. The idea was that this cleaned up all the causes of sickness and misfortunes. They also poured water over the fireplace inside the house to make sure that the fire had completely gone out for the whole day.

After the ritual, the villagers would lit *meiser* (new light) from the chief's house. Only then they resumed their normal life as before.[23] Sometimes the priest also performed this ritual in order to protect the village from the onslaught of a rampant epidemic that broke out in a nearby village.

The villagers were expected to observe the formalities of *khawtlang-in-thawi* (village sacrifice) strictly.

Ralui or spirit calling sacrifice was another important sacrifice performed by the priest. Whenever was sick, the Hmar believed that it was because the spirit of the sick person stayed back in the jhum field and it did not return home with the person.[24] Therefore, in order to cure the sick person, they performed the *ralui* or spirit calling sacrifice so that the spirit may return to the sick person at home. During this sacrifice, the whole family went to the previous *jhum* with the priest and made an altar there. The priest then killed a fowl, offered its blood to the spirit of the sick person believed to have remained there in the *jhum*. While doing this he said the following lines:[25]

Hung in lawi rawh;
Ei lo chu an hawi nawh;
Ei in an hawi lem hung rawh.

English version:

Come home;
Our *jhum* land is not pleasant;
Our home is more pleasant come home.

One more sacrifice that a priest performed inside the traditional Hmar society was that of *mihriem-in-thawi* (human sacrifice). This form of sacrifice was regarded as the highest form of sacrifice a man could make. Generally, this sacrifice was believed to serve three-fold purposes. First, it was supposed to bring glory to the person who offered the sacrifice. Secondly, it was believed that he would also get an additional slave when he goes to *mithikhuo* (abode of death).[26] Besides, it was also believed to propitiate evil spirits.

Traditional Belief in Life after Death

The Hmars believed in the existence of soul and life after death in their pre-Christian days. They believed that when a person dies, his or her soul would stay back in the neighbourhood trying to finish those tasks which he/she could not fulfil during his or her lifetime. As such, their relatives kept food on a separate plate each mealtime for the dead person. They believed that the soul would remain either in the house or its compound in the form of a rat or butterfly or bee.[27] During this period, the families of the dead would put fruits, rice, meat, etc., over the grave as an offering to the dead person's soul. If a rat was crawling in the kitchen during the day, it was supposed to be the spirit of the dead and the family would give food.

After hovering in the neighbourhood for some months, the Hmars believed that the soul would start for *mithikhuo* (the abode of the dead for common people). On the way to the abode of the dead the soul passed through a place called *hringlangtlang* (a mountain from where one could see the land of the living world). On looking back at the living world they were attracted to and attempted by their past life.[28] So the soul would stay there and view the living world. Only when their family in the living world performed a rite called *thitin* (deaddeparting rite), their soul departed from the earth.[29] During this rite, the soul would drink what is called *luonglotui* (lonesome-no-more-water) which will remove all the yearnings about the living world (look-back-no-more-flower). After this, it will have no more desire for the land of the living.[30] In this way, their ties and attachments with the land of the living was removed.

The Hmars believed that the place of the dead comprised three different abodes namely: 1. *Mithikhuo* (abode of common people), 2. *Pielral* (the abode of *thangsuos*, i.e. those who have killed different varieties of animals and performed certain public feasts) and 3.*Vanram* (heaven).The Hmars believed that except those persons who achieved the title of *thang suo* during their lifetime would go to *mithikhuo*. They also believed that just at the entrance of *mithikhuo* there was a dreadful woman called *kulsamnu* who stood at the centre of the entrance with a bow and arrows in her hands. Therefore, in order to be free from her attack, a man needs to have physical relations at least with three women in his lifetime whereas for a woman she must not have pre-marital sex. Otherwise they would be the victims of her terrible shooting. To avoid this attack, children were buried with egg. They believed that the egg would move to the gate before the spirit, and the spirit would escape punishment. They further believed that in *mithikhuo* the dead would unite again with the families who had already departed before them. There they would maintain their own families and homes, and earn their living like they did on earth.[31] The slaves they had captured and the enemies they had killed during their earthly life would serve them as their servants in this world of the spirits.[32] This place was considered to be an underground abode.

The Hmars believed that *pielral* lies somewhere beyond *mithikhuo*. Entry to *pielral* was achieved by qualifying for the title of *thangsuo*. This was an abode of bliss and the *thangsuos* were expected to be fed with rice and meat by fair maidens here. The same privilege was extended to the wife of the *thangsuo*.[33] Therefore, entrance to *pielral* was permitted only to the brave and the rich persons who could manage to kill different varieties of wild animals and arrange public feasts.[34]

Vanram or the third abode was heaven or paradise. This was abode where all the good spirits in *mithikhuo* and *pielral* would ultimately go. The Hmars believed that *mithikhuo* and *pielral* were temporary abodes for the dead before they were given entrance to *vanram*. Those who were given entrance to *vanram* would enjoy equal rights and status and there would be no distinction as on the earth in *mithikhuo or pielral*. Wicked spirits in *mithikhuo* or *pielral* would not go to *vanram*. They were believed to simply hover over the firmament restlessly through endless years after their departure from *mithikhuo* or *pielral*. All the good spirits would enjoy endless happiness in *vanram*. When a person goes to heaven, he/she would live there peacefully and enjoy eternal life.

Conclusion

In the past, the Hmars had their socio-religious life. While they believed in one Supreme God Pathien, they also believed in several other gods. Besides, they believed in the existence of a number of evil spirits. While they believed Pathien to be merciful and benevolent, they believed the evil spirits were responsible for all sorts of their miseries and misfortunes. As such they used to make a number of offerings and sacrifices to appease these spirits. However, with the advent of Christianity many changes have taken place in the Hmar society. The people have already abandoned their earlier religious beliefs. They have stopped making sacrifices of animals to appease spirits. Now they are not afraid of evil spirits whom they used to believe as responsible for all their miseries and illness. With their conversion to Christianity, they have come to believe that the gates of heaven are open to all irrespective of one's social status or accomplishments on earth. There are no longer the priests in the Hmar society. Instead there are the Pastors to perform religious functions. Christianity has also driven most of their earlier festivals into oblivion. Instead, they now celebrate Christian festivals such as Christmas, Good Friday, Easter, New Year's Day, etc.

REFERENCES

1. Liankhaia, *Mizo Sakhua*, Aizawl, 1975, pp. 1-2.

2. Lal Dena, 'Kristienna Le Hmar Nunphung' , in Thuro, *Hmar Literature Journal*, Vol. II, p. 7.
3. Louis L. Keivom, *Hmar Pi le Pu Dan*, Imphal, 1982, p. 110.
4. Salaithanga, *Mizo Sakhua* , Aizawl, p. 2.
5. Louis L. Keivom, *op. cit.*, p. 110.
6. *Ibid.*
7. L. Hranglien Songate, *Hmar Chanchin*, L & R Printing Press, Churachandpur, 1977, p. 75.
8. *Ibid.*
9. *Ibid.*
10. Ruolneikhum Pakhuongte, *The Power of the Gospel Among the Hmar Tribe*, Shillong, 1983, p. 14.
11. Rochunga Pudaite , *The Education of the Hmar People*, Sielmat, 1963, p. 52.
12. Ruolneikhum Pakhuongte, *op.cit.*, p. 14.
13. Hrangthiauva & L. Lalchungnunga, *History and Culture of the Mizos*, Aizawl, 1978, p. 14.
14. Ruolkhumzo, Traditional Administrative System and Customary Laws of the Hmars in Manipur, Unpublished PhD Thesis, MU, 2004, p. 107.
15. *Ibid.*
16. *Ibid.*
17. Louis L. Keivom, *op. cit.*, p. 16.
18. Lalkhawlien Pulamte, *An Examination of factors that led to the Conversion of the Hmar People, A Historical Consideration, 1910-1950*, Bangalore, 1985, p. 22.
19. *Ibid.*
20. L. Hranglien Songate, *op. cit.*, p. 76.
21. Louis L. Keivom, *op. cit.*, p. 91.
22. Lal Dena, The Christian Religion and the Hmar Culture, presented to Hmar Assembly, Churachandpur, 1982, p. 4.
23. Ruolkhumzo, *op. cit.*, p. 110.
24. Thangsawihmang, *A Brief Survey of the Hmars Before and After Sinlung*, Churachandpur, 1999, p. 8.
25. *Ibid.*
26. Ruolkhumzo, *op. cit.*, p. 111.
27. Thangsawihmang, *op. cit.*, p. 24.
28. Ruolneikhum Pakhuongte, *op. cit.*, p. 21.
29. *Ibid.*
30. Louis L . Keivom, *op. cit.*, p. 119.
31. Ruolneikhum Pakhuongte, *op. cit.*, p. 20.
32. *Ibid.*
33. Rochunga Pudaite, *op. cit.*, p. 57.
34. Louis L. Keivom, *op. cit.*, p. 11.

6

RELIGIOUS BELIEFS AND PRACTICES AMONG THE SIMTES OF MANIPUR

Ginneihching Simte & Danney Chara

Introduction

Before the coming of Christianity, there existed a number of beliefs among the Simte community. Most of their beliefs were based on spirits and demons. They believed that if the spirits were not pleased, they disturbed and even destroyed people. The purpose of this chapter is to bring out the many forms of spirits which were dreaded and feared by the Simtes. The Simtes, therefore, were concerned with the pleasing of evil spirits and demons so that they are less harmed in their fortunes and health. Their daily lives revolved around pleasing and offering sacrifices to the spirits and demons.

There were many forms of sacrifices and rituals performed by the Simtes. The common sacrifices were done when illness befell the people. They believed that sickness and illness were caused by evil spirits and demons. To cure, they used to offer sacrifices to the spirits responsible for the illness or sickness. The kinds of rites and rituals performed were different according to the variations of the sickness (stomachache, headache, fever etc). Each sickness required different types of sacrifices. Besides, the Simtes believed in the existence of one Supreme Being called '*Pathian*'. They believed that the *Pathian* is the creator of all. In all the religious walks of life of the Simte community, the priest played an important role in the society. His authority was next to the village chief. Nowadays the old institutions and beliefs have all been forgotten. It has been replaced by the doctrines of Christianity.

Belief in the Existence of One Supreme God

Tylor defines religion as the belief in the supernatural. Every society or group has traditional method of appeasement through the means of occultism, esoteric practices, rites, rituals, ceremonies, celebrations accompanied with offerings, prayer, sacrifices to free from a troubled life without anxieties and tensions.[1]

The term religion is known among the Simtes as *Sakhua* (Sa=animal; Khua—God). It means worship of God through animal sacrifice.[2] Another interpretation is that *sakhua* means the worship of ancestors. Pathian was a god of all humanity and goodness, and it was believed that his abode is beyond the sky. He was recognized as Tung Pathian (God above us). Sometimes the creator was also referred to as Khuazingnu or Khuanu but Khuanu may also be interpreted as Mother Nature. After the coming of Christianity, Pathian is now referred to as the Christian God. But in the pre-Christian context, Pathian was an ever-gentle God harmless to the people. They did not worship any celestial bodies. Nature was revered and worshipped for they were believed to have possessed by innumerable spirits: good and evil.

Ancestor-worship and animism were the traditional religious belief of the Simtes. They believed that if the spirits of their ancestors were not pleased, they created damages to the people particularly in matters of posterity, fertility, diseases, etc. So, to protect themselves from the wrath of the spirits of their ancestors, people worshipped them at least once a year. But, in some exceptional cases like bad dream, bad omen, sickness, etc., ancestor-worship was performed. The annual worship ceremony was performed by the head of the different clans called Tulpi[3] (Lineage head in the Simtes).

Next to the Pathian, the Simtes believed in the existence of another malevolent God called Lungzai. It is believed that Pathian and Lungzai co-existed. In some cases "Lungzai' was shown as the spiritual form of Pathian. Pathian and Lungzai, therefore, represented the highest positions in the hierarchy. Some believed that Lungzai was the wife of Pathian. Generally, Lungzai is regarded as the god of this world and Pathian as the god of above.[4]

For the sake of safety and freedom Pathian and Lungzai were revered. They were invoked to drink *zu* (rice beer) and eat meat in ritual functions. Worshipping varied from place to place. They worshipped their gods at different places like *Sumtawng* (place where mortar was kept). However, *Pathian* and *Lungzai* were considered to be benevolent beings that had little interest or influence in the ordinary human life.

Beliefs in Spirits or Demons

The Simtes believed in the existence of supernatural spirits: good and evil. These spirits were known as lesser gods. There were priests (*Siampu*) in every village which performed rites and rituals by chanting and offering sacrifices for the appeasement of the spirits. They believed that the world was inhabited by spirits: some benevolent and some malignant to man. The evil spirits dwelled in the dense forests, trees, streams, springs, mountains or any other objects which were curiously shaped or deformed. They would not attack man unless provoked. When men unconsciously encroached upon their habitation, thereby making them angry, they caused all kinds of illness and misfortunes. To recover from such illness, these spirits had to be placated by sacrifices of particular animals.[5] Passing through the forest, their names were never mentioned. Although the Simtes believed in one Supreme Being and credited to him being the creator of the universe, their daily lives revolved around appeasing the spirits and demon so as to avoid their wrath

The belief in spirits (*Gamhuais* or *Dawis* or *Siha*) dominated the lives of the Simtes. Before undertaking any task: building a new house, occupying a new village, starting a *jhum* etc., rituals had to be performed to propitiate the spirits. The Simtes believed that the spirits had a chief of their own called 'Dawimangpa'[6], which means king of the spirits or Siha Lengpa. The existence has been recollected and handed down orally through bed time stories.

Though the Simtes spent a great deal of their time and effort in propitiating the evil spirits, they did not feel the need of appeasing the good spirits. They devoted all their efforts to appease only the evil spirits, whom they feared. This was the reason why the early missionaries assumed the Simtes as devil worshippers.

Offerings were also made to the spirits of mountains, rivers, stones, trees, caves, etc. There are a number of myths and legends about mountain-spirits and river-spirits. Unless they were given due offerings and sacrifices they would harm the travellers passing their way. These myths handed down through generations shaped the people's concept. Though these myths have been forgotten by the present generation and at times rubbished as concocted stories, there is still the undeniable hold of these narrative beliefs on the subconscious mind of the Simtes. Though Christianized and modernized, there are beliefs that still persist and continue to have a grip on the people among which the myths on demons and evil spirits are quite fascinating.

Good and Evil Spirits

The Simtes believed in the existence of good and evil spirits which were susceptible of being appeased or placated through performance of *phuisam* (chanting) by the priest called Siampu during the ceremony. Some good and evil spirits are:

1. *Gamhuisia* and *Inn munsia: Gamhuisia* is the spirit of the jungle whereas *Inn munsia* is the spirit of the

house. The terms denote 'cursed place'. It is believed that souls of the deceased with unnatural death become these types of dangerous spirits. They troubled the people according to their whims, at the site where such unnatural deaths occurred. In other words, the place is haunted by the soul of the dead person.

2. *Nelhau:* These spirits are believed to be a mischievous lot. Although they cannot harm a human, they are feared for they are naughty as they teased people mercilessly. It was believed that they were the guiding force behind storms and hurricanes.[7] During the crescent moon of the month of Doupi (the lunar month of the Simtes which coincides with the Gregorian month of May) they used to roam along the banks of rivers and streams overturning each and every stone. The reason given behind was that the spirits were searching for one of their lost friends.
3. *Joumi:* It was a dangerous male spirit. People were frightened. Some even died of shock and fear. This spirit used to be active during the night. Its forms varied, though mostly it was seen very tall. It was usually up to the same height of any tree nearby. *Joumi* was fond of chicken.
4. *Kulsamnu:* It was considered to be a female spirit. All the dead spirits stayed in *Pialgal* or *Misi-khua* and they were to pass through the entrance of *Misi-khua*. At the entrance of *Misi-khua*, there was a very big giant called 'Kulsamnu' and all the spirits should necessarily pass through her. Her job was to harass the spirits who did not achieve special position in their lifetime. It was believed that harassment led the spirits to three years of torment. But this giant was afraid of the spirits of *Thangsuah*.
5. *Tomnu:* It is another female spirit. It rarely caused

trouble to mankind. It is considered to be a harmless spirit.

6. *Tan nungaah:* They were good feminine spirits who blessed the hunters and often associated with man. They were believed to be very beautiful and lived in the deep forest. It was believed that they used to fall in love with brave hunters and often helped them in their hunting.

7. *Pheisam: Pheisam* was believed to be a female spirit having one thigh only. Phei means thigh, and *sam* means deficit. Though *Pheisam* had only one leg it did not suffer from the lack of physical strength. It could fly from one big tree to another. This spirit was believed to be flying at night, so whenever one heard the sound of something flying in the air at night they called it *Pheisamleng* (a flying *Pheisam*). Its single-legged nature could be known from the fact that it left behind a trail of only one foot print on the sand bed of rivers. The foot prints were more or less same as that of a small baby. It had power to control over animals. So, hunters as a rule avoided whistling in time of hunting in the jungle lest *pheisam* would hide the beasts. Hunters could not shoot them unless they were permitted by *pheisam*. There were some hunters who had good relation with the pheisam. Such hunters could easily hunt any kind of wild animals and managed to kill not only one but even two animals in a single day. *Pheisam* also gave vested wealth in the form of property, money, cattle, rice etc., upon those who worshipped her. But if propitiation of the Pheisam was rescinded, the *pheisam* became atrocious and withdrew all the blessings which it had given to the worshipper, ultimately reducing them to a very destitute and wretched condition.[8]

8. *Siha Gamngah/Gamlahleen:* In free English translation, it means 'the spirits who keep the land'.

These spirits were of the evil kinds and were feared by the primitive Simtes. They were also known as male spirits who caused diseases, sickness and even death to hunters and travellers who ventured into their territories. They dwelt in the jungle. To appease the spirit, effigy of a buffalo made of clay was offered along with *'Zu'*.

9. *Thadam: Thadams* were the souls of dead people. As believed some souls did not go to heaven but remained on this earth. Their main work was to disturb men, threaten them when they went to the jungle and sometimes disturbed them in the village at night. So, if the Simtes heard a sound like the weeping of a man or a woman in the jungle, they would say *thadam* is weeping.[9]

10. *Dawi: Dawi* were the spirits which appeared like human beings with hands and legs. They had pointed faces like those of a deer while others had curved faces as that of a parrot. Their nails resembled those of wild animals. *Dawis* were of two genders. In one of the Simte folktales, there is a tale about a very beautiful young *dawi* lady who fell in love with a human being and even had physical relation with him .Besides this, there was a story of young *dawi* bachelors courting a young lady at night. When the young *dawi* bachelors were sitting around the fire place (*Tap-kuang*) with their faces turning away from the light, the young lady, suspecting the real nature of her visitors, suddenly brought meisel (bundle of burning sticks) to light them saying, *lenglatemelenphottadihnie* [10](let us look at the faces of our visitors). She shouted with alarm when she saw the mouth of the visitors curved like that of chicken. Instantly, the visitors run scattered and vanished through the small holes of the bamboo walls.

11. *Kau*: *Kau* or *Kausiais* was a malignant spirit and

synonymous to evileye. The evil eye was believed to be capable of causing injury, bad luck and sometimes even death to a person. But the concept and its significance varied widely from culture to culture. The person with the evil eye might cast his gaze intentionally or unintentionally. There are two types of *Kau*:[11]

(a.) *Gamkau:* It was an evil spirit of a particular area of a jungle. Anyone who encountered this spirit could fall seriously sick. Sometimes at night it was seen as fire on the hillside from a far without devastating the area. The main work of the *Gamkau* was to charm man and sucked his blood. So when such fire was seen it was believed that *Gamkau* was flying in search of food. The fire emitted was known as Kaumei-de (Kau. means evil spirits and *meide means* carrying light or fire). One interesting fact regarding the *Gamkau* is that the fire could be seen only from a far, but disappeared when one went nearer to it while it could still be seen by others from a far distance.

(b.) *Kausia:* It was a greedy spirit that could enter into a person and converted him into a different person by changing his voice, behaviour and strength. Such spirit could be released only when it was appeased with what it required. Again here *Kausia* is said to be of two types; one is having '*Ki*' (horn) and could enter inside a person's body but could not stay. The other did not have *Ki* (horn) and could stay inside forever. Hence, a person who possessed *Kau* could pass it on from generation to generation.

12. *Keuhthang:* It was a spirit which usually produced two sounds to make its presence known. The first sound means '*keuh*,' and the second sound as *thang*.

Keuhthang did not harm human beings. Sometimes it dropped pieces of mud over the beds at night from the roof of houses. *Keuhthang* could also be challenged to play the game called *Suhtum Kiheeh* where one person held one end of the Suh (rice pounding pole) and another person held the other end. The two persons turned the pole clockwise against each other to see who was stronger. Young people sleeping together at the Bachelor's Dormitory often challenged Keuhthang to play the game of *Suhtum Kiheeh*. When the young men were ready, *Keuhthang* would not come. When relaxed thinking that *Keuhthang* would not be coming, *Keuhthang* suddenly would turn the pole defeating the young men in the game.[12]

13. *Siha: Si* means death, and *ha* means ghost/spirit. Therefore, *Siha* means ghost of dead persons. The word *Siha* in common parlance is used to refer to any unseen spirit. *Siha* could be seen in different forms. It is believed that usually after a dead body was buried at the common cemetery, spirit having body like that of human being can be seen at night. Even though their physical features could not be noticed clearly, they resembled the deceased. *Sihas* are also known to exist in male and female forms.

The Role of Priests and Sacrifices

The Siampu played a very important role in the social, political and religious life of the Simtes. He could not refuse any call. Without him there could be no sacrifices or rituals associated with the spirits and gods. The Siampu used to act as mediator between men and spirits. He was believed to know all sources of problems and illness caused by the spirits and the type of sacrifices needed to appease the spirits. The priest could be from any clan in the village. He was respected next to the chief in power.

The priest is called *Siampu* in Simte, *Thempi* in Thadou, *Puithiamin* in Mizo. Every Simte village had a priest who presided over various functions relating to the spirit worshipping ceremonies and feasts. Sick persons generally consulted him as to what the spirits required. After feeling the pulse of the sick person the priest pronounced the name of animal to be killed to appease the spirit. Then the sacrifices were made under the supervision of the priest.

Dawi (magic or charm) played an important role in the religious life of the Simtes. It was a channel to communicate with the objects they worshipped The *Siampu* was the person who knew the art of communicating with the spirits and exercised it, and without him there could be no sacrifices because there would be no way to reach the ear of the objects of worship. By using this *dawi* (magic or charm) a person could harm, manipulate or even kill another person.[13]

With the coming of Christianity, the Simtes have embraced the Christian faith and have given up the worship of the spirits and related sacrifices. In place of seeking the *Siampu*, any sick would approach a pastor to pray for them. Alongside the prayer, they would seek medical help to cure their sickness. Still, the traditional and religious practices of the forefathers are recounted as part of history.

REFERENCES

1. E.B. Tylor, *Primitive Culture*, New York, 1871, pp. 428-447.
2. Tualchin Neihsial, *History and Culture of the Zoumis*, Unpublished PhD Thesis, MU, 1991, p. 88.
3. Niangdeihnuam, *The Study of the Thangkhal Tribe of Manipur*, Unpublished PhD Thesis, MU, 2008, p. 49.
4. Prim S. Vaiphei, *The Vaiphei Tribe*, Churachandpur, 1991, p. 23.
5. Jamkhothang Haokip, 'The Concept of God in Thadou/Kuki Religion', in S. Shyamkishore (ed.), *Tribal Religion*, Delhi, 2012, p. 180.
6. *Ibid*.
7. Pauliankhup, *The Traditional Beliefs and Practices of the Vaipheis of Manipur*, Unpublished M.Phil. Dissertation, MU, 2009, p. 10.
8. Interview with Mrs. Khupzavung, 90, Chiengkongpang, 2010.

9. Pauliankhup, *op. cit.*, p. 12.
10. Interview with Chinlam & Nengkhup, Beulahlane, Churachandpur, 28 August 2010.
11. *Ibid.*
12. *Ibid.*
13. Interview with T. Kaijalian, Bethlehem Veng, Churachandpur, 14 September, 2011.

7

GENESIS OF KUKI-CHIN-ZO WOMEN'S POLITICAL EVOLVEMENT

Hoipi Haokip

> *"In this age, in this island...[we have] women who would have done honour to any age or country; who in a refined taste and cultivated understanding to a feeling heart, who adorn their talents and their sensibility with sentiments of virtue, honour and humanity. We have women who could have reasoned with Locke, who might have disputed the laurel with Pope, and to whom Adisson would have listened with pleasure"—William Russell.*

In much of the Kuki-Chin-Zo written records of history, women's history is minimal. Women hardly surface as historical actors. New perspectives have emerged which changed the historical perspective. This chapter therefore, addresses the historical questions that require women's outlooks, actions and involvement as a part of the quest for these questions. Where women totally absent during the Anglo-Kuki war or the *Ina* Movement? If so why were they absent and if not what prompted them to be a part of this movement and how did they contribute towards such historical movement? This chapter hegins with a thoughtful consideration of their presence and involvement that had been for long silent? It also delves into the various women's organisations that eventually emerged in Manipur and its genesis behind their emergence.

Introduction

To cite RomilaThapar, "History was an explanation of what happened in the past, an attempt to understand the past, and of basing this understanding on 'critical enquiry' incorporated into what is also called the historical method'. Historical understanding also has to be viewed as a' process in time"[1].

Women are seen and perceived in ways the male dominated society at large projects them. Thus the chronicles of Kuki-Chin-Zo women's participation in the Anglo-Kuki war and INA has never been of much importance for a male dominated society such as the Kukis. Historians and critics agree that war and resistance have traditionally been considered as man's business... For the most part, before 1980s, women's involvement in wartime activities were either completely overlooked, mentioned incidentally, or as cases of extraordinarily heroic participation... Until this time war and resistance were defined along gendered lines and labelled as masculine.[2]

Chin-Kuki-Zo women in Manipur too have a long history of participation in the struggle for national liberation both in the traditional formal arenas and on the front line. More recently, they have been deeply involved in the vibrant civil society, promoting a respect for diverse name and in non-government organization.

Yet, so far as their political histories are concerned, they have not been included in formal power structures to any significant extent. Though, there are exceptional women, they appear to have no significant influence on political decision making either in general or with respect to issues of gender significantly. The decades of the 1950s and 60s were a watershed in the writing of history. Histories of the past continued to be written as they are to this day, and there continues to be a valuable gathering of evidences. But the more challenging trend has been to pursue answers to questions that relate to why and how something happened among those who have to be justified by evidence as well as logical argument. There is also a need to integrate a variety of facets in constructing a historical context. Behind this marginalisation lie women who hold the privilege of being the future instructress of man in his power to gain real power and knowledge. Yet, they have been pictured as a silent and weak personage, their role being hidden in subterfuge.

Pre-Colonial Period

While women are still officially not allowed in combat in almost all nations, there is a long history of female involvement in warfare. Espionage knows no gender and in fact being female it could provide less suspicio on. In the context of the Kuki-Chin-Zo society too women despite not being a participant in warfare, they somehow remain an important source of rendering help in one way or the other in the form of supplying arms, aiding in the manufacture of arms, or serving as spies.

Kuki-Chin-Women in Manipur have been playing commendable roles creating different fates for themselves, particularly before and after the British Colonial rule. Though, most of the women involve in such kind of activities have been recorded, yet it is vey much an undeniable fact that their presence have always been an unwritten account, taken for granted. Despite being illiterate in terms of modern education during the pre-colonial period, they have contributed and enhanced the socio-economic condition of their family, village and community as such.

In the Kuki-Chin-Zo society women took care of the fields, hoeing, tending, harvesting. They also haul firewood, built and maintain household chores. Men meanwhile were concerned with hunting and fishing. In such a situation the every day household management lies on her. So, she is well versed in the administration and running of her house, which have enhanced her capability to be much more diplomatic, loyal and courage than her male counterparts.

During my quest to find if women really occupy a subordinate role as depicted by most colonial ethnographers, I had gain much insight to the fact that women are well versed in the art of sorcery and magical chants, though society did not formally acknowledge their roles as priestesses. Besides, every Kuki-Chin –Zo women are well versed in the art of composing eloquent and poignant ballads and poems to inspire a community. The Kuki-Chin women are superb poets. Important events or tragedies are often chronicled in the forms of poems by the women. These remain as a source of oral history for constructing historical accounts. One such incident where the wife of Chassad composed an ode when the cap of the slain leader of the British was presented to her as a mark of respect. It goes like this:

> *"Keila Khoi ang kakiton*
> *Phung gol laitha laisim lun*
> *Khotin dong nol e"*
> (Despite all my imperfections
> My families with a remarkable token
> Honour me worthily worthwhile
> Passing through all the gates
> With well wide recognition.)

Another instance which shows the remarkable poetic composition was composition by Mrs. Haotinkhup, the queen of Kamhao dynasty on hearing the fame of Pu Ngulsong, the chief of Lonpi:

> *"Jang toni tuisong a peng mi umlou e*
> *Katoi song.....O tuilum pholngou*
> *Nang jing jen eim O"*

Free translation :
" A few are born with exception
My beloved Ngulsong, the Phulngou (Vaphol)
O.....you are my guest."[3]

Traditionally when a man participated in a successful attack on another community he may be rewarded with increased status and perhaps an added wife.[4] Thus, during those days of head-hunting a man who failed to bring a head of the enemy as a trophy was mocked and scorned by the women folks. On the other hand, a man with the most number of heads was counted as a hero. Thus, women could either deride a man as a coward or a hero. So , rather than being ridiculed by a mere woman a man often in order to save face and as an act of bravado had to prove his heroism and audacity, lesst he fails to find a bride of his choice.

Yet, despite this the most important political difference, notable was that she could neither be an inheritor of her father's land nor rise to the position of a decision maker. This fact had been reiterated by Carey and Tuck[5], "There is always a strong feeling against women inheriting anything and, unless a woman has powerful relations, she will entirely be ignored at the division of estate, and even a widow have to work hard to secure any particular property which has been specially bequeathed to her by her husband on his deathbed".

Ester Boserup[6] opines that "women made significant productive contributions in the subsistence economy.....her freedom is but in the economic where she labours and wields control over her sons and daughters but not her husbands......her prestige and value is highlighted in the traditional society when she can thus perform such ceremony or that of her ability to muster as much economic gain in the post-modern society, adding wealth and affluent to her husband's family but not to that of her own". This statement holds relevance for the Kuki-Chin-Zo women. Though she is attributed to the economic enhancement of her family or that of her community for which she is honoured by the performance of ceremonies such as the 'Chang-Ai'[7] (ceremonial rites perform in connection with harvesting of surplus immeasurable crops) the governance was in the hands of the men. Being the chief's wife did not exempt her from such economic activities. She, like all other women has to perform what is expected of a woman, i.e., to fetch water, wood, weave, tends the crops, brew wine and provide for the needs of her family. From dawn to dusk she toils hard and has to ceaselessly work with no grudges. Her task ranges from household domesticity and giving a helping hand in the clearing of forest for *jhum* cultivation to that of even constructing a house when it falls short of man in times of war raids or intra-tribal raids where she has to look after herself and her family.

The Kuki-Chin Zo traditional social structures discourage the participation of women in decision making. They are forbidden from taking part in the special gathering, primary election, and in matters pertaining to marriage, divorce, etc. She has no say. Nor is her opinion sought. Every final decision falls on her father, brothers or her uncles.[8]

Despite this when her husband dies she can remarry and if she is the chief's wife and her son is a minor then a woman can on behalf of her husband takes the mantle of authority as a chieftainess and her decision is obeyed and respected by the council of ministers and her people. As such quite a number of women emerged as Chieftainess wielding power as successful rulers well versed in the customary laws of the Kuki-Chin-Zo socio-political system. On the one hand, a common woman may not be allowed to represent her husband in the village council; however, if she is a widow then on behalf of her husband, she can exercise opinion and be a part of the village council, Though in one way married women are treated as subordinate, exceptions are allowed in the case of the widows, they are treated with respect and reverence.

Colonial Period

The Colonial period in Manipur is significant due to the Anglo-Kuki-War (1917-19) and the INA (1942-43). Movement resonant across the Kuki-Chin-Zo dominated areas. During the Anglo-Kuki War and the Indian National Army, Kuki-Chin Women were undeniably present at all levels. Like all individuals, these women performed small and random acts of resistance aiding men, encouraging them and assisting them in manufacturing gun powders (the Kukis have skills in manufacturing of gun powder). As a large quantity of gun powder was required for waging against the British, assistance of women became important. Building barricades and doing whatever they assisted men. Women were recruited for certain support task in assisting the men folks. During the war period administrative work felt upon women. The wife of the chief now acted as Chieftainess on behalf of their husband who had to fight against the British. Women took over the decision-making of the village. According to the customary rights of the Kuki-Chin-Mizo society, in the absence of the husband, the wife could act as the chief of the village, and hence, during this period she took up the mantle of Chiefship administrating on her husband's behalf and the men folks had to obey her. Her presence was always required, if any important decision was to be initiated by her council of ministers and so consent could never be taken for granted, if she as the chieftainess disagreed. Then, no further actions or policies could be undertaken and so the council had to defer it or alternative means had to be sought. She alone could also propitiate ceremonial rites in the absence of her husband by calling upon the *thempu* or shaman of the village in her husband's name. Her presence required before the shaman could commence ceremonial rites for the husband's campaign. Thus, despite allotting women an inferior position, occasion also arose wherein sole authority lied with her. She even aided in transporting arms and ammunitions.[9] As said, women were also actively engaged in manufacturing of gun powders which the Kuki-Chin-Zo are an expert.[10] When the War took place the women composed great many ballads to inspire the men in fighting valiantly against the British.

One such ballad that was composed by the "women folk of Laijang" (in Tamenglong District, Manipur), the village of the great Kuki war Hero, Tintong Haokip, before the commencement of battle field goes like this as sung by Pu Thonglun Haokip[11]:

> *"Laijang Tintong bul Lunmmang*
> *Pupa Khanggol she in lang*
> *Sitcha kaigol si-dounan,*
> *Kaigal lhingtei hen*
>
> Free translation :
> "Daring Tintong of Laijang
> May thy fame soar
> Against thy foes thine wage
> May thy force be reckon[12]

When the INA troops marched towards Manipur, the information was propagated by women by the name of Hoijakim and her husband Lunngam Kuki who brought the pamphlets of the Indo-Japanese forces for the first time into Manipur valley. It was said that while they were away their son died at home for want of care.

As far as women's role during the INA Movement was concerned, K.R. Palit[13] counts that young girls of the Kuki tribe were forced to work as spies for them against the INA. These girls occasionally approached our INA-Japanese commanders with all British Military secrets." According to Pu Thonglhun Haokip, the relation with the Kukis and Japanese force was such that there was mutual respect for Kuki women and during their occasional intrusion in the Kuki villages for their daily food supplies, the Indo-Japanese force never once tried to forcibly assault the women folks, nor such incident ever occurred rather since the Japanese were new to the terrain the women folk sometimes act as guides for the Indo-Japanese forces and thereby rendering every possible aid they could in assisting them.

Such was the sacrifice of the Kuki-Chin-Zo woman that

their her child was snatched away by the cruel fate of death and was forced to suffer numerous hardship at the hands of the British but their intelligence and tact help them turn their tables by aiding the Indo-Japanese forces.

Post-Independence Era

The introduction of education among girls in the hills of Manipur partly by the Christian missionaries[14] and the Government of India[15] (Jamini Devi, 1989) gave fillip among women to claim their legitimate rights. Eventually, the introduction of education paved the way for the formation of various Kuki Women Bodies. Reflecting the professionalization of women's movements, another arena in which women have articulated their political and social aspirations is the formation of numerous non-government organisations that have sprung up during the past decades often funded by foreign donors. Some are truly autonomous; others more or less associated with the male dominated political agencies.

These newly formed women organizations are significant. These organizations strive for the realization of the principal of equality between men and women. Its work is fundamentally grounded in "International Human Rights Covenants" as well as local customs and values which conform to the principal of gender equality. Some Kuki women organisations that stand out prominently are: Kuki Women Union, Hmar Women Union, Zomi Mothers Union.

Kuki Women Union

The formation of the Kuki Women Union has its genesis in the ethnic conflict between the Nagas and Kukis in 1993. The KWU was established initially in Motbung, Senapati District, and then later shifted in Churachandpur District in 1993. According to a founder member and secretary of KWU, Ms. Awei Haokip[16], this is her excerpt, "I was appointed as the secretary since I was the only educated woman" she added "those days communication between one village to another was difficult since there were no access to phone nor cell phone, the only sources of communication available was a landline phone at Kangpokpi, which often many a time was not so easily accessible, with the death toll escalating with sufferings and fear on the rise, a handful of women decided to take matters in their own hands and so henceforth decided to form an organisation which would aid the widows, orphans, the displaced persons. Armed only with the love and compassion for their sufferings brethren and women-folk and destitute children, they voluntarily decided to come out to the frontline from their warm hearts and simple life of domesticity by playing humanitarian services for the Kuki community.

Presently, the KWU is brought under the aegis of the Kuki Inpi (Apex body of the Kukis). The Kuki Women Union consisting of limited, dedicated members decided to come out to the frontline to play humanitarian services for the Kuki community. It has played a great role as co-ordinator between State Government and Central Government to intervene. It also played immense role as peace mission to desist from violence. Presently, the KWU is headed by Mrs. Rose Mangshi Haokip (Retired Lecturer and social worker) as the President of the Kuki Women Union. Again on 25th June, 1997 clashes between the Kukis and Paite started. The KWU started relief work, rehabilitation of refugees and medical assistance. Hapless to the continued violence that erupted women first started to pray in churches, seeking solace for a peaceful solution for both sides, as the State failed to check its escalation. Relief works were carried on a massive scale from village to village. The ethnic clashes reduced many homeless, orphaned and widowed. In 1998, they started an orphanage initially with eleven children. The numbers have increased. The orphanage is inter-denominational. Both girls and boys between the ages 5-15 years. are living there. There are more boys than girls in the orphanage. Girls are normally taken for adoption by families. Seeing the unselfish sacrifices, zeal, and passion and success of these women the Kuki Inpi decided to support them and brought them under their aegis.

Hmar Women Association

Similarly, Hmar Women's Association (HWA) was set up in 1988. In the wake of the Mizoram government (under the then Chief Ministership of Lalthwantnzhawla) issuing warrant of arrest in the Churachandpur District, Manipur declaring the Hmar Peoples convention as underground unit. The HWA resented the unlawful arrest of civilians and organized mass women procession in the death of the night towards the police station for the release of men arrested. the HWA was successful in its movement securing the release of the arrested menfolk. The association also works for the protection of women from social and political violence and atrocities against women.

The Hmar Women Association took up the cases of allegations of the mass rape of twenty-five Hmar women (victims included four minor girls) in Churachandpur district by UNLF which resulted in the statutory inquiry by the National Commission for Women (NCW). A protest rally was organized in Churachandpur district on 4th April, 2010 jointly supported by the ZMA and the KWU.

Zomi Mothers Association

The Zomi Mothers Association (ZMA) was registered in 1991 with Grace Zammi as the Secretary and Joycee as Vice President. The yeomen services of the ZMA in the ethnic violence in Churachandpur district in 1997 is promising. During the clashes, the ZMA provided relief material. The clashes took place in all villages in the hill areas. Houses were burnt down and many were killed. The ZMA distributed relief materials. They conducted their own peace building activities. The Zomi women prayed with the Kuki women. The ZMA found places and homes for Zomi orphaned children in Coimbatore. In 2003, when clashes broke out between the Karbi and the Hmar, relief measures and rehabilitation were given to the affected in Churachandpur district. The ZMA, also started propagating Self Help Groups and have eight groups at the moment. The ZMA also intervened in 1998 when an alcoholic father sold his youngest daughter without the mother's acknowledgement. The ZMA found the child and handed her back to the mother.

Conclusion

Women are "represented" than to be described. Their stories told much but less allowed to tell their own stories. Despite their contributions and achievements, society continues to ignore marginalised women. Society still deems them as incapable to manage State policies and enter the arenas of politics. Their position is always undermined by the society. In spite of constitutional equal status in social, economic and political spheres, Kuki-Chin-Zo women still have to struggle to achieve their rightful place. The numerous contributions that women made during the Anglo-Kuki War or that of the INA movement remained but a hazy often muddled up records since men had felt their contribution as insignificant. Only recently interest has been shown in this area but due to dearth of written documents it proves a big hurdle with most of the elders who have witnessed or heard the tales being told by their fathers gone but, still it is not too late and a lot of in-depth study needs to be undertaken. These heroic deeds of some women during the Anglo-Kuki War and INA pave the way for political orientations and birth of Kuki-Chin-Zo Women Association.

REFERENCES

1. Susheela Kaushik (ed.), *Women's Oppressions: Patterns and Perspectives*, Shakti Books, Delhi, 1985, p. 11.
2. Cynthoe Enloe, *The Morning after Sexual Politics after End of Cold War*, Berkeley, 1993, pp. 246-247.
3. Espirit de Corps, 1917-1919, Patriotic Souveneir, Imphal, 27 February, 2010.
4. John H. Bodley, *Cultural Anthropology: Tribes, Status and Global System*, Aeta Press, USA, 2011, p. 53.

5. Bertram Carey and H.N. Tuck, *The Chin Hills: A History of the People, Our Dealings with their Customs and Manners and a Gazetteer of their Country*, Tribal Research Institute, Aizawl, Mizoram, 2008, p. 208.
6. Ester Boserup, *Women's Role in Economic Development*, New York: St. Martin's Press, 1986.
7. T.S. Gangte, *The Kukis*, Gyan Publishing, New Delhi, 1993, p.185.
8. Bertram Carey and H.N. Tuck, *op. cit.*, p. 210.
9. Interview with Pu Thonglhun Haokip, 75, New Lambuland, 15-07-2011.
10. Tingneichong G.Kipgen, *Women's Role in the 20th Century*, Kalpaz Publication, Delhi, 2010.
11. Interview with Pu Thonglhun Haokip, 75, New Lambuland, 15-07-2011.
12. Translation is mine.
13. K.R. Palit, *My Adventure with INA Movement*, Lion Press House, New Delhi, 1946.
14. L. Jayaseelan, *Impact of Missionary Movement in Manipur*, Scholar Publishing House, New Delhi, 1990.
15. Jamini, *Education in Manipur*, Imphal, 1980.
16. Interview with Ms. Awei Haokip (founder member of the Kuki Women Union), 47, Motbung Village, 2012.

8

PROVERBIAL EXPONENTS AND WOMEN
A STUDY OF THE THADOU-KUKI WOMEN OF MANIPUR

Arfina Haokip

Introduction

As abundant as proverbs are in the pre-literate society like the Thadou-Kukis where folklores form the basis of historical records, proverbs also remain as one such important source through which the position of women can be understood by studying the existing common proverbs that had been in usage since time immemorial. Its investigation has been seriously undertaken only recently. The principal difficulty has been in the assembling of such maxims on women to base its study. Its oral nature has made it all the more impossible to collect such age-old adage commonly used in the Thadou-Kuki society.

Hence, this chapter is partly an attempt to study the existing common proverbs of the Thadou-Kukis. To highlight the position of women and its concept among the patrilineal Kuki society, it is to point out how women have always been viewed and treated in the society and the subsequent inferences and attitude towards women. Using the various terms, the chapter tries to understand the position of women among the Thadous Kukis through folk literature. According to the New Encyclopaedia Britannica, folk literature is defined as the lore chiefly of unlettered peoples transmitted by word of mouth. It consists as does as written literature, of prose, verse, narratives, poems, songs, myths, dramas, rituals, proverbs, riddles, and the like[1]. The characteristic of folk literature is the fact that it is oral. Hence, this chapter is an attempt to study the adage of the Thadou-Kuki based on proverbial exponents and traces the role and its significance in the society. How far woman is held as subordinate or how far her role is being assigned?

Conceptual Theory and its Function

According to Meander, 'A proverb is a' short generally, known sentence of the folk which contains wisdom, truth, morals and traditional views in a metaphorical fixed and memorisable form and which is handed down from generation to generation'.[2] The Wikipedia cites proverbs as 'Almost in all linguistic groups the use of proverbs gets a pivotal place in the expression referring to some context and situation. Proverbs expresses a truth, based on common sense or the practical experience of humanity. They are often metaphorical.' Through the usage of proverbs it is possible to know the importance attached to some elements of institutions and sections in the society. Proverbs serve as a specific and important intellectual function – that of subsuming the particular under the general. Hence, proverbs are important tools which can help one to gauge the level of status they occupy in the society. Given the above terms, the Thadou-Kukis too have many proverbs pertaining to their social life. They have a varied and rich number of proverbs which had definitely been unexplored as a means of historical sources. Therefore, with regard to women among the Thadou-Kukis, numerous proverbs have been in usage and passed on from one generation to another. As such proverbs serve as a function of deeper meaning, one which can be understood only through the analysis of social situations to which they are appropriate.[3]

These proverbs act as a moral and disciplinary usage of guidance instilling a sense of obedience among the women when certain acts are practised in the society. It is also referred to make women feel that they are an inferior to men and thus mentally keep them as the man wants them. In other words, to show that without men women cannot survive alone, they are kept unworth of their own. Herzog defines it thus as an important function of proverb is to smooth the social friction and dissatisfaction and to ease the individual in his efforts to adjust himself in his setting and fate. If people disagree, if they work at cross-purposes, if a person complain of injustice, an older more experienced, or less concerned person is always at hand a comforting, quieting, light shedding proverbs.[4]

Therefore, proverbs serve as a medium of instilling obedience, guidance and teaching even among the Thadou-Kuki. They are used as instruction when certain individual such as women or children fails to follow the dictum of the society. It is a means through which women are maintained under male domination. In other words, codes of conduct are transmitted through these maxims.

Conventional Aphorism

The vital role of some maxims and its dispensation in the Thadou-Kuki has been illustrated below:

In the traditional Thadou-Kuki society, weaving is regarded as a woman's work. Women unskilled in weaving are regarded as useless. She is often looked at by her weaving attributes and skill. Therefore, during her marriage, a woman is normally presented with weaving implements as part of her dowry which is gifted by her parents. Regardless of her class every woman whether belonging to the chiefs' family or the common family, she is expected to be skilled in weaving. Hence, the adage runs *'numei pon khong theilou vin akoma chapang kichem angoh'e'*[5] meaning when certain woman does not know how to weave skilfully she often blames it on the children playing nearby for she never wants to be faulted in her lack of weaving clothes skilfully or artistically. The society, especially, the men often mock it by referring to this statement whenever certain household work has not been done as she is expected to do so. Instead of taking the blame on her part she tends to blame other people or her children or *vice versa.* This maxim has been mostly coined by the men in the society implying the fickleness of women.

Another usage which is referred to women in a derogatory term *"Numei gilou le meivang nisa thoh a hahsai"* referring to a wicked woman is as unbearable as the hot rays of the sun. Women have always been viewed as wicked and so their company is unbearable. In the Thadou-Kuki society men tend to eye women as always in the negative sense, so in order to escape their presence, this term has been referred and commonly used so that the men can go out as they pleased with their male companions. It is always regarded that when a man stays too much in a woman's company, the man is always influenced by her woman. When a woman marries she is regarded as dead to her maternal family. She is tied to her husband for good or bad and her identity ceases to exist within her family. When a woman dissatisfied her husband or her relatives or in-laws, she is treated as a non-existent identity whose sole responsibility is to please her in-laws, husband, and relatives of her new family. If anything she displeases to her husband or her in-laws, she is often being scolded by this adage *'Numei gilou vin anung velsom ale e'*. It signifies that if she acts contrary against the wishes, manners or the customary norms of the society and caught the wrath of her husband, she is forewarned by this proverb, i.e., to be prudent or else she would be sent back to her parental house. Besides whenever a woman travels she is expected to carry on with her normal activities of helping and aiding in the kitchen. If she fails to do so she is regarded as irresponsible woman who does not know how to behave in her role as a guest. So her work never ceases. Woman who fails to acknowledge what she is supposed to do is referred as being untaught. The very old adage of *'numei kholjin suktum to jin'* means that a travelling woman carries with her a wooden pestle. She is expected according to normal convention to assist her host in cooking or washing or *vice versa.* This maxim depicts that despite long distant journey as a guest, it is her role not to forget her duties even in the house of her host. Her task of domesticity always follows her wherever she goes.[6]

In a patriarchal society, woman is never allowed to be politically involved in the decision making so as to strengthen this traditional maxim, *'Numei thusei le jana vadoh ham'*. This signifies that women are well known for no significant values in their talks. A woman is always accepted to have no knowledge in administration and also the running of the village and so any matter which pertains to important decision can never be sought from her. Nor she is looked at as a reliable source for seeking any kind of political information. If any advice is being sought by her husband then it is only in such matter which concerns with social matter. Her mind and thought are regarded shallow and incapable of the knowledge about the decision making, which is a man's domain. In the Thadou-Kuki society *'Numei lungthim le vohkong dong'* means that her mind and thought are as shallow as a pig's wooden pan. It refers to unimportance of her quality as decision maker, strategist or ruler, definitely hinting that she cannot become a person of village responsibility. Henceforth, in the Thadou-Kuki society, a woman is never allowed any sort of inheritance in immovable assets such as land. It runs *"Numei din gamtum aumpoi"* meaning that a woman cannot inherit land which she can call her own. Besides, when her husband dies, her next kin of the family, her uncle or son inherit the land. According to Thadou customary law, as in patriarchal and patrilocal society, woman cannot inherit land.[7] Besides, when she get married she is no longer a part of her mother's family. Giving land in her name would be akin to giving land to some other people who is not supposed to inherit it.

Woman cannot be a part of the political village assembly. Nor can she be elected as a member of the council of ministers. Her presence is only required for looking after the needs of the man and in serving food or *ju* (rice beer) to the members in council. If she is the chief's wife, even then she can only be the head of the village under the regency of her minor son. When her son attains his age, her regency ends and so as her power. Woman is not regarded as belonging to her husband until she gives birth son[s]. Only then, her position is secured and can be truly counted as a member of her husband's family. She can be easily divorced on the grounds of her inability to give birth to a son no matter how many daughters. A man can thus easily divorce her and can go for next marriage. Such instances have been found in the Thadou-Kuki society. Women are being divorced due to their inability of giving birth to a son. While, looking at the nature of such norms, one notices that even till today a man often resorts to divorcing his wife at the insistence of his family or on his inability to have a son. Since descent follows through the male line, a woman who is unable to have a son is regarded as *ingam'*[8] (extinct from the clan). The blame is always on the shoulder of a woman. Her position is arbitrary depending on the birth of a son. A proverb describes women are *'Numei le chapang simlou'*[9], i.e., women and children are never counted in the village thus signifying that women are at par with children whose words and advice can never be taken seriously. Their places are not much counted in important issues concerning the socio-political affairs of families or that of the village welfare. Their duties are to concentrate wholly in household chores. She is never regarded as a fully mature member of the community. Though, she may wield certain authority in her family, it is always behind the curtains. Even in her son's marriage or that of her daughter, it is fully under the men's domain and she has no say except in counselling or narrating her choice of preferences. When she is divorced her father, brothers, and male members do not have the full right in initiating the fines nor is she allowed whether she have any choice in the matter of her son which is decided by the family. A married woman is never taken seriously by the menfolk. If her husband died and she lives as a widow in her husband's family without re-marrying, she is honoured by the family and her community. In every village it is always the rule that every individual should always contribute any kind of assistance may be in kind or whenever she requires. A widow is exempted from paying taxes and any legal fines. She can take part in the village councils, gives advice on issues pertaining to the welfare of her village. Every man pays due regard to her and her words of council are always taken seriously. She, as a widow, can also issue words of authority in her family. Hence, when any kind of dispute which cannot be brought to any amicable solution by the villagers, a widow's help and guidance is often sought. Hence *'Meithai vangin kho alhing e'*[10] symbolises the importance of widow with an acknowledgement that without a widow a village population is never complete. It implies the role of widow complements the wholeness of a village. Without a widow a village community is never complete. A widow makes the village complete. Unlike other society where widows are ignored, in the Thadou-Kuki village, the presence of a widow is honoured and her presence is fully realised for the stability of the traditional Thadou- Kuki village life. Accordingly, saying runs, *'in to phat le vabang phat Alibang*e'[11] explaining that a widow is regarded as good embodiment of fertility like a stretch of fertile land by the side of a stream. Widow's position is one of pleasures and gratitude. She is seen as compassion, where every individual of the community takes pleasure in her company. She is free neither from ostracism nor ill-respect nor against any kind of prejudice. All weary men and women take shelter in her house and all assist her in her hardship so that she is not short of any kind of wants. Her curse is feared and so. She is regarded as a woman of integrity and honesty. None could ignore her on the ground of her being a widow. The Chief too also fears to displease her lest misfortune befall his family.

Conclusion

The nature of the available maxims on women in the Thadou-Kuki society showed how women is viewed. This age-old adage signifies the subordinate position of woman. It highlights the fact that since the primordial age woman has always been under the umbrella of such maxims. It validates to bind women within the control of men; else she would rise up against men. Just as myths are generated to explain the physical world and its inhabitants, so folklore provides support for institutions and behaviour patterns of a culture. Besides suggesting rules for conduct, folklore also drives home the need for proper social behaviour by holding up socially accepted norms and by eulogizing those who follow them. It is also referred as a form of teaching through manner. Women live under a strict conventional norms in a manner that they do not deviate from the so called accepted norms. It emphasises useful information in drawing one to analyse the mindset of male's attitude towards women in the Thadou-Kuki society of Manipur. Proverbs refer mediums of explanation of understanding the relation: men *vis-á-vis* women in the society. These adages are often referred commonly by the men folks. Hence the proverbs so available put a dent on the morals of women who normally and eventually come to identify and associate themselves with it.

REFERENCES

1. *The New Encyclopeadia Britannica*, Vol. VII, William Benton, Chicago, London, 1980, p. 454.
2. William Bascom, 'Folklore' in Sills (ed.), *The Encyclopedia of Social Sciences*, Vol. V, USA, McMillan Company and Free Press, 1968, p. 497.
3. G. Herzog, *Jabo Proverbs from Liberia*, London, 1936, p. 2.
4. Interview with Bulshi Touthang, 75, New Lambuland, 1-3-2009.
5. H.Kamkhenthang & T. Chingzaman, 'Traditional Paite Society: With Special Reference to Women', in B. Datta Ray & Ashok Kumar Ray (eds), *Dynamics of Power Relations in Tribal Societies of North-East India*, Om Publications, New Delhi, 2006, p.173.
6. Khaikhotinthang Kipgen,*The Thadou Kukis*, Motbung, 1982, p. 83.
7. Interview with Seijkhojang Singson, 75, Canaan Veng, 1-11-2008.
8. Tingneichong G. Kipgen, *Women's Role in the Twentieth Century: A Historical Study*, Kalpaz Publication, Delhi, 2010, p. 82.
9. *Ibid.*
10. Interview with Veikhoneng Haokip, 76, Game Village, Imphal, 3-8-2008.
11. *Ibid.*

9

ASPECTS OF MARRIAGE PAYMENT AND ITS RELEVANCE IN CHIKIM SOCIETY

Priyadarshni. M. Gangte

Introduction

The Chin-Kuki-Mizo are a people comprising several ethnic groups who are closely allied to one another. They have a common culture, tradition, language, custom, mode of cultivation, form of government, etc. They inhabit the entire Chin Hills State of Myanmar and are known 'Chin'. These same groups of people are known as 'Kuki' when they are in Manipur, Nagaland, Tripura, Assam, etc., in India and also in Chittagong Hill Tracts of Bangladesh. In recent times, these people inhabiting in the erstwhile Lushai Hills District of Assam preferred to abandon the term and called themselves as 'Mizo' which is recognised by the Government of India..

For the purpose of this chapter, therefore, the terms Chin, Kuki, Mizo would be clubbed together in the acronym, CHIKIM, which is, literally speaking a word that conveys 'all nationalities'.

Social institution, to MacIver[1], is the established form or condition of procedure characteristic of a group activity. Sutherland and Maxwell [2] said that it is a web of interrelated folkways, mores and laws which enter in some function or functions. Likewise, Green[3] contended that the social institution is the organization of several folkways into a unit which serves a number of social functions. And Ginsberg[4] was convinced to attribute it as definite and sanctioned form or mode of relationship between social beings in regard to one another or to some external object. Similarly, Gillin and Gillin[5] said that it is a functional configuration of culture pattern including actions, ideas, attitudes and cultural equipment which possess certain permanence and which is intended to satisfy felt social needs. Horton and Hunt[6] said that it is an organized system of relationship which embodies certain common rules and procedures meeting certain basic needs of the society.

It is clear that institutions are forms of procedure. Every organisation is dependent upon certain recognised and established set of rules, traditions, customs and usages which may be given names of institutions. They are the forms of procedure which are recognised and accepted by society governing the relation between individuals and groups. Thus, marriage, education, property, religion, etc., are some of the main institutions.

Characteristics of the concept of institution may, therefore, be attributed to the means of controlling individuals, collective activities of men, proceedings which are based on customs, dogmas, and means of social control that must be compulsorily obeyed by individuals which have symbols of material or non-material values that receive social recognition.

Marriage

There are thirteen forms of marriage prevalent in Chikim society. Marriage emerges as a social arrangement by which a couple is legitimized in their physical relationship and their child is given a legitimate position in the society that is often determined by the parenthood in the social sense.[7] The Chikims do not think of marriage necessarily as a union based on romantic love although beauty, character and health are always sought in choice of a wife.

Secondly, in the Chikim society, marriage involves making

of payment by the bridegroom or his kin to the father or close relative of the would-be bride in case the father had expired. Such system of understanding of the nature of marriage alliance was also prevalent in a great number of societies in ancient and modern times in all parts of the world. Making of payment of marriage by the bride-groom either in the form of kind or service to the bride's kin is an essential part of establishment of legality.[8] Marriage payment was held officially in South Africa as per native custom with payment of Mithun in general.

Hindu marriage customs, traditions and rituals are of interest because they not only have bearings on tribal forms of marriages but also have cross-cultural evidences all across the country. One can see Manu's *Dharmashastra*, Kautalya's *Arthasastra*, and other relevant literature and secondary sources.

Among some Chikim tribes, practice of marriage payment is prevalent and is known as 'bride-price', which is paid in cash, kind and '*mithun*'. Some people believe that 'bride-price' is a completed word of marriage payment alleged to have been coined by British administrators during the colonial period in India.[9] To avoid redundancy, the term 'marriage payment' will be consistently used to mean 'marriage price' or 'bride-price' in this work.

As case studies, we have tried to look into this practice among the Lushais, Lakhers,Thadous, Zomis, old Kukis and some minor groups. Our research has revealed that it was indeed a widespread phenomenon. It was a common practice among them and had significant sociological dimensions.

Dulien Speaking Mizos (Lushai)

Marriage payment is the most important factor in a Chikim marriage. No marriage can be performed unless part of marriage-payment is made in advance by the bride-groom to the bride's family. It was paid in terms of *mithuns* when barter system was practised. A *mithun* used to cost rupees forty as fixed by the British India administration in eighteenth century when currency system was first introduced in this part of the North East. Some clans had fixed the prices for their maids in the past.[10] It varied from four to ten *mithuns* depending upon the antecedents, blood and beauty of the bride. Marriage payment for a chief's daughter was as many as ten *mithuns* or more[11] for the Dulien (Lushai) speaking Chikims. Minor concessions could be given during the time of payment. In this connection, marriage payments were practically never paid up in full at once at the time of wedding for the reason that hardly anybody had enough money to pay the same at once.[12] Generally, there was a custom of marriage-payment only in instalments and the remaining to be paid after some time, i.e., twenty years or more. The customary laws of Thadou, Gangte, Vaiphei, Paite, etc., in this regard are widely different from the ones described above.[13]

Marriage-payment is a sacred institution prevalent in the Chikim society. It is, however, not to be understood as a sale price.[14] It is not a commercial transaction. Marriage payment was sometimes used as a weapon for a clever parent to reject a suitor.[15] If it is really felt that the usual payment of any part of the same was unduly delayed or was not intentionally paid, the aggrieved party could seek the chief's permission to seize any of the property of the debtor against the claim.[16]

The marriage payment consisted of two parts[17]: Manpui and Mantang. The Manpui is the price that has to go direct to the girl's father or in his absence, to her brother. If she has none of them, it has to be received by her nearest male relative. The general rate of Manpui is five *mithuns* or Rs. 100 if the girl had dowry or *thuam* in the Dulien language. The custom of increasing Rs. 20 was prevalent if the girl was provided with *Thuam*.

It is pertinent to mention that the Lushai, the Dulien speakers' custom is slightly different from others in dealing with matters relating to marriage payment. It happened in circumstances where the girl was adopted by a man since childhood then the price went to him. In cases where male relatives failed to receive the marriage payment, the mother of the bride did not marry again and had taken all the responsibilities for her daughter (bride) she would let her mother receive the payment or she could select anyone to receive her marriage payment. In case her mother remarried and had gone to live with her husband under whose care the girl was brought up could be entitled to receive the marriage payment.[18] In case she is a *falak* or illegitimate child, her mother could receive the marriage payment.[19]

During the course of our survey, we found that Parry was right about the *Mantang* or the subsidiary price of the bride, which was normally distributed to different categories of persons.[20]

(a) *Sumhmahruai*, Rs. 20, this price is payable to the bride's father or brother.

(b) *Sumfang*, Rs. 8 is payable to the bride's father or brother.

(c) *Pusum*, Rs. 6 goes to the bride's (the maternal uncle of the bride).

(d) *Palal*, Rs. 5 is to be received by any person, selected by the bride as adopted father. The *palal* in reciprocal has to give the bride a fowl and zubel (pot with rice beer) as *lawichal* (wedding feast given by recipients of *Mantang*).

(e) *Ni-ar*, Rs. 2 has to be received by the parental aunt.

(f) *Naupuakpuan*, Rs. 2 is entitled by the bride's elder sister in consideration of her having carried the bride about in her cloth when the child was a baby.

The above-mentioned subsidiary price or *mantang* are the integral parts of marriage payment. In addition to this, there are also two optional *mans*—they are *thianwan* and *lawichal*.[21]

(i) *Thianwan* Rs. 2 or Rs. 3 is payable to a friend of the bride, it is from the *manpui*. *Thianman* is refunded in case the bride left her husband *sumchchuah* (divorce of husband by wife) or *Uire* (adultery).

(ii) *Lawichal* Rs. 2 is a payment (not compulsory) payable only when the bride and the bridegroom are from different villages. When the bride is escorted by a group of friends and a man, who leads them to the bridegroom's residence. This man is known as *lawichal* in the language of Dulien speakers. He is sometimes rewarded Rs. 2 which is also to be refunded in case the bride later leaves her husband *Sumchchuah* or *Uire*.

Moreover, the following rates of marriage payment are realized:

(i) *Tlai* means head of one mithun's price Rs. 20.
(ii) *Tlai Sial* means half mithun Rs. 20.
(iii) *Sepui* means a full grown mithun Rs. 40.
(iv) *Seding* means a full grown mithun or Rs. 40.
(v) *Senufa* means a mithun and calf or Rs. 60.
(vi) *Puikhat* means Rs. 20.
(vii) *Puisawnsial* means Rs. 20.

The Maras (Lakhers)

Marriage payment among the Lakhers was quite high and this worked as a deterrent to easy divorce and fortified the position of the wife. Like the Lushais, marriage payment in the Lakher customs was shared by a long line of relatives even aunts of the bride have to receive part of it. Sometimes, sharing of the same was so complicated that litigations continued endlessly.[22] The main price was called *angkia*. Higher clan Lakhers also adopted the custom of taking higher rate of *angkia*, which varied from 10 to 70 rupees. The different parts of the marriage payment, are the *angkia*, the *puma*, the *nongcheu*, the *nangcheu*, etc. All these prices have their own subsidiary prices.[23]

The *angkia* means "house enter". It is the main price taken by the father of the bride. In some Lakher society, the *angkia* is received by the eldest son (brother) for the eldest daughter. Likewise the youngest daughter's *angkia* goes to the youngest brother.

The next payment is the *puma (Puma* has the same significance of that other prices.) which is payable only to the bride *pupa* who is her maternal uncle. The rate at which *puma* is payable depends on the rate of the angkia and if it is 60 rupees the rate of the *pumapi* or *puma* payment is also 60 rupees and is generally claimed when the couple settles down as man and wife.

The third marriage payment is the *Nongcheu. (Nongcheu* is found to have existed only in the *Lakher* society) which means 'the mother's price'. If the mother and father of the bride have been divorced, it is payable to the bride's mother. If they are still married, it is payable to the bride's mother's sister.

The fourth marriage payment is the *Nangcheu (*Nangcheu' is equivalent to *niman* or *Niar,* and it is sometimes replaced by tini), which means the aunt's price and is payable to the bride's eldest paternal aunt.

Here it would be significant to note that among the mainland communities, instead of cash, goods are sent across to every member of the bridegroom by the bride's party and *vice versa*.

The Thadou/Kukis

Among the Thadous, the marriage payment has an interesting legend.[24]

Chongthu was the younger brother of Nongmangpa, the Chief of the underworld. As per Thadou custom, in the presence of the elder brother called *Upa*, the younger brother called *Naopa* cannot become a chief. So, Noimangpa, being the elder, was the chief, Chongthu also intended to become the Chief. Therefore, he went out in search of a suitable land where he could establish himself separately as a Chief.[25] He found one. On his plan to become a chief, he wanted to go with his own close friends whom he could trust. Thus, he arranged for the marriage of each of his selected men. In doing so he made the marriage payments of each bride to their parents. In those days, no valuable property or cash was available. All the valuable items that one could think of was a *paigen*. This was a belt made of leather and decorated with a kind of beads, called *longchang*, in seven lines.[26] This was then considered to be a very rare and valuable item of property. This could only be afforded by the chief alone. So, traditionally it became associated with the sole property, the right of which was vested only in the chief and was venerated very much being associated with a certain amount of superstition [27].

Chongthu being the younger brother of Noimangpa, the chief, had access to it and when he arranged for the brides of his friends with whom he planned to go to his newly found land, he paid the *paigen* to the parents of the girls as marriage payment. It so happened that though the commoners dared not refuse to accept the *paigen* when offered to them as marriage payment subsequently, they could neither dare keep it with them owing to their superstitions attached to it nor could they dare refuse the bride in marriage.[28] Thus, along with the bride, the parents returned the *paigen* to Chongthu saying that being a valuable property associated with the Chief exclusively, they dare not keep it or else, the wrath of the unseen supernatural power visit them and bring misfortune to them.[29] This process went on and on until Chongthu was able to arrange 30 of his best and closest friends with the payment of *paigen* as the marriage payment.

Hereafter, marriage payment of every clan was paid in terms of seven mithuns based on the seven lines of '*longchung*' on the *paigen*. This, however, needs further investigation and confirmation, the prevailing different versions on the matter among the Thadou tribes needs specific enquiries.

Our research into ethnicity and folklores reveal that since then marriage payment came to exist though in actual practice there are variations among the clans in terms of kind and number of *mithuns*. However, one can assume that the following structure is the broad base for marriage payment as propounded by Crawford.[30]

Bride Price Structure of Thadous

	Clan		*Price*
1.	Doungel	(i)	selsom (10 *mithuns*)
		(ii)	dahpi ni (2 big copper gongs)
		(iii)	dahbu ni (2 sets of three different small sizes of
2.	Sitlhou		copper gongs)
		(iv)	Khichang ni (2 ear beads)
		(v)	Khichong ni (2 bead necklaces)
3.	Singson	(i)	Selsomlanga (15 *mithuns*)
4.	Kipgen	(i)	selsom (10 *mithuns*)
		(ii)	dahpi ni (2 big copper gongs)
5.	Haokip	(iii)	Khichong ni (2 bead necklaces)
		(iv)	Khichang ni (2 ear beads)
6.	Chongloi	(i)	Selsagee (7 *mithuns*)
		(ii)	dahpi khat (1 big copper gong)
		(iii)	dahbu khat (1 set of three different small sizes of
7.	Hangshing		copper gongs)
		(iv)	Khichang khat (1 ear bead)
		(v)	Khichong khat (1 bead necklace)

Crawford is the first and only person so far to work on the customary laws of the Thadous ever-undertaken by an authority. The work did not pretend to be exhaustive and was printed in such a form as to enable officers to make their own additions. Examples of the then existing court practice in the matter of loans and oaths were inserted even though they were not strictly speaking customs. Therefore, the book is not intended to be a legal code. He was sincerely assisted in his enquiries by William Shaw, B.C. Gasper, L.L. Peter, the Sub-Divisional Officers of Tamenglong, Churachandpur and Ukhrul respectively and by J. H. Hutton, Director of Ethnology and J.C. Higgins, Political Agent in Manipur. In his work he rendered valuable suggestions and advice. Today in hindsight we feel that though the work is not as comprehensive as it could have been, it is, however, worthwhile. *(It is also observed that the Gauhati High Court has undertaken a project on the customary laws of the Thadou-Kukis with special reference to the land holding systems, sponsored by the North Eastern Council, Shillong under the Directorship of Dr. J. Barooah, Law Research Institute Gauhati High Court, assisted by Mayonmi Shimray as Research Officer and Apem K. H. as Assistant Research Officer. It is found that the Research Institute has given a blanket acceptance to see the above marriage payment structure without slightest analysis or comment on the same.*)

Shaw[31] in his study on the Thadou observed several deviations from what Crawford had specified in his work. He contended that the question of amount of marriage payment among the Thadous was not definite and commented that the chiefs and wealthy persons usually claimed and paid the equivalent of ten *mithuns*, Rs. 200 in cash, 2 *dahpi* (large gongs), 2 *dahpu* (set of trio gongs), 2 *khichang* (ear beads), 2 *khichong* (necklaces). He did not name any specific clan of the Thadous. He further opined that ordinary persons often actually paid a couple of *mithun*, *khichang* and *khichong*. As in an instance, he said that a pig in some cases may be taken as one *mithun* and that as per his personal experience he had come across cases where Rs. 40 had stood for 4 mithuns, a jar of *ju* for a *khichang* or *khichong*.[32] Thus in actual practice the parent of the bride hardly ever received the marriage payment in full but in the form of more or less fictitious substitutes. He was emphatic in this regard to the effect that the parents loved to name large amounts as the 'man' not with any idea of getting it, but to be able to boast that their daughter was married for so much. [33] Often when enquired as to what precisely they had received, it was found that actually a much smaller amount had been accepted in full satisfaction by a system of fictitious values.[34] This is very similar to the practices among the Lushais, Zomis, etc. Fictitious values have more often created false pretensions of wealth and richness, which became bone of contentions later and led to unhappy marriages.

It must also be mentioned that Hutton[35] was convinced to have observed the fact that the first and last number of the marriage payment by *mithun* must necessarily be paid in *mithun* [*selkeng-liding* (a standing mithun with its four legs) by this it means that marriage payment has to be by live-*mithun*]. The first and the last marriage payment must in no case be substituted in any form of cash or kind.

Gangte[36] another authority working on the marriage payment of the Thadous maintains that the marriage payment of the Singson Thadou is 30 mithuns without any other items added to it unlike the other Thadou clans. The higher rate of marriage payment among the Singsons has no origin according to him. It is said, the Singsons are the direct junior collaterals of the Sitlhous. So when their senior collateral (Sitlhous) increased the marriage payment the junior also deemed it proper to follow suit. (*The contention of Gangte in regard to marriage payment of the Singson was confirmed from informants S.L. Singson[37], Dr. Seikho Singsit[38], and Reverend Kaikhosei*[39].

In order to further ascertain or otherwise, Mrs. Lunkhoneng,[40] *shared her personal experience as a daughter of the chief of Lungthulien village. She belongs to a Singson clan of the Thadou, Tipaimukh, Churachandpur District who married Thangkhopao in 1947 belonging to Kipgen of the Thadou. She claimed that she vividly remembered her marriage payment was 30 mithuns.*)

During the course of our research we found that one common conspicuous missing fact is that of 'Lutom Laisui', a very important and compulsory item in the marriage payment. It signifies the importance of father and mother of the bride. 'Lutom' is given to the father of the bride in token expression of gratitude. Likewise, 'Laisui' is an exclusive item to be given to the mother of the bride for having given birth to her daughter from her naval. Here, it must be said that, while the father is shown respect for his paternal masculinity, the mother too is highly respected for giving birth to the child.

In this regard, it is interesting to state that there cropped up differences between William Shaw and J.H. Hutton, who out of confusion literally dealt with the two terms out of ignorance of the language and meaning provided to the two items. Shaw[41] attributed 'Lutom' as a gift given to the mother and 'Laisui' to the father. Hutton[42] contended otherwise and explained that Shaw got it the wrong way round. In doing so, he explained saying that Laisui means a woman's waist-band, while Lutom is a man's loincloth. They were cloths for bride's parent and further contended that it could be accounted for a money payment of Re. 1 and Rs. 2 respectively, that a woman can claim for property and that a Thadou woman can make in her own account.

Similarly, we found another feature that has not been dealt with by the several authorities in regard to Manpi which stands for principal marriage-payment that consists of one *mithun* on the tail of which one piece of big bead *khichang* through the ear of which the tail of the *mithun* can be made to pass through as a decorative piece.[43] This bead is counted as equivalent to one *mithun*. Therefore, the Manpi or the principal *mithun* is counted as to bear the price of two *mithuns*. The principal *mithun* is expected to have given birth to as many calves as possible. It is believed that with such principal *mithun* included in the marriage payment similar number of children are in return given birth by the bride. Therefore, it is insisted that such principal *mithun* should necessarily reveal calf bearing [44].

We also observed that the broad based marriage payment as shown above is not totally followed by different clans. As for an instance, the Haokips of Chassad lineage known as the seniormost (*piba*) of the Haokip take ten *mithuns* inclusive of the principal *mithun*.[45] However, as for other junior lineages of the Haokip clan of the Thadou, the marriage payment is fixed at eight *mithuns*.

Another pertinent point we have observed is the fact that though the marriage-payments of different clans are fixed it is customarily not paid in full throughout the life time of the bride. The practice of marriage payment is the principal *mithun* accompanied by one or more subsidiary *mithun* and the remaining marriage payment may not be necessarily in terms of *mithuns*. They can be substituted in kind. Symbolically the counting could represent *mithun* depending on the agreement between the groom's and bride's parties.[46]

We have also observed that in some societies such as that of Sumatra and Malay Archipelago, marriage payment in full[47] had to be made compulsorily so as to be eligible for father-right. It implies that the children of father-right marriage payment system are of exclusive possession of the father. Similarly if no payment is made at all, the children belong to the mother and her kin. These South-East Asian social traits could have entered the Thadou social customs during their period of origination and intermingling of their culture with tribes in Manipur.[48]

The Chin/ Pawi/ Zomi

The payment of marriage price among the Zomis also forms an integral part. In their custom, it is also called *manpi* (principal price). In every society of Zomi (Chin) or Kuki or Chikim tribes, marriage ceremony takes two days: First day ,for sending off the bride by the parents and the second day for wedding which is to be performed at the bridegroom's place. A would-be bride cannot be sent-off unless and until the question of *manpi* is settled. This is paid by the bridegroom side to the bride's parents and it is received by the father of the bride. In case he is not alive, the price goes to the nearest male relative on his side preferably to the eldest or the youngest male member who is the heir-apparent.

In general, among the Zomi, marriage payment *manpi* or principal price is fixed normally on the following four factors.[49]

(i) the clan to which the bride belongs,
(ii) the amount of dowry the bride carries,
(iii) the beauty of her, and
(iv) mutual understanding.

Chief's Family or Aristocratic Family

If the bride belongs to the chief's clan or aristocratic family, the normal price of bride is ten *mithuns* or equivalent value of ten *mithuns* in rupees. Once the principal marriage payment, i.e., one live-*mithun* is paid, the rest of the price can be substituted in kind like gong, valuable household utensils (copper, silver, aluminium) etc.[50] When the marriage is solemnized the parents of the bride offer a sumptuous feast in bidding farewell to their daughter by sacrificing a pig or a cow or two pigs or two cows depending on their capacity and number of guests. This is a normal standard among the average Zomis.[51] In symbolic significance of final settlement of marriage negotiation all the elders from both the sides gather with a mug of rice beer each in their hands and take specific portions of the sacrificial meat together. This is known as 'witness supper' [52] of the marriage. This 'witness supper' is preceded with formal handing over of the marriage payment. After deliberation they have to agree finally by accepting the marriage payment or totally refunding the same in good faith (which occurs rarely).

The following is the generally accepted agreement by Zo or Zomi or Chin or Pawi so far as the marriage-payment is concerned. It is practised even today.

Sialsuam (ten *mithuns*) -	Chief or Aristocratic clan	
Sialthum (three *Mithuns*) -	Commoners.	53

Although covered virtually under the Zomi Customary Law, marriage payment of the Paites is a bit different. The marriage-payment among them is normally one *mithun* and a calf, '*sial nuta*'. As per the British administration, one full grown *mithun* costs Rs. 40 and Rs. 20 for a *mithun* calf called *tai* or *tlai*[54] (meaning half). No one is exempted from payment of marriage price. However, in the Paite customary law, deferred payment is allowed on the ground of financial hardship.[55] Non payment or inability to afford payment of the same is not considered a reasonable ground to withdraw marriage proposal or to dissolve the same.[56] Zomi clans like Zou take only *Sialnga* (five *mithuns*) . The Zous stick to maintain their customs since time immemorial. The obligation of the bridegroom towards the bride's party is significant in their social and cultural life. Any relationship between the two clans involved can also play a role in determining marriage.

Thus, we find that sometimes the marriage payment can only be symbolic. It means that the expenses of the wedding ceremony are counted as marriage payment.[57] If a poor boy is not in a position to pay he may be allowed to pay later. A boy may also be exempted from paying the same if he causes elopement of the girl and moves to the house of the girl and waits until the girl is ready to marry him.[58]

In addition to *manpi*, there are also other subsidiary marriage-payments. They are :[59]

(i) *Puchum* (Rs. 4) goes to the maternal uncle of the bride.

(ii) *Niman* is equal to that of *Pusum* which is to be accepted by the paternal aunt.

(iii) *Thaman or Palal*, equal to that of *Pusum*, is the labour or service price to be reciprocated for taking the charge of the parents of the bride and is usually given to the head of the family. It is prevalent among the Gangte, Paite, Simte, Thadou, Vaiphei.

(iv) *Thallouh 'sum'* (price goes to the nearest relative of the head of the family).

(v) *Lamman* or *Thiansum* is a small amount of money that goes to a bride's friend as a token of love.

(vi) *Nuapuan puak 'man'* is the price for the cloth used for carrying the bride when she was a child by her mother or elder sister. It varies from Rs. 4 to Rs. 20 depending on the class of the clan she belongs to. These payments in cash or kind suggest complete cessation of ties of the girl who is getting married with her family as she has to start her own family with full devotion and understanding.

Vumson[60] has maintained that throughout Zo history marriage customs seem to have been uniform with bride-prices and "wife givers" and "wife-takers" characteristics of the Zo people. Different prices are asked for different brides with social status and physical perfection determining price.[61]

Thakur[62] has contended that a wealthy commoner can often pay a high marriage price and so marries a woman of high class, and if his descendants continue this practice they will achieve high status rank with many privileges of the aristocratic class, except, of course, the same in the line of possible succession to hereditary headmanship or chieftainship.

The Old Kukis

Among the Aimol, Anal, Chiru, Chothe, Kolhen, Kom, Lamgang and Tikhup Purum, etc., the marriage payment is divided into several parts. To mention a few among the Aimol, the bride's eldest brother[63] gets Rs. 6 and each of the other rupee 1 less than his immediate senior. The paternal and maternal uncles receive Rs. 2. The aunt and the elder sister receive Re. 1 each as *niman*. Among the Anal and the Purum the marriage payment must not be less than a pig and a piece of iron (a cubit in length) but the girl's relatives try to get as much as they can.[64] The bridegroom has to feast the family of his bride three times on pork, fowls and rice washed down with plenty of Zu. A Chiru girl has a marriage payment of only one gong.[65] A Chothe girl's marriage payment comprises a spear, a *dao* and a fowl and the same is sealed by the consumption of Zu. The marriage payment of a Kolhen[66] girl is a gong and Rs. 7 to her mother and Rs. 7 to the elder[s] and younger brother[s] and the maternal uncle[s].

The marriage payment of the Kom girl is very high. The father receives one gong, four buffaloes, fifteen cloths, a hoe, and a spear. The aunt takes a black and white cloth.[67] The Lamgang bridegroom has to pay his father-in-law three pigs or buffaloes or cows, one sting of conch-shell beads, one lead bracelet and one black or blue petticoat.[68] A Tikhup father of the bride receives a gong, ten hoes, one *dao* and one spear and Rs. 7 by the maternal grand-father.[69]

Apart from paying all items of marriage payments such as *mithun*, cow, pig, gong, bead, necklace, spears, *dao*, money and whatever ought to be paid by the bridegroom, a three-year service is to be served to the bride's family.[70] This practice is prevalent among the Aimol, Anal, Chiru and Purum. During this period of service, he works with dedication as a son of the house. Likewise the Hmars, Moyon and Monsang also practised this system.[71]

Conclusion

We need a change in the mindset of the masses. Education is a vital weapon. Male participation is essential. Constraints and restraints preventing women's access to education have to be counteracted. Opportunities have to be provided to enable the women who have been traditionally marginalised.[72] The syllabus and curriculum in schools have to register the presence of women in society and also to break the stereotypes through texts.[73]

Despite the winds of change brought about by modernization, Christianity and science and technology, traditionalism is deeply rooted in the dynamics of system of marriage.[74] Summing up, marriage payment is, of course, the pivotal part in a Chikim's marriage. However, liberalization, privatization and globalisation, democratic set-up, traditional norms have somehow impacted the ethnic groups. The traditional system never recognizes the rights of women as the decision-makers in matters of community like inter-ethnic conflict crises management, social sanctions, and so forth. The customary laws prevalent among the ethnic groups though portrayed as egalitarian socio-economic structures, are discriminatory when it comes to women's right. The customary laws of the Chikims are not justifiably manifested. They are inhumane and deprived women in many ways.

REFERENCES

1. R.M. MacIver, *Society: A Textbook of Sociology*, Farrar and Rinehart, New York, 1945, p. 5.
2. Woodward Sutherland and Maxwell, *Introductory Sociology*, Oxford and IBH Publishing Co., Bombay, 1961, p. 35.
3. Arnold Green, *Sociology*, McGraw Hill Book Co. Inc., New York, 1956, p. 94.

4. Morris Ginsberg, *Psychology of Society*, Methuen, London, 1949, p. 122.
5. Gillen and Gillen, *Cultural Sociology*, Mac Millan Co., New York, 1950, p. 35.
6. Horton and Hunt, *Sociology*, McGrow Hill, New York, 1968, p. 75.
7. A.R. Radcliff Brown and Daryll Forde, *African System of Kinship and Marriage*, OUP, London, New York, Toronto, 1950, p. 5.
8. A.R. Radcliff Brown and Daryll Forde, *op. cit.*, p. 46.
9. P.M. Gangte, *Customary Laws of Meitei And Mizo Societies*, Akansha Publishing House, New Delhi, 2008, p. 135.
10. J.D. Baveja, *The Land Where the Bamboo Flowers*, Publication Board, Assam, Gauhati, 1970, p. 25.
11. Lal Biak Thanga, *The Mizos*, United Publishers, Gauhati, 1978, p. 19.
12. N. E. Parry, *A Monograph on Lushai Customs and Ceremonies*, Firma KLM (Pvt.) Ltd., Calcutta, 1928, p. 24.
13. P.M. Gangte, *op. cit.*, p. 159.
14. J.D. Baveja, *op. cit.*, 1970, p. 25.
15. *Ibid.*
16. N. Chatterji, *Status of Women in the Mizo Society*, Tribal Research Centre, Aizawl, 1975, p. 19.
17. J. Shakespear, *The Lushai Kuki Clans, Part. I*, Tribal Research Institute, Aizawl, p. 50.
18. N. E. Parry, *A Monograph on Lushai Customs and Ceremonies*, Firma KLM (Pvt.) Ltd., Calcutta, 1928, p. 24.
19. Bimal J. Deb and Dilip Kumar Lahiri, *Lushai Customs and Ceremonies*, Mittal Publications, Delhi, 1983, p. 24.
20. N. E. Parry, *op. cit.*, pp. 25-27.
21. P.M. Gangte, *op. cit.*, p.159.
22. G. Barkataki, *Tribes of Assam*, NBT, New Delhi, 1969, p. 105.
23. N. E. Parry, *op. cit.*, p. 24.
24. T. S. Gangte, *The Kukis of Manipur*, Gyan Publishing House, New Delhi, 1993, pp 92-93.
25. *Ibid.*
26. *Ibid.*
27. *Ibid.*
28. *Ibid.*
29. *Ibid.*
30. C. G. Crawford, *Hand Book of Kuki Custom*, Directorate of Printing & Stationery, Manipur, 1984, pp. 2-3.
31. William Shaw, *The Thadou Kuki*, Shillong, 1928, pp. 58-59.
32. William Shaw, *op. cit.*, p. 59.
33. *Ibid.*
34. *Ibid.*
35. J. H. Hutton, 'Notes on the Thadou Kukis', *Journal of the Asiatic Society of Bengal*, XXIV, 1929, p. 59.

36. T.S. Gangte, *op. cit.*, p. 95.
37. Interview with S.L. Singson, 70, Old Lambulane, Imphal, Manipur, 3.5.2004.
38. Interview with Dr. Seikho Singsit, 58, Tuibong, Churachandpur, Manipur, 18. 7. 2006.
39. Interview with Reverend Kaikhosie, 60, Old Lambulane, Imphal, Manipur, 7. 4. 2005.
40. Interview with Mrs. Lunkhoneng Kipgen, 80, Old Lambulane, Imphal, Manipur, 30. 6. 2006.
41. William Shaw, *op. cit.*, p. 63.
42. J. H. Hutton, 'Notes on the Thadou Kukis', *Journal of the Asiatic Society of Bengal*, XXIV, 1929, p. 59.
43. *Ibid.*
44. *Ibid.*
45. Interview with D. Letkhojam Haokip, Chassad, 19-7-2005.
46. P.M. Gangte, *op. cit.*, p. 168.
47. A. R. Radcliff Brown and Daryll Forde, *op. cit.*, p. 51.
48. P.M. Gangte, *op. cit.*, p. 169.
49. T. Gougin, *History of Zomi*, Churachandpur, 1984, pp. 36 – 37.
50. Interview with Lutcha Vaiphei, 70, Churachandpur, 4-10-2005.
51. T. Gougin, *op. cit.*, p. 37.
52. Interview with Lutcha Vaiphei, 70, Churachandpur, 4-10-2005.
53. T. Gougin, *History of Zomi*, Churachandpur, 1984, pp. 36-37.
54. *Ibid.*
55. H. Kamkhenthang, *The Paite— A Transborder Tribe of India and Burma*, Mittal Publication, Delhi, 1988, p. 110.
56. *Ibid.*
57. Vumson, *Zo History*, Aizawl, undated, p. 14.
58. *Ibid.*
59. T. Gougin, *op. cit.*, pp. 38-40.
60. Vumson, *Zo History*, Aizawl, undated, p. 14.
61. *Ibid.*
62. K. Robin (ed.), *Chin: History, Culture and Identity*, Dominant Publishers and Distributors, New Delhi, 2009, p. 222-223.
63. *J. Shakespeare, op. cit.*, p.152.
64. *Ibid.*
65. *Ibid.*
66. *Ibid.*
67. *Ibid.*
68. *Ibid.*
69. *Ibid.*
70. *Ibid.*
71. *In Search of Identity*, Kuki Baptist Convention Press, Imphal, 1986, p. 7.

72. Malini Bhattacharya, *'Woman and Education'* in P. Krishnaprasad (ed.), *Women and Society in India*, Vol. 31, Issue No. 2, February, 2002, Delhi, p. 5.
73. *Ibid.*
74. P.M. Gangte, *Institution of 'Neilah' and 'Kong-Lo' Marriage for Maintenance of Social Order And Cultural Identity among the Chin-Kuki-Mizo Society*, presented at a national seminar on "Indigenous Knowledge Tradition in North East India, Guwahati, 27-29 March, 2006.

10

BRIEF ANALYSIS OF THE MARRIAGE SYSTEM OF THE BIATES

S. Lhinghoijem

Introduction

The Biates, a small community also known as Biete and Bete, is regarded as one of the oldest hill tribes of the Mizo umbrella groups of people mostly inhabiting the Tuiral, Saipung constituency of Jaintia Hills (Meghalaya) and Khartlong constituency of north Cachar Hills of Assam.[1] They are found separated by the river called Kopili or Kangkalang or Tuipidung, which is the boundary of Assam and Meghalaya. On the one side is the Kharthong Bial, Kharthong Constituency, North Cachar Hills (now known as Dima Hasao) Autonomous Council, Assam and on the other side is Saipung Bial, Saipung Constituency, Jaintia Hills District Council, Meghalaya. Thus, the Biates are found living in the border area of the three States, viz., Mizoram, Assam, Jaintia (Meghalaya). According to Pakem[2], the Biate is one of the Mizo tribes (known as the Lushai- Kuki-Chin).

The Biate Marriage System

The traditional marriage among the Biate was arranged once. This is the most common one unlike the preferential marriage prevalent among the Kuki-Chin-Mizo. Though these practices are no longer adhered, parents in the days of yore had the sole authority to choose a boy or girl of their liking. Marriage within the clan or sub-clan was not prevalent. According to Rema Nampui, marriage within the clan or sub-clan was not practised though a few could be seen in the present day.[3] Monogamy was generally the accepted rule. Love marriage was almost absent in the olden days. But, it could be visibly noticed that younger generation now prefers love marriage rather than the arranged one. Data collected shows that the rate of love marriage crossed 70 per cent while the remaining followed the arranged marriage. C.A. Soppitt mentioned that child marriage is allowed in the Rangkhols though the custom is not very common. Thus, a man may bespeak the newly born daughter of another for himself or his son; but until the girl is full grown, the couple is not allowed to live together.

Accepted Norms of Marriageable Age

Marriage is usually solemnized after they attain maturity. The age as to when a person is to get married is actually fixed. People consider that for a girl the ideal age to get married is 20-25 years but according to census collected it could be noted that girls usually get married as early as 15 years. Late marriage is rare to be noticed.

From the various interviews conducted, it has been noted that majority of the people feel that one should first be financially stable such as getting a salaried job or is capable enough to run the household before one plans to get married. It could be noted that people though have an idea, view, choice for age of marriage; it is not a must or compulsion to follow that particular age.

Normally, when a Biate boy reaches a marriageable age; it is the responsibility of the parents to look for a suitable bride of their preferential choice as their daughter-in-law. When the parents of the boy have this kind of thinking and view for their marriageable son, it is a norm as well as the customary rule for the Biates to share their feeling with the other members of the family, friends and well wishers whom they consider as permissible to know their plan for the marriage. They select the members by themselves according to the circumstances they face.

Norms of Seeking a Bride

While seeking a bride, it is a norm for the boy's parents to serve *zu* (rice beer) to a few selected members. The *zu* or wine is served to the members as a kind of supplicatory offering for seeking the girl's hand. If anyone of the members present rejected the cup of *zu*, it means that he/she does not agree to be the eligible member taking responsibility for seeking a bride. Therefore, the family members have to look for someone else to replace him/her. If all the members present drink as the *zu*, it symbolizes the consent. Once the *zu* spree is over and when all the members consume the *zu*, the boy who is supposed to be the groom is called forward by the members. Peculiarly, the Biates, after seeking the consent of the girl's parents, the boy is questioned whether he agrees with his parent's choice of girl to marry. If he nods his head, a particular day is fixed at the place for going to the girl's house for seeking her hand. If in case disagrees, then another choice is put forward by the members as well as by his parents.

Rituals of Seeking a Bride

In the Biate marriage system, the procedure for seeking a bride takes place in three phases of visits to the girl's house. First, a day should be fixed by the members' convenience to visit the girl's house for seeking the daughter. All the members gathered at the boy's residence and discuss how they would approach and who would lead the conversation. Usually, the conversation is led by the father of the boy.[4] Pre-information is given to the girl's parents that they are coming though the reasons are not usually mentioned.

These kinds of visiting a girl's house solely for the purpose of seeking her hand was normally done in the evening in the olden days as people used to go to their fields or *jhum* land to work during the day time. Till today this kind of tradition is still practised as people used to leave for work in the day time and usually came back home at night. On their first visit, the boy's family or so to say the selected members go to the girl's house to pass the information that they want their daughter for their son. On this first visit, the boy's family members do not carry any gift or wine with them. They proceed empty handed. When the request is being made known; the girl's family/parents will not give them a reply of their request. They are rather informed to come again on another particular day so fixed. In this visit, the girl's family do not expect for any response from the girl's side. The girl's family hence decides to seek their daughter's. The girl will give her approval or disapproval. In most cases the choice is usually done by the parents without consulting their daughter.

In the second, preparation is made to prepare a special kind of *zu* that is meant especially for this purpose. Flavour of *zu* signifies a kind of status and dignity among the Biates. When the day is fixed for the second visit, both parties meet at the girl's residence to hear the decision of the girl as well as her parents. In this visit, the boy's relative members especially the ladies poured *zu* serving first to the girl's father, mother and move on till the last member. As they drink *zu*, the negotiation begins. If the girl's parents or relative members do not drink *zu* or do not even touch the glass, it symbolizes rejection of the proposal. If all take the glasses and drink *zu* , it welcomes proposal. This *zu* offering and drinking is a ritual participated by the girl's parents to show their approval of the forthcoming nuptials. Though this *zu* they offer in this occasion it describes love, agreement and respect of both parties. This particular offering of *zu* is called *Lenkhamzu* in the Biate language which means 'Reservation Wine' or 'Engagement Wine' signifying that the girl is engaged to that particular boy and that no one is allowed to court her anymore. In case if the girl or her parents reject the proposal on this day, the boy's parents have to take back their pot of *zu* where all the members who are involved in asking the girls hand will gather together at the boy's residence. Here, all the members will drink *zu* along with the boy's family members to show that they are a loser and unsuccessful in their endeavour to seek the girl.[5]

On the third and final visit (in case if the boy's party receives an approval from the girl's party), the boy's family will carry with them a pot of *zu* again. This time the pot of *zu* they carry with is a *zu* of joy and happiness as they are finally on the verge of getting the girl. On this day, both the parties gather. Festive celebration for making the family boundary bigger is seen. In this, wedding date is fixed by both the parties with the consent of the priest.

Persona of Choosing a Bride

Parents sometimes try to control the choice of their children as to what qualities one should look for in a partner. When there was no class division, marriage used to be settled on the basis of quality of the boy and girl, i.e., a person should be hard working, amiable behaviour and at times even physical character. A girl is chosen based on her skill and family background besides her industriousness. Elders often eye the physique of a girl by her legs. Girl having skinny legs is assumed to be weak hence a girl with good sturdy legs is preferred. She would be strong and can assist in carrying out numerous duties. In the past, industriousness of the person was the most preferable quality. At present, education, job and economic status are deciding factors.

Ceremonies and Rituals

Marriage ceremonies are usually carried out with much pomp and grandeur though may not be in all the cases of marriage. For the Christians in general, marriage rituals are conducted in the church and are usually presided over by the pastor or priest. The traditional form of marriages differs from the Christian one. In the past, when people followed animism, marriage ceremonies or rituals were performed in the Bualkuang. Nowadays, Bualkuang is more or less replaced by a place called church after conversion to Christianity.

Marriage Payment

Marriage payment is still compulsory among all the tribals of the north-eastern region. The Chin-Kuki-Mizo groups have been following this rule very strictly till today. The marriage payment is strictly followed among the Biates till today. It is a compulsion to clear the marriage payment at the time of the marriageThe bridegroom's family has to pay the price of the bride to the bride's family. The bride's price consists of a round brass plate called 'Mairang' measuring around one and a half metres. But the Biates do not do the measurement in modern measuring rather they still follow their traditional form of measurement called *khap* where the finger especially the thumb and the point fingers are stretched at the maximum where one stretching is called *khap*. The *mairang* or brass plate should measure six *khaps* meaning that stretching should be six times. The size of the brass plate should be accurate and if in case it is smaller than six *khaps*, the bride's family rejects it and the groom's family is requested to replace it with the accurate size. The payment of the brass plate is called *mannai* which means bride's price. Unlike other Kuki groups, the Biates have three categories of bride price. The real bride price is *mannai*,then there is another price the groom has to pay called *sersut*. The '*sersut*' is paid so that the husband could have sexual relation with the wife which is just 1.25 rupees. The amount still remains the same.[6] With the passage of time and the decrease of money value the other Kuki tribes have increased the amount equivalent to the past amount. But the Biate's who used to pay rupees 1.25 still follow the traditional pattern thus the money value of 25 paise is still very much in the society. *Sersut* is paid on the wedding day itself. The third category of the bride price is *sinmaksin* which is Rs. 2. *Sinmaksin* is also paid along with *sersut*. *sinmaksin* is paid to the bride's family so that the husband while staying in the bride's place enjoys the status of family member. It could be mentioned that the Biates followed the residential pattern of matri-patrilocal. The husband has to stay in the house of the wife for some time and only after that he can take her to his house. In return of the bride's price, the bride's family has to follow some formalities of payment in return. The bride's family has to give the groom's family a cotton blanket woven in hand called *ponpui*, 'Ril' cane basket, *sumduk* a wooden box and *bem* a kind of basket .

Marriage Gift

At the end of the groom's stay in the bride's residence, the couple has to inform the parents of the groom that they are ready to leave. Before they leave the bride's residence, the parents of the groom will pay a formal visit to the girl's parents requesting them and appealing them to release the couple from their house and send them to their residence. If the parents of the wife agree to the request, a day is fixed for taking the son and daughter-in-law to their house. On the fixed day a feast used to be arranged at the groom's residence to welcome the couple. This ceremony of welcoming feast for the couple in the groom's residence is called *moithrui*. Here relatives and friends are invited to attend the ceremony. The gifts include axe, spade, hoe, bamboo basket, blanket, mattresses, etc., that are needed to set up their new house.

Divorce

Divorce is rare among the Biates. But it is allowed if circumstances compel. The reason for divorce can be adultery, infidelity, want of children, ill treatment, etc. According to data collected, there are fifty female divorcees and twenty male divorcees. The divorce cases are taken up by the representatives of the five clans or the Namringa Dewan. They summon the couple and interrogate them so that judgment is done without any bias. A fine of Rs 300 is imposed as a court fee and is supposed to be paid by the person who commits the mistake. Whosoever found guilty is supposed to kill one pig at the residence of the spouse. It has been noted that either spouse can initiate divorce. Children have to stay with one of the parents. There are no particular rules that the children have to stay with their mother or father after divorce. They can stay with one of the parents.

Some of the main causes of divorce among the Biate's are:

(a) *Divorce by Mutual Consent:* In this type of divorce, the causes of divorce may be due to incompatibility of the husband and wife to meet the family economic requirements; lack of satisfying the physical needs between the spouses. For such cases divorce is decided by the husband and wife themselves. All the parents and relatives try their best to solve the problem.

(b) *Adultery or Infidelity:* In case of the husband leaving his wife and having sexual relationship with another woman, wife may complain to her relatives and this may end up in a wife divorcing her husband. After the divorce, the children may live with the mother or father. One committing the mistake cannot take the custody of the children.

(c) *Want of Children:* If the wife does not bear any child, the husband often seeks divorce. If no male child is born to take heirship of the father, there is a tendency of the husband divorcing his wife to marry another girl to get male heir.

(d) *Ill-Treatment:* In many cases, we find wives subjected to ill-treatment and harassment by their husbands or in-laws. In such instances, they, with the help of their relatives and clan members, seek divorce. If justified, they can have custody of all their children.

Role of the Clan Council on Divorce

When divorce takes place due to wife's infidelity or other reasons, punishment to the wife was so severe that she has to leave her husband's home without taking anything except the clothes she wore. Not only this, the wife has to pay Rs 300 to the *khua namtin'* (clan council) with *maktha* where she has to kill a pig; a fine of Rs 10 to the husband's maternal uncles for defaming and exploiting the life of their nephew; another fine of Rs 10 to the headman called *vaifak* for diminishing the village prestige. This form of divorce from the wife's side is called *nupuisut.*

If the divorce takes place because of the husband's fault, the children go to the mother but they have to retain their father's title. In some cases, the children take the mother's title as they are fed and brought up by the mother. All the properties, movable or immovable, are divided into two equal parts between the husband and the wife. The fine imposed is same as that fine in *nupuisut* (divorce by the wife) though the term used is different. Here it is called *pasalsut* (divorce by the husband).

Remarriage

Remarriage is not prohibited among the Biates in general. Both man and woman whether divorcee, separated, widow or widower can remarry. The *sinmaksin* which was paid at the time of marriage to the bride's family by the groom's family is reduced to half and the actual amount of Rs 2 is reduced to Re. 1 which they called *thlanthlan napinim* which means spitting mucus on the grave of the deceased spouse. But getting married after a gap of one or two years or getting married in old age, the bride price is same and usual as a new bride: *sersut* of Rs. 1.25 paise and the *sinmaksin* of Rs. 2. The price is same as usual and called *semeihol* meaning 'unburned charcoal' since the couples have grown old and there is no possibility for them to get or beget a child from their own. This marriage was called unburned charcoal because even if it is blown it will not produce any heat and will not burn to give light anymore. Even though remarriage is allowed, the people hardly practise it. It was mainly due to the fear that they would be disfavoured by the villagers and the status which they achieved in the society might be affected.

Pre- Marital Sex

It has been observed that only one case of pre-marital sex has come to my notice during my fieldwork. The Biates in general do not approve pre-marital sex. The church elders usually cancel the names of such doers from the church register. Even though the doers are not exactly chased out of the village they are outcasted by the villagers. If a girl gets pregnant before marriage the Namringa Dewan summons her and questions the identity of the child's father. When the girl mentions the name of the father of the child, the man is again summoned in the court of the Nam Ringa Dewan and is asked whether he will marry the pregnant girl or not. If he agrees to marry her, he has to pay the *sersut* of Rs1.25 and *sinmaksin* of Rs 2 and the brass plate called *mairang* to the girl's parents. But if he refuses to marry her, he has to pay a fine of Rs. 300 to the Nam Ringa Dewan or the village authority and has to kill one pig at the girl's residence.

Extra Marital Sex

Extra-marital affairs are rare. It has been observed that there are only two cases found while undergoing my entire fieldwork. In such cases, divorce is the solution to the problem. If a woman commits, her husband never forgives her. If *vice versa* the wife tries to adjust with him for the sake of the children and financial support she receives from him. She rather requests him to sever such relation with the other woman. In some cases the wife does not tolerate at all about her husband action. The Biates believe that the first wife has all the legal rights and blessings of the house and gets the sole authority over her children and hence no one can occupy her place unless she dies.

The Biates, part of the Kuki-Chin-Mizo groups, have many similarities in the traditional marriage system; yet slight differences are also noted. These changes may be due to the fact that they are so dispersed and also acculturated.

REFERENCES

1. Aaron Lungleng, Food Habits of the Biates of Saipung Village, Jaintia Hills, Meghalaya Hills, unpublished MA dissertation, NEHU, Shillong, 2001, p. 8.
2. Pakem, 'The Biates', in Dey Sreema Mudram (ed.), *The Tribes of North East India*, Vendrame, Shillong, 1984.
3. Rema Nampui, 57, Saijol village.
4. R.P. Liana, 74, Lura village.
5. Narrated by Rebgpuia Ngamlai, 37, Saipung village.
6. Lalduhoma, 51, Saipung village.

11

IMPACT OF CHRISTIANITY ON THE KUKIS OF MANIPUR

Salam Irene

With the advent of British rule, the tribals of North-East India were exposed to Christianity and significant numbers embraced it. The question of religious conversations often occupies centre stage in politics. Faith in God and adherence to a particular religion is entirely a matter of conscience and a subject of individual freedom. Change of faith and informed choice are constitutional rights that guarantee personal choice.[1] James Johnstone, the Political Agent of Manipur, however, regarded Christianization of the people as the only effective means for mutually attaching them to the government.[2] The tribals of Manipur for the most part have no written history. They depend greatly on oral tradition they rely heavily on arts and culture, songs and dances, legends and stories. The Kukis-Chin-Mizo believed in the existence of Supreme Being or God, Pathan/Pathian/Pasian.[3] They believed in the existence both benevolent and malevolent spirits whom they propitiated through the offering of sacrifices. Inn-doi-Indawi or Doi-bom was the house God or deity of the Kukis. Critical scholars of the *Bible* state that "beneath much of the *Old Testament* there remained a residue of older tradition which had originated in folktales.[4] In other words, God encountered his people, the Israelites through their folk culture. What is noteworthy in folk culture is that most of its values are also found in tribal cultures. In the pages of *Bible,* one finds folk cultural features and values. When the evangelist Mathew wants to tell us who Jesus is, he started by listing a long list of genealogy (*Mt* 1:1-17). Tribals would understand the logic of Mathew. In folk and tribal cultures, the people are intimately tied to their lands. This is what we find in the *Bible*-words of *Psalm* 137:1,4-1, By the rivers of Babylon.

> There we sat and there we wept
> When we remember Zion
> ....
> How can we sing the Lord's song in the foreign land?

Folk cultural features like group/clan loyalty and control, economics of sharing, social dimension of sin are tribal as well as Biblical.[5] The Kukis before their conversion to Christianity believed in the existence of a Supreme Being, Creator and Lord of the world. Some members of the *Zo* in Manipur believed that they are descendants of one of the lost tribes of Israel, and some have in recent decades migrated and become citizens of Israel. The second Vatican Council wrote: From ancient times to the present, there is found among various peoples a certain perceptions of that mysterious power abiding in the course of nature and in the happenings of the human life; at the times some indeed have come to recognition of a Supreme Being, or even of a father. This perception and recognition penetrates their lives with a profound religious sense.

The Kukis society is like other tribal societies, a service oriented society. Christianity is a very community oriented religion much in harmony with tribal outlook and mentality in general. Christianity is also equally a religion of personal discipleship and loyalty to Christ. This is evident in the celebration. 'The value implies in the sharing of one's wealth is a conspicuous gospel value.[6]

The religious belief that binds people also facilitates the spread of the gospel— the belief in life after death. The Kuki Chins believed that the soul of the deceased goes to *Mithikhua/ Misikhua* (Land of Dead) the tribal concept of two worlds for the dead — Pialral and Mithikhua, and the Christian belief in heaven and hell differ, yet the former was transformed by the Christian teaching of Heaven and Hell, and the Christian hope of salvation to all, rich, poor alike.[7] The primary mission of the Church is to make available the message proclaimed by Jesus Christ, the message that God is love, the loving Father who created us, loves and cares for us. The Christian missionaries found the Kukis open to this message. Moreover, the sacrifices as also the offerings of the chosen people of God as narrated in the *Old Testament* bear a strong resemblance to the offerings of the Kukis on festivals especially those related to the agricultural cycle as also to the propitiation of spirits. Although Christianity came to the Kukis just a century ago, the Kukis Christians are committed Christians observing Sunday as a Holy Day, a day of obligation, prayers and thanksgiving for blessing received. There are several local churches where services are conducted both in English and local dialects. Moreover the process of inculturation has also ensured that the Kukis remain devout Christians. Inculturation is the effort to inject Christ's message into a given socio-cultural milieu thereby summoning that milieu to grow in accordance with its own values so long as they can be reconciled with the Gospel message. Inculturation seeks to naturalization the Church in every country, region and social sector, while fully respecting the native genius and character of each human collectivity. The basic cosmological structure of the indigenous religion was the concept of lesser spirit (Khuovang) and the concept of Supreme Being (*Pathien*), a God of all humanity and goodness. The lesser spirits underpinned events and processes in the microcosm of the local community and its environment, whilst the Supreme Being underpinned events and processes the macrocosm, i.e., in the world as whole. Since the microcosm formed part of the macrocosm, the lesser spirits were thought of either as manifestation of the Supreme Being or as entities ultimately deriving their power from him. Ironically, the people also saw Christian God and the Supreme Being of their tradition religion were addressed by the same name "pathien". There was thus an indigenous concept of the Supreme Being which was continuous in its essentials with the Christian concept. In the minds of the converts there was a close association between the specificity of their new faith and the modern from which it came, including education, technology, material well-being and eventually material consciousness.[8] The impact of Christianity on the Kukis religion is evident from the change in belief (commitment to the Gospel), practices and customs associated with their primeval religion. In the first place, Christianity offered the people the promised of Eternal Salvation. This in practice meant that is freed the Kukis from the fear of spirits, especially those that they believed brought sickness, misfortune and death. It also freed them from the constant need to slaughter birds and animals for sacrifices which was a major drain on their income. However, Christianity did impose a 'tithe' on all the Kukis Christians, but the amount contributed in tithe is negligible to their previous expenditure on animal sacrifices. Secondly, the Gospel message of God as a Loving Father of all his children meant that in matters of prayer, fulfilment of religious obligations, church services, community events, *Bible* camps, all Kukis, rich or poor, were treated on equality. No distinction was made between the Kukis Christians. This inculcated a sense of pride and dignity and rid them of that fear and uncertainty that possessed them when their lives were ruled by spirits. Traditional gennas which governed their daily lives were also abandoned. Since the missionaries looked askance at the Kuki custom of rice-liquor brewing and drinking, the Kuki Christians for the most part abandoned this traditional practice, and commenced drinking tea or soft drinks at public events especially associated with religious and church activities.

Above all, Christianity replaced the traditional Kuki religion: Evangelization was born of transfiguring religious experience. This experience was the experience of conversion of being born again as 'Culture, it is the vital space within the human person comes face to face with the Gospel'.[9] Moreover, the singing of hymns in the Christian churches especially in the local dialects greatly appealed to the Kukis who possessed great proficiency in song and dance. Tribal music varies according to the nature of the song but folksongs contain the treasure of literature of the people. It depicts the people's philosophy of life, personal character. After embracing Christianity, many of the original lyrics containing romantic and derogative expression have been modified to the tune of the Gospel message.[10] Christianity lifted the Kukis from the old world to the new especially through the medium of education. To a great extent Christianity was synonymous with western or modern education. Although the British colonialists had made attempts to introduce western education in Manipur prior to the advent of the Christian missionaries, it was the latter who engaged in a massive education through a vast network of schools and colleges. In the eyes of many, it is almost an expression of her identity.[11] Christian education can be understood in the context of the decree issued by Vatican 11: 'Since every man of whatever dignity of a person has an inalienable right to education corresponding to his proper destiny, and suited to his native talents, his sex, his cultural background, and his ancestral heritage. At the same time this education should pave the way to brotherly. For a true education aims at the formation of the human person with respect to his ultimate goal and simultaneously with respect to the good of those societies of which as a man, he is a member, and in whose responsibilities as an adult he will share. The single foremost agent of social change is education. Prior to the advent of colonial rule, the Kukis did not have a formal syatem of education. It was education more than anything else that shaped the new tribal Kuki society. Previously illiterate, the Kukis were first hesitant to attend Christian schools. As T. Luikham stated : Our fathers living in caves and jungles were blind to the advantage of education and averse to its introduction. The tribal believed that education would result in young people becoming alienated from their roots, but they gradually accepts the maxim that education is the path to progress and development. Educational institutions while acting as a medium for the propagation of the Gospel also trained the Kukis for future service both to the Church and State. Several Kuki Christians educated from primarily Christian schools. This is equally true for Kuki engineers, doctors, nurses, lawyers, teachers, researchers, academicians, social workers and so on and of course for Kuki pastors, priests, catechists and missionaries. Education U.M. Fox trained native workers in practical skills[12] or sustainable livelihood. Catholic missionaries established *Grihini* schools which imparted vocational training in many disciplines. The missionaries gave priority to the study of local vernaculars as the basis for the formulation of their education programmes'. The Protestant missionaries exalted the *Bible* as the ultimate source of authority and made it as a condition that if an individual had to worship God aright, he must be able to read. Education and evangelism were interlinked.[13] One of the most important results of education was the imparting of a sound moral character to children, instilling in them a sense of purpose, a value in life. These values continue to guide through life. It also taught the Kukis a sense of co-operation, forgiveness, and abandonment of the idea of revenge even though elimination of all forms of factionalism could not be achieved. It taught to reject evil without sacrifices the good, and in holding together in one, things which elsewhere are incompatible.[14]

The reasons for the success of the Christian missionaries in education can be attributed to the fact 'that they can command the services of a group of men ability and devotion who have given themselves up for a long term of years specifically to the service — the missionary teachers have as a body, exceptional qualification. They have laboured with the greatest earnestness to cultivate the humane side of student life. They have obviously undertaken their work from no motives of self-interest.[15] Another major impact of Christianity on the Kukis was the introduction of education of girls and women both formal and vocational. This was illustrated not only in the rise in the standard of living of the Kukis, but in the emphasis on personal hygiene, sanitation and drainage, as also imparting of scientific and technical knowledge in the fields of agriculture, animal husbandry, fisheries, etc. Education brought to the Kukis a new world view all its attendant ramifications. It opened new doors to the previously isolated tribals, especially because the Kukis for the most part often embraced Christianity become proficient in the English language which gave them a cutting edge in competitive examinations. They also abandoned inertia and superstition, adopted new thinking and practices which raised their socio-economic status. They were also introduced to modern medicine with all its attendant advantages. A change was evinced in the field of house construction, more durable materials were used and animals were no longer housed in the family home but kept in separated pens or enclosures.

The language was now given a written form in the Roman script produced a vast repertory of literature in their own dialects. One perhaps inadvertent effect of Christianity and modern education was the emergence of a middle class in Kuki society. Although the missionaries and their educators treated all tribals alike, as a result of education, educated Kukis forged ahead in nearly every discipline whether pastoral ministry, government service, education, health sector, etc. The newly educated Kukis became an 'elite' group who successfully altered the balance of power in tradition society, by capturing political leadership (e.g., Phuzathang Tonsing who has been a Cabinet Minister in all Congress formed governments), and thus rendering partly or wholly redundant, the position and responsibilities of tradition Chieftains who found their power eroded. By virtue of their power they also dominated the social hierarchy, and the ordinary Kuki Christian tried to emulate the ways of the life and standard of living of the Kukis elite, even in matters of etiquette, speech, dress, food habit, etc., the tendency of the middle class towards consumerism has permeated to the less privileged Kukis who emulating this consumerist lifestyle fall into debt especially with reference to celebrations in connection with rites of passage, like marriage, where all Western trappings are included, from an expensive bridal gown to a huge wedding cake. Education in part paved the way to social inequality and calss differentiation and enabled the educated Kukis to replace the traditional elites in decision making. The middle class have become greatly urbanized, they have built residences in town, adopted an urban lifestyle which has resulted in severing or decreasing kinship ties with family and relatives living on villages. As N.K. Bose noted: Christianity has undoubtedly brought the message of a richer life, a wider companionship, and a new sense of dignity to converts. But it is interesting of a note that the Christian religion has always been attended by the beliefs of modern civilization. Up to now the principal agent of westernization among the tribal folks has been the Christian missionary enterprise.[16] The educated class remained in constant contact with the rulers, both in colonial and post-colonial Manipur, and their missionary education as also proximity to those in power, paved the way for their emergence as leader in Kuki society. Contrary to the reasons for growth of a middle class in India or elsewhere, the middle class of the Kukis emerged not from an economic base but because of Christianity and Western education.

The impact of Christianity was greatly apparently in the field of health care, hospitals, dispensaries, medical centres were started to catch the need of all. Some of the prominent institutions are the Catholic Medical Centre at Imphal, Sielamt Christian Hospital in Churachandpur and Kangpokpi Christian Hospital at Kangpokpi. The introduction of modern medical medicine greatly reduced the incidence of disease and shortened the time of physical affliction. Moreover subsidises charges were levied for the use of these facilities which rendered yeoman service to the Kukis. The missionaries also taught modern remedies for common ailments like, cold, cough, fever, diarrohea, and introduced the concept of a balanced diet. Christianity introduced the Kukis to modern attire, especially western attire, in schools, workplaces, homes, social gatherings, weddings, etc., western hairstyles and fashion accessories gained prominence, especially ties for men and western gowns for women. The early Christian missionaries were accused of destroying much fabric of social life and culture of the Kukis. This was true to a large extent in the first phase of missionary activity. But now the Church is interpreting the Christ even in today's culture context. In the early days, the missionaries were unfamiliar message in the light of their own theological categories and assumptions. But, in the Gospel narratives are found several occurrences of 'Jesus' experience with ethnicity. The objective of Christian missionaries is to make experience with ethnicity. The objective of Christian missionaries is to make experience of God more meaningful in the variety of cultures and ethnic multiplicity.[17]

REFERENCES

1. Salam Irene, The Attitude of the Catholic Church towards Society and State in Manipur (A paper), p. 7.
2. Lal Dena, *Christian Missions and Colonialism*, Vendrame, Shillong, 1998, p. 19.
3. Salam Irene, Ginneiching Simte, Thenkhogin Haokip, The Impact of Modernization among the Tribals of Manipur (A Project Report), 2011, p.29.
4. P.G. Kirkpatrick, The *Old Testament* and Folklore Study, *Journal for the Study of the Old Testament Supplement Services* ,62, JSOT Press, 1988, 26.
5. Peter Haokip, 'Folk Culture: A Medium for the Spread of the Gospel', in L. Jeyaseelan (ed.), Culture, Mission and Contextualization, 2000, pp. 136-138.
6. Salam Irene, Ginneiching Simte, Thekhogin Haokip, *op. cit.*, p. 31.
7. *Ibid.*, pp. 16-19.
8. Lal Dena, *op. cit.*, pp. 87-88.
9. Jeyaseelan, Culture, Mission and Contextualization, *Preface*, p. xi.
10. Linus Neli, 'In Search of Christ Experience through Culture', in L. Jeyaseelan (ed.), *op.cit.*, pp. 163-164.
11. Salam Irene, Catholic Education in Manipur, Delhi, 1989, p.68..
12. Lal Dena, *op. cit.*, p. 37.
13. Lal Dena, *op. cit.*, pp. 90-91.
14. Salam Irene, *op. cit.*, p. 195.
15. Salam Irene, *op. cit.*, pp. 197-198.
16. R. Simon, Social Structure and Rise of Middle Class among the Manipur Tankhul Naga Tribe, Unpublished PhD thesis, MU, 2010, pp. 153-154.
17. Linus Neli, *op. cit.*, p. 173.

12

THE KUKI WOMEN

ROLE AND STATUS

Tingneichong Gangte

The Kukis are an offshoot of the Tibeto-Burman race. *Kuki* is the term applied in India and *Chin* in Burma for the same nationality.[1] The names which have only denotation in the beginning began to acquire connotation.[2] Journal of the 69th Anniversary of the Kuki Rebellion, 1917-19, 1985, p. 10. They are classified as *Old Kuki* or *New Kuki* according to the date they migrated into Manipur. The term *Kuki* is a generic word covering a number of tribes, sub-tribes, clans and sub-clans. All these tribes have close affinity with each other in terms of language, culture, dress, mode of living, food habits, etc. However, they prefer to be identified separately by the names of their respective tribes. Despite the fact of their divisions into many tribes, sub-tribes, clans and so on, they have no language barriers as they could communicate in their respective dialects. The Kuki-Chin is a linguistic sub-family of the Tibeto-Burman group comprising the Kuki-Chin-Mizo (Zo) and the Meitei. There were no monumental inscriptions to trace their past history. Folk tales, oral genealogy, songs, legends, poems are the materials for the Kukis. Another point worthy to be noted is that the role and action of men has been recorded, but there is no record of the Kuki women in the history writing.

Women in every society play certain roles and enjoy

statuses different from the men. The position of women in a society can be identified by examining the roles performed by them in different fields. In the Kuki society there are activities which are performed exclusively by the women and some are performed by both the sexes. It is written that 'the duties of a Thadou housewife are much less in comparison with those of her husband. The wife is responsible for the household chores'. Women take the role of nurturing while the men take the role of bread earning. Yet, they have no power and position in the society. From childhood she performs her roles throughout the days. On the position of the Paite women it is written that 'mother was loved by all but was not given even position in the home. She occupied the third place at home. The lots of mother in the past were deplorable. They work day and night, yet they were rebuked and insulted rather than praised and honoured for the services'. There is a saying in the Thadou society: *'Numei leh chapang simlou'* meaning to exclude women and children. The burden of looking after the interests of the family in the home fronts lies on her shoulders. She has every right without consulting anybody of the family to sell animals like pigs, hens and ducks reared by her. A close study shows that the Kuki women participated in decision making in the privacy of the home and also in the society level. The Kuki society is a close knit institution of family and is very important. It is casteless society. According to T.S. Gangte, 'The class composition of the Kukis and their political organizations were so independent of each other that the Kukis were obsessed with the idea of inter-clan rivalries being helped and fomented by the designing political organization'. It is further mentioned that 'according to their culture and tradition the social system of the Kukis was so segmented that every individual was made consciously aware that he or she belonged to a particular clan or sub-clan'.[3] The Kukis follow the patriarchal system of family structure. Customary laws and obligations in the society are extensive. The Kuki society is well organized. It is made possible by the institutions of Becha and Tucha. Becha is a person who belongs to a different clan but in the event of any social functions like birth, death, marriage, etc., Becha assumes the 'responsibilities of managerial work' and implements the decision of the head of the family on his behalf. However, some old Kuki groups like the Chiru, Kom, Chothe, etc., the Becha system is not practised but in its place the maternal uncle is given due importance in all similar matters.[4] In the traditional Kuki society, the maternal bond is not broken as there are many cultural rites and ceremonies which are observed even after a woman got married and left her maternal home. It is the Tucha Sungao relation which has become an indispensable part of the social life of the Kukis. 'Nephew' in the Kuki language is *'Tu'* and a 'child' of one's sister is *'cha'*. Therefore, *Tucha* means a child born of a sister and in turn the mother's brother's children are called *sung-gao*. The *Tucha Sung-gao* relationship is purely based on blood connection which expresses loyalty and solidarity of the blood relationship and mutual voluntary obligation. It is a by-product of matrimonial alliance and can have no other consideration whatsoever. The position of a *sung-gao* in relation to his *tucha* is nothing but to give. In a society where mother's brother's daughter's marriage is preferred, the *sung-gao* relative of an ego occupies a high position. Also, the *sung-gao* relative (the eldest son) has the right to claim the 'Long-man' (death price or corpse price) of his *tute* who were born of his sister. This death price is taken not as a punishment, but as proof of the love bond relationship between the brother's and sister's children. This signifies the good will of the *tute* and opens the door for cross-cousin marriage called *neite-kilah* (maternal uncle's daughter). The Kukis believed that this form of marriage ensures good health for the married couple and their children and it also establishes a continuous and permanent link between two groups of families. In spite of traditional prescription for this type of *neinu-neipa* marriage, its popularity among the younger generation is on the wane. The new generations of youths marry outside the clan group.

In the marriage system of the Kukis whatever the type of marriage, a bride price has to be paid by the boy's side to the girl's family. It varies from clan to clan. This bride price is said to have a social value as it is not to be paid in full even if one is able to do so. Bride-price, however, does not lower down the status of women in the Kuki society. It rather enhances her status as much as an accomplished bride fetches higher bride-price. The bride price received is matched by the dowry given by the parents. The standard of the dowry and the bridal feast given by the bride's parents enhances her prestige among her friends and among women in general. It appears to be a safety value for good economic relations between the wife given and wife-taker family, besides guarantying good conduct of the bride whose failure to satisfy the groom may lead to the forfeiture of the bride price to be received by the wife giving family. It also implies that the man should have obligation, love, respect, etc., for his wife and her relatives. It is to build a good relation with his wife's side.

Gangte further suggested two reasons for paying the bride-price. One is for compensation to the economic loss of the girl's family as she is the main pillar of the family's economy. The other reason is that she is the bearer of children for the expansion of family line of generation. Here, one can understand one of the important roles played by the Kuki Women. Traditionally, divorce was allowed. If a man divorces his wife without any cause, he does not get back the bride price he had paid and he is also fined one *mithun* as *daman* (divorce). If it is the woman who divorces her husband, the husband can take back the bride price he had paid to her. There is a saying among the Kuki which shows that a husband could divorce his wife at any time. It says *'Numei Phalou le honpal phalou chu khel ding mong ahi'* which means a bad wife and a bad fence can always be replaced. There is another unique custom at the death time of the Kukis where women are given prominent place. If a man has paid the full price for his wife during the marriage, he has on her death and the death of her sons to pay a further sum called *long-man*[5] (corpse price) to the nearest male relative. This shows an important position held by the Kuki women in the family. Therefore, in the Tucha-Sung-gao relation the bride price and Longman have social values. Traditionally, Kuki women were not socially aware. By observing the ethnological ways of the Kuki tribe one can safely assume that a Kuki woman within her family configuration and social setting remains a 'patriarchal woman'. A patriarchal woman, in the words of Lois Tyson,[6] can be defined as 'a woman who has internalized the norms and values of patriarchy'.

Patriarchy can be defined, in short, as any culture that privileges men by promoting traditional gender roles. Traditional gender roles cast men as rational, strong, protective and decisive and on the other hand they cast women as emotionally (irrational) weak, nurturing and submissive. The cultural habit of patriarchal dominance as universal still plays an important role in successfully excluding women from equal access to leadership and decision making positions both in the family and beyond the household. However, in contemporary times a considerable transformation has begun to surface both within the four walls of the home and in the society. By observing the nuances of fluctuating family values, fluid inter-personal relationships and the influence as well as the inevitable affects of western science and capitalism, industrialization, Kuki women no longer hesitate in attempting to negotiate their traditional feminity with the needs of modern times which is an ever-pressing reality. The Kuki women started to take part in movements which are burning topics of the present society, be it political, social and economic issues of the society from time to time. They no longer remained silent spectators when anti-State violence against women and anti-Manipuri activities threatened their Manipur State. On August 4, 1997 when OCTIM (Organising Committee of Territorial Integrity of Manipur) organized a mass rally, the Kuki women also joined the mass rally. Again they, in their traditional dresses, participated in the rally organized both by the AMKIL (Apunba Manipur Kanba Ima Lup) and NIPCO (National Identity Protection Committee) on 28 September, 2000. The Kuki Women for Human Rights Network Manipur and the Kuki Mothers Association condemned the uncivilized act of the security forces for firing upon anti-cease fire protestors on 18 June, 2001. Even the Human Rights Network also expressed its strong opinion for basic rights of the people. Today, Kuki society will no longer castigates her like it would have years ago if she wishes to pursue "unwomanly" vocation in present times. The future looks bright for young. The budding Kuki women are ready to step out of their societal 'cocooning'. Traditionally, the Kuki women had no role to play in politics especially in the village administration. Women were not allowed to utter even a word in the meeting of Haosa-upa (village elders). Their role was only to distribute red-tea in the meetings. Widows having no son were allowed to attend the annual village meeting. She was not allowed to have an effective say in any important matter. It was considered to be an exclusive domain for the male counterparts. Chief or Chairman of a Village Council is the only male. However, a striking feature we discovered from our empirical research is that there are some women who held Chieftainships or Chairmanships of the Village Councils after the death of their husbands. One held chieftainship for about 15 years. She is Mrs. Lamkhoneng Haokip of Vakan village, Manipur (1985-2000). Another woman named Vahjaneng Mate of Tengnoupal village of Chandel District held chieftainship after her husband's death.[7] Mrs. Lhaikhohoi Haokip of Kotlen village, New Cachar Road (Senapati District) and Mrs. Nemjating Gangte[8] of Santing village in Churachandpur District held chieftainships since 1992 till date. In Chandel district, there are four women chiefs.

Apart from Mrs. Vahjaning Mate, Miss Ating (Christina) Haokip, daughter of L. Jamson Haokip became the chief of Saivom village. Villages like Bongli and Chahmol of Machi Block in Chandel District are all headed by women: Neikhochong Haokip and Vahneng Haokip respectively.[9] In the village Council, women were included. For example, in Molnom village, Churachandpur district, Mrs. Ngainei, wife of Ngangam Haokip and Mrs. Thenneng, wife of Rev. L. Lhunkholet were elected in 2007 as Village Local Committee members. In modern politics women have started involving themselves in casting votes and also some have stood for political leadership. The Kuki women enjoyed adult franchise for the first time in 1948. They have started participating in the political process of the State both as voters and candidates.

Their number of voters always outnumbered men voters. Mrs. Lhingjaneng Gangte was nominated as the Member of the Territorial Council, 1957 to 1963 and nominated to the Territorial Assembly,1963-1969. There was also another woman who was nominated along with Mrs. Lhingjaneng Gangte. She was Mrs. Akim Angnal. In the mid-term Assembly Election in 1974, Mrs. Lhingjaneng Gangte contested from the Saikot constituency but was defeated. Mrs. Lhingjaneng Gangte received Padma Shree Award. [10] In the Parliamentary election, Miss Kim Gangte was elected as the Member of Parliament in 1998 as a C.P.I. Candidate. Many Kuki women contested in the assembly seats but could not succeed. There is no Panchayati Raj system in all the hill districts and District Autonomous Councils have been defunct.

The general attitude of males towards inclusion of women as authority member is not encouraging. Moreover, women in the hills are generally not concerned with this issue except for a few enlightened women who discuss the matter occasionally in an informal discussion. Individual women progressing do not carry women's issues unless these issues enter the political process. Women, generally, are ignorant of their rights and also the importance of women's participation in decision making bodies and levels. The important role placed by the Kuki women as a decision maker can be seen even during the Anglo Kuki War of Independence of 1917-1919. It was the Kuki women who guarded the villages, looked after their homes and families. They suffered silently the pangs of separation from their loved ones when their men folk went to war against the British. It is unimaginable the hardship, emotional trauma they faced when the British took their men for labour corps to France. Not only this, the Kuki women suffered untold miseries during and after the war when the Kuki chiefs and leaders of the war were imprisoned and punished. Villages suspected to have been involved in abetting and sheltering the so called 'Rebels' during the war were burnt down. It was the woman and children who suffered the most and the loss of life on the part of the Kukis might perhaps be no less than that of the government though the exact figure of the dead and wounded on the side of the Kukis are not available. Those brave women who went through the untold miseries can be called 'forgotten heroines' of the Anglo Kuki war of Independence of 1917 because they are the ones who bravely shouldered the responsibilities of guarding their villages, supplying food to the men, looking after the wounded warriors. Asking the Kuki warriors to go to France simply as labourers in the war front was considered an insult of the highest degree. Their pride was hurt when their women took over the decision making in the village administration and in their homes. The proud Kuki warriors thought that 'menial labour falls within the realms of women's domain'.[11] The struggle of the Kukis for freedom from the British rule in Manipur continued even after their defeat in Anglo-Kuki war of 1917-19. The Kuki men and women joined the INA (Indian National Army) forces and served in intelligence as reporters, guides, sepoys and others. The gifted skills of the villagers enabled them to produce simple forms of weaponry tools and implements for both aggressive and defensive purposes. Consequently, chiefs' fighting-men possessed guns (which had flint-locks ......). They manufactured gun powder.[12]

In 1944, a Kuki woman named Hoijakim and her husband Longjangam Kuki carried the letter of Netaji Subhash Chandra Bose to Imphal and delivered to Thokchom Angou Singh. It was suggested by Dr. Gulabjao who was posted at Sugnu during that time. They also met Potsangbam Tomal Singh and Laishram Kanhai before they returned back.[13] Mrs. Hoijakim and her husband acted as spies for the Indian National Army. The INA under the leadership of Col. S.A. Malik hoisted the Tri-colour flag for the first time on the sacred soil of liberated area at Moirang. In fact, the soil of 'Moirang' was sanctified by the blood and tears of the Indo-Japanese forces.[14] Onkholet Haokip known as Japan Pakang followed the Japanese upto Japan as he could not stay in his own land in the face of enemy's domination.

The main occupation of the Kukis is agriculture: terrace and *jhum* cultivation. They settled in almost all the entire hill areas of Manipur and the adjoining regions of the North-Eastern India, Myanmar and Bangladesh. The Kukis are surmised to have arrived in Manipur between 14th and 15th

century A.D.[15] They were followed by Thadou, Khongsais and his cognate groups at the end of 16th century and the beginning of 17th century. The Kukis shifted from one place to another in search of suitable terrain for settlement. The Kukis solely depended on mode of agricultural economy. In as far as *jhuming* cultivation is concerned, majority of the Kuki tribes sow their seeds without upturning the soil.[16] The Kuki women work side by side with their husbands in the fields. Their source of livelihood is provided by the land they inhabit and the forest around them. With the primitive technology at their command they feel at home in the midst of forest life which is inseparable from high landish society. They form groups called *lom* where they work together taking turns to work in their fields. *lom* is said to be one of the most important organizations concerned with the economic relations among the Kukis. The literal meaning of *lom* is understood as collective labour force. This collective service gives the Kuki women a sense of responsibility, fraternity and peaceful co-existence among them. This contributes greatly to the socio-economic development of the village in particular and the society in general. This *lom* system helps the poor and needy people like the widows. *lom* was practised by the Kukis and continued till today.

The Kuki women cultivated various types of crops by using an implement of dibbling stick made of bamboo or wood and a small hoe called *tucha*. The soil is dug, seed inserted and covered with the soil. Weeding is done on the basis of the growth of the weeds. Other than rice, Kuki women cultivated varieties of cash crops : cucumber, maize, beans, gourds, ginger, turmeric, taro or yam locally known as (*paan* or *baal*), etc. In Manipur *jhum* is heavily practised in the areas where the Kukis inhabited predominantly than the areas inhabited by the Naga.[17] The Kuki women started coming to the market in Imphal to sell their vegetables grown in their own fields. There are women who opened small shops to sell meat, tea, second hand clothes in Imphal areas and in the hill areas. They formed themselves into societies or self-help groups. Each society has at least 20 women. They focus on making the best use of the local resources and making the maximum possible uses. Since there is a great availability of fruits like oranges, pineapples, lemon, passion fruits, etc. they make squashes, jams, achar and sell in the market. The profit they shared contributes in the economy of the family. The traditional economy of the Kukis is subsistence economy. They manufactured almost anything from bamboo baskets to gunpowder for their socio-economic requirements. The Kuki women are expected to learn the art of weaving from childhood. In the past, women who were expert in the art of weaving were considered to be better brides as her services strengthened the domestic economy. The Kuki dresses in general are the identity of a nation or a tribe. Dresses are like the unwritten code where one's social status and culture can be determined. The Kuki ways of dressing are often artistic, well adapted to the working condition of the hills. Not only the Kukis but the different tribes of the Nagas have special shawls with symbols of animals, objects, etc., for their festive occasion."[18] The Kuki women did careful handicraft work and artistic designs. These beautiful shawls and wraps around are much in demands among the elite Kuki women. Patterns and designs of some of the Kukis like the Thadous are taken from the colours of animals like python, fish bone, elephant knee, jungle bamboo tube, mortar, etc. It is believed that a lady who operates the work of weaving without performing ritual or offering will not last long. Since there was no major industries among the hill tribes most of their day-to-day domestic needs were met by themselves. Pottery making was considered the work of women folk among the Kukis. The Kuki women used to sell rice-beer liked by all. But this custom is not in practice now as most of the Kukis have converted to Christianity. It is used at times of religious ceremonies and social functions. The most popular smoke used in the traditional days was *tuibuh* (tobacco juice) and *dumphol*. The Kukis are rarely seen without a pipe in their mouth. In the Churachandpur district, women come to the market and sell *tuibuh*. With such a small amount of money she gets from selling this tobacco juice she contributes in family. Hodson described, 'I have travelled with Kukis who ate nothing all the day but kept up their strength by constant sips of this juice, which they retained in the mouth not more than three minutes at a time'.[19] The Kuki women are expected to engage themselves in lighter part of the domestic works whereas the more difficult jobs are done by their male counterparts. Spinning, weaving, cooking, rearing of poultry and pigs, etc., are exclusively women's domain. In exceptional cases, widows without adult sons engage in activities which are normally tagged 'male'. There are women who spent their days toiling hard in the river banks to gather sand and shingles but given a meagre sum that is hard to sustain the daily needs. In the first half of 20th century under colonial economy, rice became a prospective commercial crop in Manipur. Consequently, the British authorities began to take interest in expanding terrace cultivation. Besides, Potato cultivation by Kukis and Nagas in the hills was encouraged by the British.[20] Traditionally, the only trade known among the Kukis was barter which was carried out within the village circle. The only assignment in which they were engaged in their day- to- day life was Vaikon/Loukon (field appointment). Money system of trade and commerce was not known until they came in contact with other neighbouring tribes. The advent of British introduced the Kukis the knowledge of currency system. They had no other concerns other than agricultural activities. But things have changed with the coming of the British. Western education opened the eyes of the Kukis and they realized the importance of having material possession and the importance of education. In a Kuki family the presence of one talented and skilful woman could extend her support economically to the whole family. The labour inputs and time spent by both male and female is comparatively the same with that of agricultural activities.

The Kukis led a measurable socio-economic life more so during and after the Anglo Kuki War 1917-1919. The British had exploited the resources. The continuance of the war for more than two years meant complete draining away of their economic resources. There was a total breakdown of agricultural economy. As a result of starvation, the Kuki warriors surrendered to the British. The introduction of money economy and the expansion of markets had a far reaching impact on the socio-economic life of the Kukis. They began to think of producing goods to sell in the markets. It is the women folk who took larger share of the responsibility in it. Now-a-days, Kuki women in many cases are the bread earners. There are many educated Kuki women working as employees in different departments of the Manipur Government.

Unfortunately, during the early 1990s on account of the ethnic cleansing, economic condition of the Kukis worsened. Many Kuki women became widows and a large number of children orphaned. The Kukis became landless and were reduced to mere wage earners or hired labourers. To sustain their daily needs they took up different occupations not by choice but out of necessity. Many young girls became vulnerable. Many youth became drug addicts. The ethnic tension led displacement.

Like any other tribal society Kuki society is also patriarchal. In spite of the tremendous contributions they have no right of inheritance. Our research has shown that a few thoughtful parents do share their property among daughters and sons. With the introduction of Self-Help Groups, the Kuki women are now introduced to awareness programmes ranging from conflict resolution to prevention of HIV/AIDS, how to stand on their own feet, how to become economically independent. They are on their way to viewing the world with new eyes.

The Kuki customs, culture and traditions establish the superiority of men over women. But, improvement through education has changed the man-woman relationship and brought about the emancipation of women in Kuki society. Above all, the Kuki society has become more liberal and tolerant than it was before.

REFERENCES

1. J. Shakespear, *The Lushai Kuki Clans*, Delhi, 1994, p. 147.
2. Journal of the 69th Anniversary of the Kuki Rebellion, 1917-19, 1985, p. 10.
3. T.S. Gangte, *The Kukis of Manipur – A Historical Analysis*, Gyan Publishing House, New Delhi, 1993, p. 26.

4. Tarun Goswami, *Kuki Life and Lore,* Assam, 1985, p. 19.
5. Longman is a customary duty consisting of one *mithun*, claimable by the maternal uncle of the heir on the death of his nephew and their mother. It is paid by the father or the eldest son. However, Longman cannot be claimed in the case of unnatural death and women who bear no male issues.
6. Lois Tyson, *Critical Theory Today*, Routledge, 2006, New York.
7. Reported by Paokhohen Haokip, Chief of Sita Village, Chandel District, Manipur.
8. Nemjating Gangte is the sister-in-law of the writer.
9. Interview with Mrs. Ating Haokip,Chief of Saivom Village, Chandel District, Manipur.
10. Interview with Mrs. Lhingjaneng Gangte, Member, Manipur State Commission for Women.
11. S. Kipgen, Political and Economic History of the Kukis of Manipur, unpublished PhD Thesis, MU, p. 158.
12. E.W. Dun, *A Bridged Gazetteer of Manipur*, Vivek Publishing House, Delhi, 1975, pp. 32-35.
13. Laikhuram Ibobi Singh, *Manipur Praja Sanmelani Amasung Anisuba Nupi Lan*, Imphal, 2003 p.123.
14. Quoted in Souvenir – Golden Jubilee Celebration.
15. Vumson, *Zo History*, Aizawl, 1986, p. 64.
16. K. Kipgen, *op. cit.*, p. 114.
17. T.S. Gangte, Seminar Paper, MUTSU, 2001, p. 2.
18. Sina Khayi, 'Cultural Significance of Tribal Costumes in Modern Times', Seminar Paper, MUTSU, March, 1996.
19. T.C. Hodson,*The Naga Tribes of Manipur*, B.R. Publishing Corporation, New Delhi, 1974, p. 61.
20. Manipur Administrative Report, MSA, Imphal, 1913-14.

13

CHIN-KUKI-MIZO ETHNIC NATIONALITY TRANSFORMATION

A CRITICAL OBSERVATION

Paul B. Chonzik

Introduction

Anthony D. Smith in his *The Ethnic Revival* (1981) observed, "The dissolution of ethnicity. The transcendence of nationalism. The internationalisation of culture. These have been the dreams, and expectations, of liberals and rationalists in practically every country, and in practically every country they have been confounded and disappointed".[1] Benedict Anderson also told us that the old nations once fully consolidated 'find themselves challenged by sub-nationalisms within their borders — nationalisms which, naturally, dream of shedding this subness one happy day'.[2] Indeed, in almost every corner of the world, nation-states are fighting wars against *national struggle* of sub-nations for self-determination demanding autonomy and often than not seeking independence from the parent state. *Nationalism* for sub-nations is *anti-national* for the nation; *national struggle* for sub-nations is a *rebellion* or *insurgence* for nations; *patriot* to a sub-nation is a *renegade* to the nation. There are many examples of such 'contesting nationalisms' in the history of nationalities in North-East India.[3] In the case of *Chin-Kuki-Mizo* nationality, members of which are dispersed over a wide area yet more or less confined in a rather compact area of Manipur, Mizoram, Assam, Tripura in North-East India, Chittagong Hill Tracts of Bangladesh and Chin Hills of Myanmar, history witnessed that they had undergone division resulting in many of the tribes (sub-nationalities) within the nationality claiming to be distinct. Even the smaller marginal nationalities belonging to the sub-nationalities wanted to break away from the sub-nationality they belong to. Each of these sub-nationalities are dreaming of shedding their 'sub-ness' one happy day. In the mean time, sections of the *Kuki-Chin-Mizo* nationality had been and are trying to re-unite and even fought for integration under one administrative unit. Thus the *Chin-Kuki-Mizo* nationality is facing claims and counter-claims of national affiliation giving way to contesting nationalisms. This chapter tries to contextualize empirical data within global theoretical framework.

It may first be noted that the *Chin-Kuki-Mizo* nationality presumably a single group not very long time ago had divided into several tribes over the ages. Grierson in 1904 had already listed 32 tribes dividing them on the basis of dialect differences and tribal nomenclatures.[4]

Grierson put the following tribes under *Chin languages:* 1. *Northern Group* – (a) Thādo, (b) Soktē, (c) Siyin, (d) Rāltē, (e) Paitē; 2. *Central Group* – (a) Tashn, (b) Lai, (c) Lakher, (d) Lushei, (e) Banjōgi, (f) Pānkhū; 3. *Old Kuki* – (a) Rāngkhōl, (b) Bētē, (c) Hallām, (d) Langrong, (e) Aimol, f) (Anāl, (g) Chiru, (h) Hiroi-Lamgāng, (i) Kolrēn, (j) Kōm, (k) Pūrūim, (l) Mhâr, (m) Châ; 4. *Southern Group* – Chinmē, Welaung, Chinbōk, Yindu, Chinbou, Khyang or Shō, Khami.

Liangkhaia, one of the earliest native writers, in 1938, in his *Mizo Chanchin* (Mizo history), also listed 32 such tribes, some names of the tribes different from that of Grierson's.[5]

Liangkhaia's list included Pawi (Lai), Matu, Paihte (Paite), Thahdo (Thado), Hmar, Kawm (Kom), Zo, Chiru, Aimawl (Aimol), Khawl, Tarau, Anal, Purum, Tikhup, Rangte, Vaiphei,

Lakher (Mara), Langrawng, Chawrai (Chorai), Bawng, Mualthuam (Muolsuom or Molsom), Kaihpēn (now Kaipēng), Pangkhua (Pâng), Tlânglau, Biate (Biete), Hrangkhawl (Hrangkhol), Bawmzo, Miria, Dâwn, Takam, Kumi (or Khumi), Darlawng (Darlong). All brackets are mine showing the way the clans/tribes are known today.

L. Keivom, writing in 1991 observed that there were not less than 47 tribes from this original group.[6] Some of the tribes from this original group have even changed their ethnic affiliation (migrated?) to other nationalities. Cases in point are — sub-tribes of the *Kuki-Chin-Mizo* group such as Aimol, Anal, Chothe, Chiru, Maring, Monsang, Moyong (also Lamkang) who have now identify themselves as Naga, and Koloi and Rupini tribes of Tripura state of North-East India who have now identify themselves as Tripuri.[7] Why? There must have been push factors from the parent ethnic group or conversely there must have been pull factors from the other nationalities to which these tribes feel belonging to. We shall not go into this. We shall however, look into the factors promoting ethnic division.

Chin-Kuki-Mizo Groups as a Nation

Treating the group, given a hyphenated nomenclature, *Chin-Kuki-Mizo,* consisting of three collective proper names of groups of tribes as a composite whole and as a nation may be questioned. Yes, presently there are groups of people in North-East India who identify themselves separately as *Chin, Kuki* and *Mizo*. To this may be added another collective proper name *Zomi* which became popular among some of them during the 1980s. It may, therefore, be more proper to refer to them as *Chin-Kuki-Mizo-Zomi.* While *Kuki* and *Chin* are names given to them by others (their exoethnonym), *Mizo* and *Zomi* are names they themselves coined (endoethnonym) for their collective proper name.

The ethnonym *Mizo* literally means 'hill people' (Mi = people; zo = hilly region). This includes the *Luseis* (*Lushais* or *Lhoosais*) and kindred tribes, and the ethnonym *Zomi* (literally meaning the same as *Mizo*) includes the Paite and cognate tribes.Thus, there are *Mizo, Kuki, Chin* and *Zomi* nationalities having practically the same tribes within their respective nationalities. That the people representing these collective proper names are one and of common origin is clear from the writings of British administrators who left valuable records of the people. When the British first encountered the tribes belonging to this group, they referred to them variously as *Kuki (Kookie or Cuci), Chin,* and *Lusei (Lushai* or *Lhoosai),* which are names given to them by others (exoethnonym). Thus, T.H. Lewin, writing in 1869 observed:

> *"The Lhoosai, commonly called the Kookies, are a powerful and independent people, who touch upon the borders of the Chittagong Hill Tracts. They extend in numberless hordes, north and north-east, until they reach Cachar on the one hand, and the frontiers of Burmah on the other. They cannot be considered as a nation for they have no coherence of government or policy, but, with slight differences, they speak one language and follow the same customs."*[8]

G.A. Grierson, in 1904, also wrote:

> *"The vast mountainous region, from the Jaintia and Naga Hills, is the home of Kuki-Chin tribes. We find them, besides, in the valley of Manipur, and, in small settlements, in the Cachar Plains and Sylhet. The denomination Kuki-Chin is purely conventional one, there being no proper name comprising all these tribes."*[9]

Grierson further said:

> *"Kuki is an Assamese or Bengali term, applied to various hill tribes, such as the Lusheis, Rangkhols, Thados, etc." and*

> *"...Chin is a Burmese word used to denote the various hill tribes living in the country between Burma and the Provinces of Assam and Bengal... The name is not used by the tribes themselves, who used titles such as Zo or Yo or Sho."*[10]

Shakespear (1912), after dwelling on the confusion on terms like *Kuki, Lushai* and *Chin*, etc., concluded:

> *'Nevertheless, there is no doubt that the Kuki, Lushais and Chins are all of the same race'.*[11]

Probably early British writers were unable to distinguish one tribe of the group from another and simply believed that they were one. The *Luseis* (*Lushais* or *Lhoosais*) have abandoned their exoethnonym and, along with kindred tribes have chosen to adopt *Mizo* for their ethnic identification. It is interesting to note that historians belonging to *Chin, Kuki* and *Mizo,* and also *Zomi* groups, listed practically the same tribes as belonging to their respective groups. Hence, all of them are one and of same origin.

This group can be called a nation in the *eastern* or *ethnic model*. This is one of the two models of conceiving 'nation' as Anthony D. Smith discusses.[12] The other is the *western model* or *civic model,* according to which the term 'nation' is equated with a political entity or a political-territorial unit like India, Pakistan, France, Brazil, United States of America, etc. According to this *eastern* or *ethnic model,* the term 'nation' refers to human collectively marked off from the rest of other human collectivities by certain common culture, similar traditions, common myth of origin, linguistic affinity and common historical memories the group shared.[13] Yulian Bromley, in his study of the ethnic nationality formations and transformations of the troubled Soviet Union, observed that even when one ethnic group is transformed through the various processes, its 'predominant traditional properties are preserved, though in a greatly modified form'.[14] This is also true of the *Chin-Kuki-Mizo* people. Though this group had undergone ethnic transformation through the ages, they still retain some of the basic elements of their culture and language. Language in particular is dynamic and new words are formed almost every season, so that local variations could easily develop. Of the tribes from this group, there are some who had lost '*r*' in their syllable in the course of such developments.[15] However, from the surviving language there is no doubt that they are from the same family. The 'predominant' traditional properties of their culture and languages and folktales that they retained indicated that they are of the same ethnic group of same ancestry, of the same origin. They shared similar cultures unique to them such as the prevalence of various types of *darkhuong* (gong), *sathu* (fermented pork), and their style of *jhum* cultivation, etc. They also shared many similar traditional folk tales such as a folk hero whose stories are the same but known by different names, viz., *Sura* by *Hmar* and kindred tribes, *Chhura* by *Lusei* speaking group and *Penglam* by non-'*r*' groups. They also shared common myth of origin from a cave or pit or stone enclosure believed to be somewhere in southern China, which again is given different names such as *Sinlung* by Hmar and Darlong, etc., *Chhinlung* by Lusei (Mizo), *Chinlung* by Thadou-Kuki, *Khuul* or *Khul* byTiddim and Paite, *Khur* by Kom, etc., *Khurpui* by Chorei and Hallam groups and *Khol* by Anals, etc.[16] They also have strong linguistic affinity, as indicated above, which is why Grierson in his *Linguistic Survey of India* put them under one group he called 'Kuki-Chin' due lack of 'proper name comprising all these tribes', belonging to the greater Tibeto-Burmese linguistic group.[17] Thus, we can safely say that the group qualifies to be called a 'nation' in the ethnic model. The slight differences in the cultural practices and languages (or dialects) must have been future developments due to geographical divisions. New words and practices are developing every season even today. T.H. Lewin appears to have conceived 'nation' in the *civic* or *western model* when he contended that the *Chin-Kuki-Mizo* group could not be considered a nation because of their lack of 'coherence of government and policy' (see *f.n.* 8 above).

Transformation—Coalescence or Division?

There are mainly two ways in which nations in the ethnic model are formed or transformed, namely *coalescence* and *division.*[18] In the case of *coalescence,* an ethnic nation may be formed through the coming together of ethnic communities following the process of amalgamation of separate units or absorption of one unit by another, as in the process of assimilation. In the case of *division,* ethnic group may be divided and subdivided through fission, as with sectarian schism, or through 'proliferation', when a part of the ethnic community leaves to form a new group.[19]

Chin-Kuki-Mizo nationality had undergone division. The process of *division* appears to have produced two levels of division within the nationality. At the *higher level,* division happened broadly on the basis of the different collective proper names such as *Chin, Kuki, Mizo* and later on *Zomi* with which some of the tribes or part of the tribes of the nationality chose to identify themselves. This is to say that while some tribes or part of the tribes integrate using one of these collective proper names as their collective proper name, the other tribes or section of the tribes integrate using the other collective proper names. In other words, we may say that a process of *coalescence* happened on the enlarged groups such as *Chin, Kuki, Mizo* and also *Zomi,* the leaders of which have formed organizations to mobilize the tribes under their respective banners. No wonder, there is *Mizo* nation (Mizo National Front), *Kuki* nation (Kuki National Assembly), *Chin* nation (Chin National Army), *Zomi* nation (Zomi National Council), each trying to mobilize the same groups of tribes within their fold. These organizations have been able to absorb the sub-nationalities (at least sections of some of them). Smaller, marginal groups were more prone to be absorbed into such enlarged nationality. It thus happen that many *Hmars, Raltes, Pawis (Lais)* and *Paites* and others were ready to identify themselves as *Mizo,* whereas some sections among them steadfastly chose to be distinct. In the same manner, some sections of *Paite, Zo, Thadou, Vaiphei* and *Gangte* tribes and others readily identify themselves as *Kuki,* while some chose to identify themselves in their respective 'separate' tribal nomenclature. This is also true of the *Chin*, a collective ethnic nomenclature more commonly used by section of the groups mostly living in Myanmar (Burma) as Chittagong Hill Tracks of Bangladesh such as the *Tiddims* (*Tedims*), the *Dapzar*, etc., while some chose to identify themselves in their separate tribal nomenclature. This is also the case with *Zomi* groups consisting of sections of *Paite, Gangte, Vaiphei, Jou, tribes*, etc. It may be said that each of these collective proper names have become names of 'base ethnic group' on which coalescence is taking place and also is being consciously attempted. It so happened that those who readily identify themselves as *Chin* sought to unify or re-unify the fragmented groups into single *Chin* nationality. In the same way, those who readily identify themselves as *Kuki, Mizo* and *Zomi* sought to unify or re-unify the divided tribes into single nationality as *Kuki, Mizo,* and also *Zomi*, respectively.

At the *next level*, division percolated down to the sub-nationalities, so that there are *Paite* nation (Paite National Council), *Hmar* nation (Hmar National Congress), *Kom* nation (Kom National Union), *Vaiphei* nation (Vaiphei National Organisation) and so on. It may percolate down to the marginal nationalities belonging to the sub-nationalities in the long run. The process appears to have already started when one finds that tribes such as the *Biete, Hrangkhawl, Darlong*, began to separate themselves from their Hmar ethnic affiliation and started asserting being distinct. Division at the first place happened due to various factors while coalescence also did take place as discussed below.

Ethnic Processes Operative within Chi-Kuki-Mizo Nationin

The *Chin-Kuki-Mizo* nationality had undergone ethnic division and integration to reach the present status.

The nationality might have undergone division from a larger group, as many nationalities did, long time ago in their history. The present study, however, confine to more recent period, when the group began to disperse into several geographical pockets, leading to their settlement in their present habitations. Till the British colonization of their areas, division in the *Chin-Kuki-Mizo* nationality had taken place without external force.

Factors helping Ethnic Division during Pre-Colonial Period

There are certain factors which helped ethnic division in the *Chin-Kuki-Mizo* nationality during this period. We shall briefly discuss some of them as follows:

1. Geographical Division, Inter-clan and inter-village Warfare

Without going into the various views on the movement of the group back into their history which were mainly based on legends and traditions, suffice it to say that the *Chin-Kuki-Mizo* tribes were believed to have begun moving out of Kabaw Valley in the Chin Hills of Myanmar from the beginning of the 12th century A.D. probably afraid of the Ahom army who consequently conquered the indigenous rulers of Assam in 1228 A.D. (This needs further historical survey). B. Lalthangliana believed that by 1200 A.D. most of the tribes from the *Chin-Kuki-Mizo* group have left Kabaw Valley.[20] The groups were said to have moved out in batches, one after another, following different directions, each group consisting mainly of the same clan.[21] In the long run this separation gave way to tribe-based division since clan enlarged begot tribe which ultimately could become basis for claiming distinct ethnic identity whereby concretizing the walls of division. According to some Hmar historians, basing on traditional folk song, this dispersion started after their forefathers from their Shan settlement due to famine.[22] Whatever, dispersed they did.

Lt. Colonel J. Shakespeare gave the common title 'Old Kuki' to the group who moved out of their Chin Hills settlement and 'New Kuki' to the groups who moved out later.[23] Some of the *Old Kuki* groups moved to Tripura and some to Cachar and North Cachar Hills of Assam, and some to Manipur and some to Chittagong Hill Tracts of Bangladesh. It appears that the *New Kuki* group who moved into Lushai

Hills, also were themselves driven out by the Luseis soon after.[24] Many of the *New Kukis* tribes moved into different regions in Manipur, Cachar and North Cachar Hills of Assam, and most of them retained *Kuki* as their ethnic nomenclature.

It is difficult to determine the date of their migration into these places. One source in which reference to *Kuki* was made in the land grants in Tripura suggests that the *Kukis* were already in Tripura sometime in the late twelfth century. In the history of Tripura mention is made of Raja Dharmadahar of Kailagadh who granted land to a Kanauj Brahmin. The inscription in the copper plate marking this event bears the name of 'Kuki-land'; the land bounded in the east of Longoi (Langkaih) River and the date is mentioned as 1195.[25] Reference to *Kuki* is also made in the *Rajmala,* the Chronicles of the Tripura Rajas, whereby Raja Dhanya Manikya's (1490-1515) reign is said to have witnessed a quarrel over the possession of a white elephant with the *Kukis* who occupied the deep forest lying to the east of Tripura and the west of Lushai Hills.[26] In the same chronicles, reference is made about the *Kukis* in connection with the Tipperah Raja Chachag, who flourished about 1512.[27] Thus, even if the date suggested by reference to *Kuki* in the land grant made by Raja Dharmadahar to a Kanauj Brahmin dating 1195 is considered doubtful, it is evident that the *Kukis* had already settled in Tripura hills in the middle or late 15th century.

The last batch of migrants into Lushai Hills (now Mizoram) consists of the many clans of the *Lusei* tribe, the most prominent among them being the Sailo clan probably around later part of 15th century or early part of the 16th century A.D.[28]

It is also not certain at what point of time the *Chin-Kuki-Mizo* clans and villages started fighting against each other. But there is enough proof that their forefathers had been fighting among themselves. Bringing home enemies head used to be considered a great achievement which each adult male member was vying for. While some of the fights were over land for cultivation, there were also wars fought just for prestige. *Assam Administration Report* (1921-22) tells us about the inhabitants of Lushai Hills and adjoining areas:

> *"From the earliest period of which we have any knowledge, the hills lying to the south of Manipur, Cachar and eastern Sylhet have been inhabited by various tribes known to the Bengalis by the common name of Kukis. These tribes have always, so far as we knew, been divided into numerous families, each family acknowledging a chief or ruling house, and these houses being generally engaged in warfare with one another. Each village had its chief, whose object it was to extend the fame and power of his village by fighting with his neighbours...."*[29]

In 1869, Lewin wrote about the Lusei raid on the Pâng (The Pâng, written as *Pankho* by the British writers, is one of the lesser tribes belonging to the *Lusei-Kuki-Chin* nation and resides mostly in southern Mizoram and Chittagong Hills tracts of Bangladesh.) chief Ardung Raja's village as narrated by a Pâng young man, who said :

> *"....About four in the morning..., the sentry saw something moving in the jungle outside the stockade, and he thought it was a guyal or jungle pig, and threw a stone at it, then up sprang the Lhoosai, about 200 Lhoosai men, and gave a low guttural shout, hoarse and deep. All our villagers abandoned their houses, and fled for their lives down a concealed path. My mother took me on her back and ran. The Lhoosai only got two of our people, and they were too drunk to move. They hauled one fellow up, but he only grunted and lay down again; then they prodded him with a spear, and he only grunted the more. So they cut him to pieces as he lay. Then they plundered our village and went away".*[30]

These inter-clan and inter-village feuds furthered the process of internal division of the people.

2. Lack of Good Road Communication

About their communication Major A.G. McCall had written about Lushai Hills sometime between 1939 and 1944

> *"Contemplate a country about the size of Wales with no ordinary roads, even for bicycles, with but one small lake, rivers as yet too dangerous for boats, except in the hands of experts from a far distant land, all composed of steep and rugged hills lacerated by these same whimsical rivers and we have something like Lushai".*[31]

If this was the condition as seen by the British officials in around 1939, it must have been really bad before the British came since there was no historical record about a stable governance in the history of the *Chin-Kuki-Mizo* by the time they began to disperse. Lack of road and other communication systems between one area to another added to the furtherance of division.

3. Chieftainship

It is not certain how chieftainship developed among the *Chin-Kuki-Mizo* people. But it is certain that the people were divided into several chieftainships, each consisting of one or more villages. The ultimate result of this was that loyalty to the larger nationality shifted to loyalty to chief and the chiefdom. And relationship between them was not always cordial. Rather they were almost always at war. This further strengthened the process of disintegration which had already started due to disperse geographical settlements.

Intra-Ethnic Consolidation under Sailo Chiefs

In the process of ethnic nationality transformations, intra-ethnic consolidation often happens, whereby large ethnic groups were formed through the 'smoothing over' of local internal differences that exists between member-units which have lost their self-awareness but endowed with individual specific culture components and the 'evening out' of dialectical differences and cultural everyday life distinctions as the general ethnic self-awareness is strengthened.[32] Intra-ethnic consolidation may operate either consciously or unconsciously of the members concerned. Consciously when participating member-units chose to forget or discard their individual ethnic attributes in favour of the general enlarged ethnic group to which they have now been integrated because they gain than lose to do so. It more often operate unconsciously because the participating member-units have lost their distinct ethnic self-awareness.

In the history of *Chin-Kuki-Mizo* nationality intra-ethnic consolidation took place under the strong influence of Sailo chiefs.

Selesih, a Sailo village with seven thousand households

The Lusei clans were the later group among the *Chin-Kuki-Mizo* people to move across the Liau River into Lushai Hills from Kabaw Valley and Chin Hills (now in Myanmar). After the Luseis moved into Lushai Hills, there were still a large group of warlike Pawis (Lais) who stayed back in Chin Hills of Myanmar. Apprehensive of the possible Pawi attack from across Liau, seven of the Sailo chiefs decided to live together in one big village and they chose the village run by one of them, Pukawlha (or Pu Kawla).[33] The name of the village was **Selesih** which lies between Khawbung and Zawlsei village in southern part of Champhai district of the present Mizoram.[34] The village grew so large that it was said to have 7000 households. This might have been an exaggeration, but still, with seven chiefs the village must have been a big one. The setting up of such a big village (town?) under the Sailo chiefs is of historical significance for certain reasons such as:

- Many *Chin-Kuki-Mizo* tribes came under their sway which had a homogenizing impact on the nationality.

- Lusei (Duhlian) language developed as a common medium of communication among *Chin-Kuki-Mizo* people who came under their influence. This language is now developing as a *lingua franca* among the various tribes of the nationality consisting of those who readily identify themselves as *Mizo*.
- The Sailo chiefs with so many subjects to rule over developed better administrative system.
- They also developed more standardized customary laws.

All these helped the operation of the process of intra-ethnic consolidation within a section of the *Chin-Kuki-Mizo* nation. And it is also at this time and the following years that assimilation of various tribes into the *Chin-Kuki-Mizo* nationality took slow and sure steps.

Division and Coalescence during Colonial Phase

The British expansion into areas inhabited by the *Chin-Kuki-Mizo* tribes came at different times. The expansion into these hills mostly resulted from British reaction to the incessant raids perpetrated by the tribes on the outlying plains of their habitation which had come under British administration such as Cachar, Assam and Bengal and not so much because of imperial economic considerations. The British first tried checking these raids through punitive expeditions. But even after several successful expeditions, the raids continued, so that of policy "pacification through permanent occupation" was adopted from 1889 onwards. Thus the *Chin-Lushai Expedition of 1889-1890* was launched. This expedition resulted in the establishment of posts and communication systems.[35] On the administrative side, these operations led to the creation of the two districts of the North Lushai Hills and South Lushai Hills, with headquarters at Aizawl and Lunglei respectively. North Lushai Hills came under Assam administration along with Cachar and North Cachar Hills. South Lushai Hills along with Chittagong Hill Tracts were under Bengal administration. Chin Hills was under British Burmese province, and part of *Chin-Kuki-Mizo* settlement areas in Manipur and Tripura were under their respective princely states.

Knowing that people from Chin Hills, Arakan and Chittagong Hill Tracts and Lushai Hills were of the same tribal group, the desire to unite all territories they inhabited was voiced in 1891. In forwarding their views to the Secretary of State, the Government of India, in their financial despatch No. 191, dated the 14th July, 1891, stated their views that,

> *"It is probable that ultimately it may be found possible and desirable to consolidate under one administration the whole or the greater part of the territory in the occupation of the various tribes now separately controlled from Bengal, Burma and Assam".*[36]

It was in this spirit that the **Chin-Lushai Hills Conference** was held at Fort William, Calcutta during January 27 – 29, 1892. Final recommendations of the conference include:

> *"The majority of the Conference are of opinion that it is very desirable that the whole tract of country known as Chin-Lushai Hills should be brought under one administrative head as soon as this can be done. They also consider it advisable that the new administration should be subordinate to the Chief Commissioner of Assam....*
>
> *"The Conference is agreed that North and South Lushai Hills, with such portions of the Arakan Hill Tracts as may hereafter be determined, should be placed under Assam at once on condition that —*

(1) Complete transport and commissariat equipment for supplies from Chittagong to South Lushai, and from Cachar to North Lushai are provided;

(2) Funds are granted for roads and telegraph from Aijal (Aizawl) to Lungleh (Lunglei)."[37]

In accordance with the proposal made by the conference, the Governor-General in council made the following conclusions—

(1) The whole of Lushai country should be under the Chief Commissioner of Assam, and the transfer of the Southern Lushais from Bengal to Assam should be made as early as possible...

(4) The Northern Arakan Hill Tracts should be transferred from Burma to Assam..."[38]

However, such progressive move for administrative unification of area inhabited by the *Chin-Kuki-Mizo* tribes was foiled apparently by Alexander Mackenzie, the then Chief Commissioner of Burma, who persuaded the Government of India against 'too much administration' for Assam.[39] Thus, except for the amalgamation of North and South Lushai Hills, the desire to bring all territory 'occupied by the various tribes' did not materialize. On 1st April, 1898 a proclamation by the Government of India No. 591-E.B.[40] placed the South Lushai Hills under the administration of Assam. Another proclamation on the same day placed the amalgamated Lushai Hills under the charge of an officer who will be styled "Superintendent of the Lushai Hills" and appointed Major John Shakespeare, C.I.E., D.S.O., to be the first superintendent.[41]

Thus, although some of the British administrators wanted to unite the *Chin-Kuki-Mizo* inhabited areas under one administration, they could not do so. Instead, they put their country under several political and administrative units, which became next to impossible to undo after they granted independence to India, Pakistan (including East Pakistan which in 1972 became Bangladesh) and Burma in 1947. This administrative division helps in promoting further division of the nationality.

Division and Coalescence in Post-Colonial Phase

This period saw ethnic division fomented by political aims. Towards the mid-20th century, when the British withdrawal from India was certain, the hill tribes of North-East India, including the *Chin-Kuki-Mizo* tribes, began to wonder what their constitutional status would be after the British withdrawal. This bred intense political strife. This political strife found expression in parallel movement for integration and disintegration within the group. On the one hand political dreams were to bring the divided tribes under single administration, while, on the other hand, individual tribes sought recognition and separate treatment for political and economic ends. In other words this period saw a kind of tussle between division and coalescence within the nationality.

This trend was clearly demonstrated by the formation of many political organizations. Some of them were formed with integration policy, trying to bring as many of the *Chin-Kuki-Mizo* tribes as possible together under one administration. Among them, mention may be made of the *Mizo Union* (1946), *United Mizo Freedom Organization* (formed in 1947), *Kuki National Assembly* (formed in 1946), *Khulmi National Union* (formed in 1948), *Chin National Union* (formed in 1965), *Zomi National Council* (formed in 1972), and then *Zo Re-unification Organization* (formed in 1988). On the other hand, there were political organizations started by individual tribes such as *Paite Tribe Council* (1949), *Hmar National Congress* (formed in 1954) later *Hmar National Union* (formed in 1958), *Jou National Council* (formed in 1954) later *United Zomi Organization* (formed in 1961), striving for separate individual tribal political aims and claiming distinct ethnic identity. The formation of such organizations clearly demonstrated that there had been parallel movements for integration and disintegration among the various *Chin-Kuki-Mizo* tribes in this phase.

Why should the Individual Tribes within the Chin-Kuki-Mizo *Nationality assert their Distinct Ethnic Identity?*

There could be many reasons. Among them may be the inborn

desire to be recognized which every individual tribe had which in turn promoted the desire for self-determination and political, economic and cultural rights for the tribe. These assertions broke loose a whole series of division on narrow tribe-line enhancing the process of ethnic division that had already taken roots.

Attempts for Coalescence

In the midst of this, a strong movement for re-unification of *Chin-Kuki-Mizo* tribes is continuing. Seed for ideologies of integration and re-unification had been sown by the earlier political organizations with integration policies.

Forces helping **Chin-Kuki-Mizo** *Integration or Re-unification*

There are certain forces helping the process of re-unification. Some of these are unconscious developments while some conscious attempts are also made.

Unconscious Developments

Of the unconscious developments, one stood out as a prominent factor for integration and that is history writing.

History Writing

The British administrators had written few books alongwith administrative reports on which were found sketches of histories of the *Chin-Kuki-Mizo* people. And after the introduction of modern education indigenous writers began to write their own history. One of the earliest native history writers, as cited earlier, was Liangkhaia, who wrote *Mizo Chanchin* (Mizo History), first published in 1938. Many others soon followed. In recent years individual tribes like Hmar, Paite, Darlong and others also began writing histories of their individual tribes. All these writings, more often than not, points to oneness of the *Chin-Kuki-Mizo* tribes, that they were of common origin. Some native historians even treated the different tribes as belonging to single nationality. Among these, mention may be made of Vumson's *Zo History* (1987), B. Lalthangliana's *History of Mizo in Burma* (1980), and *India, Burma & Bangladesh—A Mizo Chanchin* (2001) and L. Keivom's series of travelogues called *Zoram Khawvel* dealing with the *Chin-Kuki-Mizo* tribes in broad spectrum. All these have helped the *Chin-Kuki-Mizo* people to understand deeper that they are one and of the same origin.

Conscious Attempts

Conscious attempts were made from several angles at different levels with varying degree of success. Few of these may be discussed as follows:

Role of Mizo Zirlai Pawl (formed in 1935)

Although *Chin-Kuki-Mizo* integration or re-unification is not their expressed objective, the Mizo Zirlai Pawl (MZP) General Headquarters in Aizawl, Mizoram, the largest students' organization of the *Chin-Kuki-Mizo* people had been consciously trying to integrate the member tribes within one nation. Some of their attempts may be discussed here:

1. In 1993, per the MZP central executive resolution, several students' organizations of individual *Chin-Kuki-Mizo* tribes were affiliated to MZP such as Hmar Students' Association (HSA), Mizoram Bawm Students' Association (MBSA), Mara Students' Organization (MSO), Lai Students' Association (LSA), Pang Zirlai Pawl (PZP), Ralte Students' League (RSL), Zomi-Paite Students' Federation (ZPSF). Zomi-Paite Students' Federation became Siam-Sin Pawl-Pi (SSPP), and got affiliated to MZP as such in 2002.[42]
2. MZP General Headquarters. had been organizing biennial broad based festival which they named ZOFEST. All the *Chin-Kuki-Mizo* tribes were invited

and expected to be represented in these festivals. The first ZOFEST was held at Churachandpur, Manipur in 2002. The second and third ZOFEST were held at Aizawl in 2004 and 2006 respectively. In the 2006 ZOFEST, 22 tribes belonging to the *Chin-Kuki-Mizo* nationality from different places participated representing the different tribes such as Paite, Gangte, Hmar, Vaiphei, Zou, Thado-Kuki, etc., from Manipur, and Darlong, Hrangkhawl, Molsom, etc., from Tripura.[43] And there were 15 members from Assam and 2 members from Bangladesh representing the *Chin-Kuki-Mizo* tribes of these areas. The aim was to inculcate sense of brotherhood and it has had positive effects towards *Chin-Kuki-Mizo* integration.

Role of Zo Reunification Organization (ZORO)

Zo Reunification Organization (ZORO) was formed in 1988 by a joint conference called *First World Zo Convention* held at Champhai, Mizoram. What was significant in the event was that it was formed at the initiative of Zomi leaders from Manipur and was fully supported by many organizations and individuals from Mizoram, Assam and Tripura including the then ruling Peoples Conference of Mizoram Assembly headed by Brig. T. Sailo. This organization is now taking up the task of consciously integrating the *Chin-Kuki-Mizo* nationality, even taking up the case to working group on indigenous peoples under United Nations Organization (UNO).

Conclusion

With the ethnic division within the *Chin-Kuki-Mizo* nationality having taken place, the various tribes belonging to the nationality began to assert their distinctness. In their midst, the protagonists of integration and re-unification of the group are trying to inculcate the idea of integration and hope to see re-unification of the nationality. Meanwhile, four collective proper names, namely *Chin, Kuki, Mizo* and *Zomi* have taken the place of 'base ethnic group' on which sections of the group are integrating. In the mean time, some students' organizations are striving to bring the divided nationality together under one umbrella. Zo Re-organization (ZORO), a non-political organization is also strongly propagating the cause ofre-unification of the divided tribes under single nomenclature —ZO and possibly under one administrative umbrella. Whether or not the divided *Chin-Kuki-Mizo* nationality will re-unite or further disintegrate, time will tell. The ultimate deciding factor, as R.S. Peters[44] and Ernest Renan[45] would argue, is the sense of belongingness of the individual tribes to the nation or nationality.

REFERENCES

1. Anthony D. Smith, *The Ethnic Revival,* Cambridge University Press, London, New York, New Rochelle, Melbourne, Sydney, 1981, p. 1.
2. Benedict Anderson, *Imagined Communities Reflections on the Origin and Spread of Nationalism,* Verso, London, New York, 1991, p. 3.
3. For a detailed study of contesting nationalism or contesting marginality, read Sajal Nag, *Contesting Marginality Ethnicity, Insurgency and Sub-nationalism in North-East India,* Manohar Publications, New Delhi, 2002.
4. G.A. Grierson, *Linguistic Survey of India Vol-III Part –III,* Motilal Banarsidass, Delhi, 1967 (Reprint of 1904), pp. 2-3.
5. Liangkhaia, *Mizo Chanchin,* (1938), Part-I & II compiled and reprinted by L.T.L. Publications, Aizawl, 2002, p. 17.
6. L. Keivom, *Zoram Khawvel,* MCL Publications, Aizawl, 1991.
7. B. Lalthangliana, *India, Burma & Bangladesh—A Mizo Chanchin,* Aizawl, 2001, pp. 141-145.
8. T.H. Lewin, *The Hill Tracks of Chittagong and the Dwellers Therein,* Tribal Research Institute (Reprint of 1869), Aizawl, 2004, p. 138.
9. See G.A. Grierson, *op. cit.,* p. 1.
10. *Ibid.*
11. J. Shakespear, *The Lushai-Kuki Clans,* 1912), Tribal Research Institute, Aizawl, 1988 (Reprint of 1912)), p. 8.
12. Anthony D. Smith, *National Identity,* Penguin, London, 1991, pp. 8-15.
13. *Ibid,* p. 8.
14. Yulian V. Bromley, *Ethnic Processes,* 'Social Science Today' Editorial Board, USSR Academy of Sciences, Moscow, 1983, p. 9.

15. See Paul B. Chonzik, *Nationality Question of North East India — A Case Study of Mizo*, unpublished PhD thesis, MU, 2009, p. 55.
16. R. Zamawia, *Zofate Zinkawnga – Zalenna Mei a Mit Tur a ni lo*, Aizawl, 2007, p. 2.
17. Grierson, *op. cit.*, p. 1.
18. Anthony D. Smith, *op. cit.*, p. 24.
19. *Ibid.*
20. B. Lalthangliana, *op. cit.*, p. 73.
21. Rochunga Pudaite, *Education of the Hmar People*, Churachandpur, 1963, pp. 26-27.
22. See Hranglien Songate , *Hmar Chanchin*, Mao Press, Imphal, 1956; Rochunga Pudaite, *The Education of the Hmar People*, Navan Press, Calcutta, 1963.
23. J. Shaekspear, *op. cit.*, pp. 147.
24. L. Keivom, *Zoram Khawvel – 4*, MCL Publications, Aizawl, 1997, p. 218.
25. Subhas Chatterjee, 'Early History of the Mizos', *Proceedings of the North East India History Association* , 1988, p. 102.
26. A.C. Bhattacharya, *Progressive Tripura*, New Delhi, 1930, p. 19.
27. Grierson, *op. cit.*, p.1.
28. Sangkima, *Essays on the History of the Mizos*, Spectrum Publications, Guwahati/Delhi, 2004, p. 53.
29. *Report on the Administration of Assam for the Year 1921-22*, Mittal Publications, Delhi, 1984, p. 46.
30. T.H. Lewin, *op. cit.*, p. 149.
31. A.G. McCall, *Lushai Chrysalis*, Tribal Research Institute, Aizawl, 2003 (Reprint of 1949), p. 19.
32. Yulian V. Bromley, *Theoretical Ethnography*, Nauka, Moscow, 1984, p. 95; Bromley's articles in *Social Sciences*, 1/1983, p. 103, quoted in S.K. Acharya, *op. cit.*, p. 84, n. 34.
33. B. Lalthangliana, *op. cit.*, pp. 212-214.
34. C. Chhuanvawra, *Sangsari Khawpui*, Aizawl, 2012.
35. Robert Reid, *The Lushai Hills*, Firma KLM Private Ltd., on behalf of Tribal Research Institute (Govt. of Mizoram), Calcutta, 1978 (Reprint of 1942), p. 17.
36. *Ibid.*, p.42.
37. Robert Reid, *op. cit.*, pp. 53-54.
38. *Ibid.*
39. *Ibid.*, p. 56.
40. *Assam Secretariat, Foreign Department- A*, May 1898, Nos. 13-14.
41. Robert Reid, *op. cit.*, p. 60.
42. *The 13th MZP Assembly 2005 General Headquarters Report*, prepared by P.C. Laltlansanga, General Secretary and Lalrinmawia, Assistant General Secretary, MZP Gen. Hqrs., Aizawl, 2005, p. 10.

43. A Media Report from Department of Information & Public Relations, Govt. of Mizoram, entitled "ZOFEST – 2006 TAN A NI TA" 13 December 2006.
44. R.S. Peters, *Social Principles and Demographic State,* London, 1950, p. 249.
45. See Ernest Renan, *Quest-ee qu'une nation?*, translated by Ida Mae Snyder, Calmann-Levy, Paris, 1882, pp. 26-29. Renan said, 'the existence of a nation is an everyday plebiscite'.

14

UNCERTAINTIES IN THE KUKI IDENTITY TILL THE TWENTIETH CENTURY

Aheibam Koireng Singh

The Etymology of Kuki

Tribes belonging to the Chin-Kuki-Mizo have close socio-cultural affinity in terms of their culture, tradition, language, custom and traditional administrative system. They are one and the same people who were collectively called 'Kuki' in India and 'Chin' in Myanmar. They are one of the native ethnic communities in Manipur having its glorious past and rich cultural heritage. The genesis of the word 'Kuki' merits discussion. Like the term 'Naga', the term 'Kuki' was also given by the outsiders. The origin of the word is not known. The first reference to the term 'Kuki' was made in 1777 A.D. in connection with the tribesmen who attacked the British subjects in Chittagong when Warren Hastings was the Governor General of Bengal.[1] According to William Shaw, the word Kuki first appears in Bengal, Rawlins writing of the "Cucis or Mountaineers of Tipra" in *Asiatic Researches* (II, xii) in the year 1792.[2] According to Grierson:[3]

> *"Kuki is an Assamese or Bengali term applied to various hill tribes, such as the Lushais, Thados, etc. It*

> *seems to have been known at a comparatively early period, in the Raj Mala, Siva is stated to have fallen in love with a Kuki woman and the Kukis are mentioned in connection with the Tippearah Raja Cachang who flourished about 1512 A.D)."*

For E.W. Dun, the term 'Kuki' was derived from a word applied to a system of cultivation adopted by the Bengalis.[4] There are many more conjectures and theories about the origin of the word 'Kuki'. Some believe that it has been derived from the Baluchistan word 'Kuchi' meaning wandering people. And some say that it comes from the British word 'Kooky' meaning peculiar or unusual people. S. Prim Vaiphei believes that it was a derogatory name given by the outsiders to an ethnic group of people living in Western Burma, North East India and Bangladesh.[5] Lal Dena contends that all the oral traditions and local sources point to the mainland China as the original home of the Chin-Kuki-Mizo.[6]

The term "Kuki" was first heard of in Manipur between 1830 and 1840 though tribes of same race had long been subjects to the ruler of Manipur.[7] All the new immigrants came to be known as 'Khongjais' to the Meiteis. The British ethnographers and administrators, in order to distinguish them from those who were already there before them, used the term "New Kuki". The census of 1891 gave the total population of Khongjais or New Kukis as 17,204.[8] The old Kuki clans of Manipur are Aimol, Chothe, Chiru, Koireng, Kom, Purul, Anal, Lamkang, Moyon, Monsang, Gangte and Vaiphei, etc. The new Kukis are Paite, Simte, Zou, Hmar and Thadou.

The recognised tribes during colonial period in Manipur who were known as Kukis are as follows. [9] They are: 1. Aimol 2. Anal, 3. Chothe, 4. Chiru, 5 Gangte, 6. Hmar, 7. Koireng, 8. Kom, 9. Lamkang, 10. Lushai, 11. Moyon, 12. Monsang, 13. Paite, 14. Thadou, 15. Vaiphei, 16. Zou, 17. Purum, 18. Simte, 19. Sukte, and 20. Ralte.

Fragmentation of Kuki Ethnicity

The tribes who were identified as belonging to the Chin-Kuki have started disowning the term 'Kuki' and 'Chin'. With the advent of Indian independence and implementation of Constitution of India, the Kuki identity undergoes a process of miniaturisation into various similar intermediary identities. According to Dr. H. Kamkhenthang, people identified themselves willy-nilly either as 'Chin' or 'Kuki' or 'Lushai' in order to be accepted in military service before India and Burma got independence. After India's independence, the Government of India recognized the various tribes of Chin-Kuki group and they could get their services as members of a recognized tribes in India no longer requiring the mention whether he was a Kuki or not. He further contends that Kuki or Chin are terms used only in reference to outside world but not in use among and within the group.[10]

The ethnoses belonging to the Chin-Kuki group did not have a common name anymore after it was disowned by the ethnoses who were once known as Kuki. Excepting Thadou, most of the tribes now want to identify themselves by their individual tribal names and not as Kukis.[11] Gangmumei Kamei contended that the appearance of William Shaw's Notes on Thadou Kukis in 1929 claiming the primacy of the Thadous revived the old rivalry among the Kuki tribes and caused the disintegration or break-up of the Kuki fraternity. Added to this rift was the tension created by the over emphasis given to the Old and New Kuki syndrome.[12] Some of the Thadou leaders also regarded other non-Thadou Kukis as 'Kuki Siki' and 'Kuki Makhai'.[13]

It was said that the Kukis had war rites known as 'Hansa-Neh' and 'Sajam-Sha' which symbolic oath are taking ceremonies involving the sacrifice of a *mithun* (a bison). It was normally performed by the seniormost head of each clan or sub-clan. Pieces of flesh of the *mithun* so sacrificed were distributed to all the junior chiefs of the clans who cannot participate in the oath taking ceremony. The junior chiefs normally do not refuse to accept it. Refusal amounts to opposition to the decision taken and may consequently lead to social ostracisation and even physical elimination unless repented.[14] The very practice of such tradition itself shows the authoritarian and coercive nature of the senior Kuki clans in their relationship with the junior clans. In the colonial past, the Kukis in Manipur in opposition to sending them as Labour Corps in France have fought gallantly against the British rule during the year 1917-1919. According to D. Letkhojam Haokip, negative outweighs the positive as regards the impact it had on Kuki society. It shattered the Kuki society into pieces, disintegrating and fragmenting them to the extent that they never come together as they did before and during the war.[15]

The Kuki National Assembly (KNA) was formed in 1946 with the primary objective of fostering consciousness of common identity and making a single political unit of the Kukis. The constituent tribes of KNA were Thadous, Paites, Vaipheis, Gangtes, Simtes, Zous, Anals, Koms, Hmar, Guites, Chirus, Monsangs, Koireng, etc.[16]

The fragmentation of Kuki polity started with the formation of Khulmi National Union (KNU) by a breakaway faction of the Kuki National Assembly in 1947 because of Thadou arrogance. Thus another generic group 'Khulmi' constituted by the Vaiphei, Gangte, Paite Simte, Zou and other non Thadou tribes from the Kuki-Chin who claimed to have originated from a 'Khul' meaning a 'cave' came into existence.[17] According to Prof. Nabakumar, it was evident from the contents of a memorandum submitted by Teba Kilong, the then Forest Minister of Manipur state, to the Dewan of Manipur that in the pre-independence period, the people were ethnically categorised into three main groups, namely, the Khulmi, the Kuki and the Naga.[18]

In 1951, the unification of different non-Naga tribes under the nomenclature, Khulmi received a fatal blow as it was not granted recognition by the Government of India.[19] The Government of India notified the Scheduled Tribes list of Manipur as - (i) any Kuki Tribe; (ii) Any Naga tribe; and (iii) any Lushai Tribe; without mentioning the ethnic names of different communities.[20] At such a point of identity crisis, the rising armed Naga expansionist movement engulfed many of the kindred tribes of non Thadou Kuki-Chin group. Though pan tribal concept of Khulmi disappeared, none of its member tribes except the 'Mates' returned to the Kuki fold.[21]

As the aftermath consequences of following the British policy of polarizing the ethnic diversity of Manipur as – 'Any Kuki Tribe'; 'Any Naga tribe'; and 'Any Lushai Tribe'; without mentioning the ethnic names of different communities, Manipur had her first experience of considerably large inter-community clashes in the form of Hmar-Kuki conflict (1959-1960). The post independence Government of India introduced scheduled lists for certain tribes and castes of the country and all the then tribes under Kuki ethnic group got separate recognition in the scheduled list under the Constitution of India in 1956. After this, political formation in the hill areas of Manipur assumed narrow community interests and it consequently led to the emergence of tribe-wise political parties like the Hmar National Council, the Vaiphei National Organization, the Zou Ntional Congress, etc. Suprisingly, while driving out the non-Thadou tribes from the Kuki fold, the Thadou political leadership still clung to the term Kuki as its common nomenclature and adopted a policy of re-Kukiazation of the erstwhile Kuki tribes.[22] One of the fundamental causes of the Hmar-Kuki conflict in 1960 was the direct outcome of this policy. Another factor responsible for the Hmar-Kuki conflict was the question of re-grouping of different tribes of Manipur into two groups, namely, Naga group and Kuki group. Disturbed by the rising Naga movement, the then Manipur administration perhaps felt the necessity of regrouping the hill tribes into Naga or Kuki and submitted the strange proposal namely, the regrouping of all the non-Naga tribes of Manipur as Kukis to the union government for endorsement. Any non-Naga tribes unwilling to identify themselves as Kukis were to be regarded. As a matter of fact, this issue came up sometime in the month of October, 1959 for secret discussion and decision and the question was said to have come up at the instance of the Union Government. For this purpose, the Manipur administration invited public opinion of all tribes concerned as to whether they would join either of the two groups — Naga or Kuki. The Hmars strongly protested the proposal for regrouping the tribes in Manipur into Kuki or Naga on the grounds that — the Hmars never called themselves even from their forefathers and would never do so in future; the term 'Kuki' was wrongly given to them much against their will, consent or interest by the British officers; and grouping or terming various communities as Kuki or Naga against their consent was quite unconstitutional and was clearly against the fundamental rights conferred to them by the Constitution of India and it was, therefore, legally objectionable. Coupled with it, the movement for creation of Kuki state by forming Kuki National Volunteer (KNV) and also imposing 'Kuki fee' of Rs. 10 per household among the various non-Naga tribes. The spark of the Hmar-Kuki communal war was ignited when armed Kuki volunteers first forced Hmar villagers at Rovazawl of Tamenglong district to contribute the 'Kuki fee'. The demand of the Kuki fee was perhaps based on the notion that many Hmars, though given a separate recognition, were still regarded as the subjects of Singson chiefs and had to pay the fee as a token of their loyalty to the Kuki leadership. On failing to get the fee, the whole village was completely burned down on 8 February, 1960. In consequence of this incident was electrical as armed clashes and serious incidents took place not only in Manipur but also in some districts of Assam and Naga hills and Tuensang areas.[23]

T.S. Gangte stated two main reasons for the near extinction of the ethnonyme Kuki.[24] They are political and social. According to him the class-composition of the Kukis and their political organization were so independent of each other that the Kukis were obsessed with the idea of clan rivalries, being fostered by the socio-political structure so designed. As a consequence, despite their being one and the same, clan rivalries for supremacy over each other strained their relationship. But such polemics could not raise its ugly head during British rule that recognized Kuki Chieftainship and administered the bill people through efficient functionaries.

However, after independence in India, when the public became conscious of modern political trends that espoused the principles of democracy, the inherent but the process of disintegration came to a lead. Another factor was social. It was intertwined intricately with political factor. The social system of Kukis was so segmented that every individual was made consciously aware that he or she belongs to a particular clan or sub-clan. It obviously became a fertile breeding ground for hatred, rivalry enmity factionalism, etc. Afterwards when the Government of India started preparing a list of scheduled tribes in Manipur, every conceivable group or clan aspired to get recognition by inclusion in the said list as scheduled tribes. Later this resulted in antagonism between recognized and unrecognized tribes.

The year 1947, also witnessed the birth of another socio-cultural association of the non-Nagas called the Kom Rem Association. The Kom, Aimol, Chini, Koireng, Purum and Kharam were the tribes who were members of the association.[25]

Another attempt of the Kuki Chin kindred to find an acceptable nomenclature was the formation of the Aizawl based 'Mizo Union' in 9 April 1946 at Mullangthu Conference. It was initiated by those who wanted to replace the word, 'Kuki' by 'Mizo'. The term Kuki was disowned on the ground that it was a name given and imposed by the outsiders.[26] The said Mizo Union submitted a memorandum to the Constituent Assembly of India on 22 April, 1947 entitled "The Case of Mizos". Among the tribes mentioned as 'Mizos' in the memorandum, Hmar, Paite, Kaum (Kom), Thadou, Chiru, Anal, Purum, Vaiphei, Rangte (Gangte) were found in Manipur.[27] The Lushai speakers who were formerly parts of Kuki and Chin had completely succeeded in disowning the term 'Kuki' and 'Chin' by adopting the nomenclature 'Mizo' for their identity.[28] But many of the kindred tribes of the Kuki-Chin group felt betrayed when the leaders of the Mizo Union were satisfied with the granting of Lushai Hills District as it fell short of their dream for unification of other kindred tribes outside it into one political unit. Those who did not enjoy the fruits of their hard-bitten movements began to feel ashamed to call themselves Mizos. The attempts made by the Aizawl based Mizo Union to unite the Kuki-Chin Lushai tribes under the banner of a common name 'Mizo' were ignored in Manipur except the Hmars who launched a boycott movement in 1949 for the integration of their areas into the former Lushai Hill.[29] 'Mi' literally means 'Man' and 'Zo' means 'hill'. So, the use of the term 'Mizo' was also opposed on the grounds that it was grammatically and philologically not correct to precede 'hill' by 'Man'.

Some sections wanted to adopt the term 'Zomi' as the common nomenclature of the Kuki-Chin-Lushai tribes. It came into prominence "during the period from late seventies to mid-eighties". One Zomi National Council was also there about this time which stood for the unity and re-unification of all those tribes who belonged to the Kuki-Chin-Lushai.[30] It sought to foster unity the framework of socio-cultural affinities among the old and New Kukis.[31] L.S. Gangte contended that the term 'Zomi' was the oldest and generic name of the "so called Kuki-Chin Group." Dr. Vumko Hao also maintained that 'Zo' was the progenitor of the people known as Kuki-Chin.[32] In this connection, Dr. Vum Ko Hau remarks:[33]

> *"Had the word Kuki been changed to Zo at that time the right word for calling the various tribes and clans of the Zo race inhabiting the area joining Burma, East Pakistan and Assam would have been answered a long time ago."*

Within the State of Manipur, it (Zomi nomenclature) has varied response. Its impact transcends the national boundary. Large sections of the Chins of Burma have responded favourably to this call.[34] Another group proposed a new ethnic appellation, which they claimed to be accommodative, and the most compromising formula. This group proposed the phraseology, "Chin-Kuki-Mizo". Exponents of this phraseology gave the acronym, CHIKIM, as common nomenclature that literally means "whole tribes" or "all Nationalities". This also has not gained much currency so far.

In 1971, a controversy started between the Thadous and their non-Thadou cognates due to publication of the *Holy Bible* who was a non-Thadou Kuki. It had serious social and political ramifications. This led to a long-drawn political battle between the Thadou protagonists and the Kuki protagonists. The issue was that the Thadou protagonists objected the publication to be described as one in Kuki, saying that the dialect in which it was translated is entirely in Thadou dialect. In a law suit filed against Dr. T. Lunkim, he was alleged of advocating the book as a translation in Kuki as he was a non-Thadou even though he spoke Thadou dialect.[35] The Thadou protagonists contended that the language had been known as Thadous and nothing else. On the other hand, their cognates claimed that the language in question was not the exclusive possession of the Thadous only.[36] One organisation called Kuki Tribes Recognition Demand Committee was formed by the speakers of non-Thadou Kukis, speaking Thadou dialect but in conflict with the Thadous to press upon the State Government as well as Central Government to make a revision of the list of Scheduled Tribes of Manipur. A rejoinder was submitted to the Government of India (GoI) through the Government of Manipur. However, the Thadou National Council (TNC) opposed the demand and requested the GoI to reject such a claim on the following grounds:[37]

> *"Firstly, it fails to draw distinction between a tribe and a clan....*
>
> *Secondly, there are certain communities the bulk of whom are strongly opposed to the term 'Kuki' being used and in fact this led to the deletion of Kuki in the 1956 when the order was issued.*
>
> *Thirdly, the term Kuki is not an indigenous word. It has no meaning at all. There is no dialect/language/ custom/tradition/ culture to be called 'Kuki'. These same people are known as Chins in Burma which is a*

> *Burmese name applied to them; in Mizoram they are known as Paites, Hmars, etc. At present, some leaders suggest to adopt Mizo in lieu of Kuki while some other again prefer Zomi. In the situation of uncertainties amongst themselves, to bring the name 'Kuki' back by the backdoor and that also through the government machinery is most undesirable."*

The tribes in the Kuki-Chin group present a picture of diversity in unity. Despite their socio-cultural affinities, they were not able to come under the fold of a unified common nomenclature. In the last decade of the twentieth century, Kukis have faced various hardships and atrocities in the process of evicting them from their habitual residence for the realization of aspired homeland of the Nagas led by the faction of its rebel groups. It had miniaturised the Kuki identity further as some tribes belonging to the Chin-Kuki-Mizo group, either out of fear or at their own volition had denounced the Kuki identity. Also in 1997-1998 there were instances of violent ethnic clashes between the Thadous and the Paites in Churachandpur district both of which are kindred tribes of Kuki.

One of the main reasons for the eruption of the said clash was the disagreement over the adoption of nomenclature. The non-Thadou Kukis spearheaded by Paites wanted to adopt Zomi nomenclature in opposition to the term 'Kuki' preferred by the Thadous. The Kukis including the non-Thadous as well were greatly inconvenienced by the 'Kukiland tax' levied by the armed Kuki outfits. The non-Thadou Kukis also doesn't want to be a part of 'Kukiland' under Thadou hegemony. The clash was finally concluded with an agreement to mutually respect the Zomi and Kuki nomenclature and leave it to the choice of the individuals or groups concerned. The Kuki Inpi Manipur (KIM) and the Zomi Council were authorised by the respective armed groups to sign the peace accord on their behalf so as to end the clashes. The first point of the agreement in the Peace Accord between the KIM and the Zomi Council says that "the nomenclatures 'Kuki' and 'Zomi' shall be mutually respected by all Zomis and Kukis. Every individual or group shall be at liberty to call himself or themselves by any name, and the nomenclature Kuki and Zomi shall not in any way be imposed upon any person or group against their will at any point of time."[38]

In fact, despite their close socio-cultural affinity, an acceptable nomenclature that encompasses all the tribes belonging to the Chin-Kuki-Mizo group is still eluding them. Furthermore, fragmentation is being heightened because of inherent idiosyncrasies on the basis of the hierarchical order of genealogy and other endogenous factors as well in addition to the activities of the armed outfits.

REFERENCES

1. Gangmumei Kamei, *Ethnicity and Social Change: An Anthology of Essays,* Imphal, 2002, p. 25.
2. William Shaw, *Notes on the Thadou Kukis,* Spectrum Publications, Guwahati/Delhi, 1997, p. 11.
3. G.A. Grierson, *Linguistic Survey of India,* Vol. III, Part III, Motilal Banarisidas, Delhi, 1967, p.1, cited in Senjam Mangi Singh, A Study of Some Selected Socio-political Problems in Manipur, unpublished PhD thesis, MU, 1996, p.4.
4. E.W. Dun, *Gazetteer of Manipur,* Manas Publications, Delhi, 1992 (1886 reprint), p. 32.
5. S. Prim Vaiphei, 'The Kukis', in N. Sanajaoba (ed.), *Manipur: Past and Present,* Vol. 3, Mittal Publications, Delhi, 1995, p. 126.
6. Lal Dena, 'The Kuki-Naga Conflict: Juxtaposed in the Colonial Context', in S Aggarwal (ed.), *Dynamics of Identity and Inter-Group Relation in Northeast India,* IIAS,Shimla, 1999, p. 185.
7. M. Bhattacharjee, *Gazetteer of India: Manipur,* Calcutta, 1963, p. 161. Sir James Johnstone also said that the Kukis were first heard of in Manipur between 1830 and 1840. He further said that they were causing anxiety and soon poured into the hill tracts of Manipur in such a number so as to drive away many of the earlier settlers. Also cited in Shakespeare: *The Lushai Kuki Clans,* Lancers, New Delhi, 1971.
8. E.W. Dun, *op. cit.,* p. 32.
9. S. Prim Vaiphei, *op. cit.,* p. 126
10. Dr. H. Kamkhenthang, 'Grouping for Identity', Dr. H.

Kamkhenthang (ed.), et. al, *In Search of Identity,* Kuki Chin Baptist Union, Imphal, 1986, pp. 1-16.

11. *Ibid.*
12. Gangmumei Kamei, *op. cit.,* p. 37.
13. S. Prim Vaiphei, 'Who are We', in Dr. H. Kamkhenthang (ed.), *op.cit.,* p. 22. 'Siki' and 'Makhai' are fractional denomination of the Rupee currency equivalent to 'Quarter of a Rupee' and 'Half a Rupee' respectively.
14. Such war-rite was performed at the outset of the Anglo-Kuki war, 1917-1919. Cited in, *Untold History of Manipur,* Imphal: Anglo-Kuki War Patriots Memorial Foundation, p. 8.
15. D. Letkhojam Haokip, 'Significance of the Anglo-Kuki War 1917-1919 AD', *The Orient Vision,* Vol. VIII, Issue 1 & 2, 2012.
16. W. Nabakumar, 'The Inter Ethnic Relationship of the Different Communities of Manipur: A Critical Appraisal', *The Orient Vision* Vol. 2, Issue 1, 2004, pp. 29-32.
17. Aheibam Koireng Singh, 'Growth of Sub-nationalism and Displacement in Northeast India with special reference to Manipur', *The Orient Vision,* Vol. 2, Issue 3, 2005, pp. 6-13.
18. W. Nabakumar, *op. cit.,* pp. 29-32.
19. Aheibam Koireng Singh, *op. cit.,* pp. 6-13.
20. W. Nabakumar, Communalism and Ethnic Divide: Anathema to Secular Society, paper presented in the *National Seminar on the Indigenous Tribal Religions of Manipur of the North East India,* Imphal, 21-23 March, 2005.
21. S. Prim Vaiphei, "The Kukis", eds., N. Sanajaoba, *Manipur: Past and Present, Vol. 3,* N. Delhi: Mittal, 1995, p. 126.
22. Laldena, *In Search of Identity: Hmars of North-East India,* Akansha, N. Delhi, 2008, pp. 102-104.
23. Laldena, *In Search of Identity: Hmars of North-East India,* Akansha, N. Delhi, 2008, pp. 104-107.
24. Dr. T.S. Gangte, "Whither Kuki Ethnicity: Is this a Centrifugal Force", *Tri-Millennium Souvenir Kuki Students Organisation,* Manipur: KSO Souvenir sub-Committee, 2000.
25. W. Nabakumar, "The Inter Ethnic Relationship of the Different Communities of Manipur: A Critical Appraisal", Vol. 2, Issue 1, *The Orient Vision,* Canchipur: National Research Centre, Oct-Nov-Dec 2004, pp. 29-32.
26. S.Thankhangin, "Why should We be called Zomis?", Dr. H. Kamkhenthang, *et. al, In Search of Identity,* Imphal: Kuki Chin Baptist Union, 1986, p. 61.
27. Gangmumei Kabui, "Genesis of the Ethnoses of Manipur, eds., N. Sanajaoba, *Manipur: Past and Present,* Vol. III, N. Delhi: Mittal, 1995, p.22
28. S. Prim Vaiphei, "The Kukis", eds., N. Sanajaoba, *Manipur: Past and*

Present, Vol. 3, N. Delhi: Mittal, 1995, p. 126. Cited from Dr. H. Kamkhenthang, "Grouping for Identity", eds., Dr. H. Kamkhenthang, *et.al, In Search of Identity,* Imphal: Kuki Chin Baptist Union, 1986.

29. Gangmumei Kabui, "Genesis of the Ethnoses of Manipur, eds., N. Sanajaoba, *Manipur: Past and Present,* Vol. III, N. Delhi: Mittal, 1995, p. 22. Cited from Hmar People's Boycott Movement, Imphal: Resistance, 1975.
30. Senjam Mangi Singh, A Study of some selected Socio-political Problem in Manipur, unpublished PhD thesis submitted to the Dept. of Political Science, Manipur University, Imphal, pp. 57-59.
31. R.K. Ranjit Singh, "Emergent Ethnic Processes in Manipur", eds., B. Pakem, *Nationality, Ethnicity and Cultural Identity in Northeast India,* N. Delhi: Omsons, 1990, p.247.
32. L.S. Gangte, "Who are we?", Dr. H. Kamkhenthang, *et. al, In Search of Identity,* Imphal: Kuki Chin Baptist Union, 1986, p. 48, 49.
33. *Ibid.* Cited from dr. Vum Ko Hau, Profile of Burma Frontier Man. Bundung, Indonesia, p. 301.
34. R.K. Ranjit Singh, "Emergent Ethnic Processes in Manipur", eds., B. Pakem, *Nationality, Ethnicity and Cultural Identity in Northeast India,* N. Delhi: Omsons, 1990, p. 247.
35. Dr. TS Gangte, "Whither Kuki Ethnicity: Is this a Centrifugal Force", *Tri-Millennium Souvenir Kuki Students Organisation,* Manipur: KSO Souvenir sub-Committee, 2000, p.44.
36. *Ibid.*
37. Dr H. Kamkhenthang, "Identity Crisis among the Tribes of Manipur", eds., B. Pakem, Nationality, Ethnicity and Cultural Identity in Northeast India, N. Delhi: Omsons, 1993, p. 285.
38. The accord was signed on 1 October 1998, with Chief Minister, Deputy Chief Minister of Manipur, Member of Parliament (Outer Manipur Parliamentary Constituency) and all the Members of Manipur Legislative Assembly and some prominent tribal leader as witness. It can be recollected that there were other two alternative nomenclatures proposed by the members present at the time of forming Kuki Inpi Manipur (KIM). One of it was Kuki Zomi Council.

15

PROBING CIVIL SOCIETY :
ORIGIN AND ROLE OF THE KUKI INPI

Sanasam Amal Singh

Introduction

The Kukis of Manipur had been the major tribe spreading their authority over a wide range of hill areas surrounding the valley of Imphal during the hey-days of the Maharaja of Manipur and subsequently during the British period. The Kuki society has its own very old socio-economics, political and religious institutions. In all the three spheres, the role of the Kuki-Inpi, a civil body of the Kuki society took an important part. In the north-eastern states where the Kukis settled there are the Kuki Inpi: Assam, Nagaland and Manipur respectively. However, in this chapter, the Kuki Inpi Manipur (KIM) will only be focused and emphasized as an institutional civil body. Before we go into the details of the Kuki-Inpi, it is necessary to analyze the general view of the civil society.

Historically, the development of civil society in the modern age took place as a major component of the citizen's movement in the Western Europe and Northern America to secure civil rights by over-throwing repressive absolute rulers. Civil society as a concept received attention in the writings of the 19th and 20th century thinkers in relation to the growth of capitalism. For Hegel, civil society (or bourgeois society) is a phase or moment in the historical succession from the family to the State. As long as any institution expresses the ethics of freedom, it is said to be within the domain of civil society.[1]

In the present day, civil society is a concept that has been much discussed and variously defined by the social theorists and observers. In the broadest possible terms, Gellner describes civil society as one form of social order among other forms.[2] In a broader aspect, civil society has both institutional and qualitative dimensions. Institutionally, civil society consists of all the associations to which people belong, including families, religious organizations, social movements, parent-teacher associations, neighbourhood associations, sports leagues, labour unions, volunteer groups, professional or occupational associations, clubs, support groups, and so forth. These associations entail connectedness and commitment to others. It is not based solely on instrumentalism. The networks and bonds forged by such memberships are vital for communities for prevention of crime, education and development of young people, promoting tolerance of social differences, and economic growth.[3] Civil society also contains a qualitative dimension that includes social attitudes such as loyalty, trust, social practices such as civility, cooperation, health and safety of the members of a society.

Kuki-Inn

The Kuki-Inn was built in memory of the Kuki warriors who fought bravely and suffered war against the British Government.[4] The British writers acknowledged this war with the Kuki Chiefs as the Kuki Rebellion of 1917-1919 and treated it as a part of the World War I. There was fighting around in the Jampi area, Henglep area (the Southern Sector), Lonpi area (South -Eastern Hills), Chahsat area (the Eastern Sector) in the rebellion ended in May 1919.[5]

The War spread out in all the hill areas surrounding the Manipur valley contiguous to the Thoungdut state of Sagaing Division in British Burma. In other words, the Kuki Chiefs and their cognate clans fought the British without any fear with the commitment to die in honour rather to live as slaves under the British authority. Today, in honour of the brave Kukis, the Government of India sanctioned the Kuki Inn to be built in honour of the Kuki Freedom Fighters and that stands at the heart of Imphal City as a monument of honour and dignity for the undaunting warriors among the Kukis to be witnessed by one and all.

The Emergence of Kuki-Inpi

Regarding the origin or emergence of the Kuki-Inpi, we need to understand two schools of thought amongst the Kuki chiefs and scholars. First, it is expressed that the Kuki Inpi is a traditional form of government and it existed since time immemorial but revived and empowered to protect the Kukis in modern days. Second, it is that the Kuki-Inpi is a recent development, i.e., after the Kuki-Naga clash in 1993. According to the first school of thought, the Kuki-Inpi is the traditional Kuki Government which has been in existence since time immemorial. It is the highest Court of appeal for the Kukis. Unlike contemporary world governments, the Kuki Inpi of the Kukis was inborn and inherited from the forefathers. It is formed through the conglomeration of all the Kukis inhabited areas: ancestral territories and the present settlements. The customs and cultures being the constitution, its basic or fundamental principle cannot be altered *in toto* but slight modifications and codifications can be made by the Inpi from time to time in order to suit the changing times or situations as and when necessary. It is noted that so far for several generations the practicability, adaptability and suitability of the Inpi to the Kuki society unchanged. Thus, the Kukis considered the Kuki-Inpi as a pragmatic, dynamic and a living constitution/government in the truest sense of the term.

Composition of the Kuki-Inpi

Traditionally, the Kuki-Inpi has the following structural composition.[6] They are:

1. Kuki-Inpi Kumpi (Emperor)
2. Nampi Semang (Home Minister)
3. Nampi Pachong (Foreign Affairs Minister); and
4. Nampi Lhangsam(Information& Broadcasting Minister) and many other secretaries and committee either appointed or elected by the Inpi to assist the execution of the multifarious functions of the Inpi.

The Kuki-Inpi-Kumpi and the Semang-Pachongs are not drawn from hereditary kinship lineage. They were chosen or elected by an electoral college consisting of all Gamkai Haosas (State Chiefs) and their Semang-Pachongs (Council of Ministers) amongst themselves who distinguished themselves in the fields of administrative skills, leadership, judgment, and possesses the qualities of statesmanship, wisdom, honesty, courage, sense of love, dedication, sacrifice, commitment and well versed in customary laws. The Kumpi though not drawn from hereditary chiefs, once elected to the post, the Kumpi is regarded as the head of all Kuki clans and the Kuki people. Moreover, whosoever is elected to the post of Kumpi is considered God's appointed person to be their chief and, therefore, high reverence and honour is attached to him. Besides, the Inpi has the power and authority over the administration, control, supervision of the Kukis : the people as well as their territories internally or externally.

Gamkai Kivaipohna

The Gamkai of State is the next tier of administration. It is formed through the amalgamation of all the Kuki districts (Lhanshung) and villages (Khosung) which fall within the topographical limits of the Gamkai. The easy understanding and effective implementation of the Inpi lies in the fact that the same principles and procedures governing the districts and the villages formed the guiding principles for the administration of the States as well. All district chiefs and village chiefs with their respective Council of Ministers collectively constituted the electoral college for the election of the Gamkai, Haosas and Semang-Pachongs. The Gamkai Haosa is either chosen or elected amongst the Lhangsung Haosas (District Chiefs) who possess the wisdom and ability to scrupulously carry out the onerous functions of the Gamkai.

In the actual functioning of the State administration, the chief is assisted by a group of elected persons who are in the local term designated as 1. Gamkai Semang, 2. Gamkai Pachong, and 3. Gamkai Lhangsam respectively. This Council of Ministers is responsible for the smooth and efficient functioning of the State administration. They also issue, from time to time, directives to the Lhangsung administrators in matters relating to the proper utilization of the available natural resources, protection or safeguarding of human rights, etc. Some of the major functions of the Gamkai administration are promotion of art and culture, communication system, human resources, health, sanitation, mutual understanding, co-operation, collection of taxes and peaceful co-existence of all irrespective of caste, creed, colour and religious differences within the Gamkai.

Lhangsung Kivaipohna

Yet, another peculiar feature of the Kuki-Inpi is the hierarchical form of Government with a decentralization of power and authority to the local units. Lhangsung Kivaipohna or district administration is the third tier of administration which is formed through the amalgamation of all the Kuki villages within the district. The post of Lhang Haosa is elected by an electoral college consisting of all village chiefs and their council of ministers amongst the chiefs for a specific period of years. In the past, elections were done through consensus but in case of a tie, voting by a secret ballot method is also adopted. It is very rare. The district councillors are called: (1). Lhangsung Semang, (2). Lhangsung Pachong and (3).Lhangsung Lhangsam respectively. The main functions of the Lhangsung administration are promotion of cordial relations between district and villages, improvement of inter-district highways, rejuvenation of cultural values, etc.

Khosung Kivaipohna

A Kuki village is the grass root level political unit. The institution of chieftainship is the highest political, social, economic and cultural institution. Theoretically, chieftainship is hereditary drawn from kinship lineage but the chief is elected or chosen by his own brothers to be their chief. The chief in return for having chosen by his own brothers does not act tyrannically. Instead, the chief considers all the villagers as his own family members and treats them with equal love and affection. In the execution of his duties, the chief is assisted by a group of trusted councillors who are either nominated or elected by the village assembly consisting of all the adult members for a fixed tenure which is normally one year term. In the local term, councillors are called: (1) Khosung Semang (2) Khosung Pachong, and (3) Khosung Lhangsam respectively. The number of Semang-Pachongs varies from village to village depending on the size of the village concerned. These councillors are collectively responsible for the smooth functioning and development of the village in all spheres of life: social, political, economic, cultural and religious.

This traditional form of the Kuki was suppressed and replaced by the colonial administration in 1919. More elaborately, it is also stated that the Kuki inhabited areas were invaded by the British India in 1700 AD. They fearlessly resisted the invading forces in all the areas including Chittagong Hill Tracts, Arakan Hills, Chin Hill, Somra Tracts, Kabo valley, Tripura, Lushai Hills, Naga Hills and Manipur Hills. The last and fieriest battle took place during 1917-1919.[7] The British forces subdued the Kuki warriors and took over the administration of the Kuki land which brought far reaching effects on the Kukis. For instance, their country was bifurcated into Burma and India so that the Kukis could no longer combine themselves to wage another war against the British regime.

Later, when India attained freedom from British regime in 1947, the Kukis readily accepted citizenship of India as free nation. However, they claimed that the British policy in India still continued till date and the Kuki people and their country have further been divided into many factions. On the other, the uprising of the Naga secessionist movement further threatened the Kukis to the extreme point of extermination. Thus, the Kukis felt that due to negligence of the Government of India and the non-stop communal war of the Nagas they were on the verge of extinction. In such a prevailing condition, the Kuki-Inpi has been revived with a view to restore communal harmony, peaceful co-existence and justice to all. It was revived at the special tribal Kuki Leaders' conference at Kuki Inn, Imphal on the 29th June, 1993 at the backdrop of the NSCN(IM) led Naga communal atrocity against the Kukis in Manipur, Assam and Nagaland (of the present North-East India) with the primary aim to initiate direct peace talk with the Naga leaders.[8]

The above mentioned view is rejected by another school of thought on the basis that there was no Kuki-Inpi at all before 1993. It is propagated that it is formed newly for the purpose of defending the Kukis from ethnic cleansing of the Nagas. Accordingly, in the early period, all the Kuki villages are interdependent to each other so there was no civil body called Kuki-Inpi. Further, it is stated that before 1993, there was civil society called Imphal Kuki Welfare Committee and the Kuki National Assembly (KNA)[9]. The latter converted into a political party.

However, in general, the first perspective is more accepted. Underlying it is that the Kuki-Inpi is an old institution which has its own historicity and in course of time has certain modification. According to them, the Kuki-Inpi is not a new organization. It is rather a rediscovery and reawakening of the past heritage where every Kuki is subjected to this institution.

The Role of the Kuki-Inpi

The basic principles of the Kuki-Inpi are —

1. Non-communal;

2. Rule of Justice; and
3. Peaceful coexistence.

As mentioned above, the role played by the Kuki-Inpi is to protect and defend the Kukis and their lands. In a nutshell, it represents the socio-political interest of the Kukis in cases that concerned the Kukis with the governments and other ethnic groups. The first Kuki-Inpi, Manipur (1993-95) under the leadership of T. Kipgen had initiated direct talks with the Naga leaders which had resulted in the formation of a Committee for Restoration of Normalcy (CRN). Though its main objective seemed far from achieving, it was a move towards the right direction for restoring communal harmony between the two tribes. The CRN has also taken up certain relief measures to the affected people by incurring grants-in-aid amounting to more than Rs. 60 lakhs through VVD, Ukhrul.[10]

The second KIM (1995-96) under the leadership of Onkhothong Haokip was rather a short-live as new executive council was inducted hardly after four months in office. However, during this short period, the Kuki traditional form of Government has been re-introduced along with decentralisation of KIM administration. The third KIM (1995-97) took charge w.e.f., 1st May, 1995 under the leadership of Holkhomang Haokip. It re-affirmed the traditional form of Kuki Government and successfully decentralized the organization by opening 16 Lhang (Block) Inpi. It has been functioning till date.[11] On the 18th October, 1995 the KIM has declared its directive principles and policy stands to bring back all the communities and the neighbouring tribes, the Nagas in particular. Based on these principles and policy-stands, the KIM approached the Government, the majority Meiteis and otherco-tribes for creating an atmosphere for peaceful solution of the continuing ethnic violence in the region. The main policies of the Kuki-Inpi :

(1) Communal Harmony with all the communities;
(2) Peaceful co-existence with all peace loving ethnic groups of people or nations; and

(3) Justice in all governance irrespective of castes and creeds.[12]

A historic protest day was observed on the 10th February 1996, in which 80,000 Kukis from all over Manipur participated the biggest ever procession of the Kukis in Imphal city mourning more than 700 Kukis killed and their coffins displayed in full view of the public at Mapal Kangjeibung (Polo Ground) with traditional doleful song and cymbal sound. The congregation stood up in silence for two minutes in solemn prayer for the departed souls. The Kukis also stayed away from Manipur festivities. For instance, the five-day centenary celebrations of Manipur Baptist Convention (MBC) held on December 1996 was without the Kuki tribes. The functions whose theme is "Christ the hope of ages" was participated by the Christians, mostly Nagas. It is also said that choirs have come from all over the State to attend the festivities as Baptism is the dominant Christian faith here with majority of Nagas and Kukis following it. However, with the Kukis not attending it, the religious function has acquired a political dimension. It appears that this stand was strengthened by the warning given by ethnic based Kuki militants like the Kuki National Front (KNF) and Kuki National Organisation (KNO) against attending the celebrations. The outfits boycotted the function saying this was not the time to indulge in celebrations keeping in view of the ethnic tension prevailing in the State. They questioned the sincerity of the Baptist convention and termed the function an "eye-wash".[13] Later, on 12th December, 1996, the second Kuki-Inpi General Assembly held at Kuki Inn, Imphal with full delegates, adopted four firm political resolutions.[14]

According to such resolutions the KIM has strengthened its role in bringing conflict resolutions in the State. For example, during Zomi and Kuki conflict, the KIM and Zomi council(s) exerted a big effort on behalf of their respective parties pledge to forgive and forget the past mistakes committed against each other. Both these civil organisations highly appreciated the State Government for all its official commitments for peace and reconstruction programmes.

As a token of customary apology for mowing down ten innocent persons and injuring other four persons on the night of the 24th June, 1997 at Saikul village by the KNF dragging the two communities into conflict, the Kuki-Inpi offered a feast by killing a four legged animal, a Bull (*bawngtal*) on the 29th September, 1998. In a very cordial atmosphere and mutual trust, the feast was happily shared together by leaders of the Kuki-Inpi and the Zomi Council. In response to the good gesture shown by the Kuki-Inpi, the Zomi Council showed their goodness and love for peace in the form of killing another four legged animal, a Pig (Voktal) the following day, the 30th September, 1998, which was happily shared together by both community leaders.

In regard to the connection with international bodies, the KIM approached the UN, UNPO, Amnesty International London, etc., seeking their humanitarian intervention on the inhuman atrocities against the Kuki tribes. It is stated that such human right approaches have been quite fruitful in decreasing the trend of violence against the Kukis since 1998. The violent activities of Naga militants against the Kukis subsided to a great extent since 1998 following the NSCN(IM) cease fire with the Government of India. The leaders of Kuki-Inpi Manipur in cooperation with Kuki-Inpi Assam and Nagaland staged a rally on the 19th January, 2001 at New Delhi protesting against the Union Government's apathy towards the Kuki problem. The Kuki leaders submitted a strong memorandum to the Prime Minister and Home Minister. The Home Minister promised to take up necessary action on the demands of the Kukis.[15]

The demands are:

(a) Constitution of High Powered Commission to assess the extent of loss and damages caused to the Kukis by NSCN(IM);

(b) Rehabilitation of displaced Kukis in their respective villages before the 2001 Census;

(c) Compensation for Kuki victims of NSCN(IM)'s atrocities; and

(d) Satisfactory solution of the Kuki problems.

It is also stated that the KIM initiated Sadiya Project since 1999. Sadiya in Upper Assam is the location where ten Kuki chiefs were exiled by the British for waging war during 1917-19. The Kukis living in many parts of the present North-East and Myanmar waged war against the British colonial power of domination policy. Further, the KIM approached the Government of Assam for allotment of land at Sadiya in commemoration of their war heroes. A trust body has also been formed under the name and style, the Anglo-Kuki Patriots Memorial Foundation. The Trust Deed has already been registered with the Registrar Act, Government of Manipur, Imphal.[16]

After observing all these activities, it can be said that the KIM has been involving more in institutional roles, determining laws, adjudicating civil and criminal disputes. Their political roles have become more strengthened when its counterpart Naga civil body, United Naga Council (UNC) served quit notice to the Kukis, and NSCN(IM) ethnic violence. As a reason of this Naga secessionist movement, the Kukiland demand also gained momentum. The leaders of KIM with a strong political consciousness also adopt the policy of separate Kukiland thinking that it will solve the Kuki problem. This political realization has not been a development overnight. It has taken time for the Kukis to realize their identity and know their needs and wants. The missionary work or the movement of Christianity has definitely contributed a lot towards the arousal of this consciousness which was not there before. People have become consciousness of their life and status in the world. They have very clearly understood that politics is a medium and politicians are the tools to attain many things for themselves and for others. History also has been one of the important factors. The Kukis from different sections were vehemently indebted to the past 'Kuki Rebellion' that is considered as the Kuki movement. This popular incident has been a vital instrument for identity assertion and in socio-political demand of the Kukis.

ANNEXURE - A

TRADITIONAL POLICY AND STANDPOINT OF KIM

After prolonged deliberation the Kuki-Inpi felt it necessary to declare the traditional Kukl-Inpi policy and the standpoint regarding the present crisis:

(a) Traditional Kuki-Inpi Policy

1. That Kukl-Inpi is non-Communal;
2. That peaceful co-existence with other tribes/ communities has been and continues to be the Kuki- Inpi policy; and
3. That Kuki-Inpi stands for justice for all.

(b) Naming of the Present Trouble

The Kuki-Inpi Manipur has been observing carefully the present turbulent situation in the North-East and Manipur in particular and unanimously come to the conclusion that the root cause of all the troubles in this is the NSCN (IM)'s claim of secessionist movement and its subsequent drive for the so called "ethnic cleansing". It is hereby resolved that the all concerned should note the cause of the present trouble and avoid wrongly using the term "Kuki-Naga conflict" henceforth.

1. That till today the Kukis have no intentions, plans nor have they made any preparations to wage war against the Nagas. It is only a section of the Naga tribes that has been waging war against the Kukis. It is only consequence to that the Kukis have been caught unprepared; have had to organize themselves for self defence and to protect their kith and kin and hearth and homes.

2. That, there has been a concerted propaganda by some sections of the Nagas that Kukis are nomadic tribes who do not have rightful claim to the land. Dictionary meaning of nomadic is gypsy. Kukis are either nomadic nor gypsies and these terms are at best a deliberate attempt to mislead to serve their sinister designs. It is simply an abuse of the English Dictionary word "nomadic". Further, the Kukis have been compared with flying birds without roots in the land. This analogy is misplaced as human beings cannot be compared with birds. If Kukis are referred to as birds then so would be the Nagas and everybody else.

   (i) That the Nagas, the Meiteis and the Kukis all have the same origins. All three claim their origins to China/the East.
   (ii) That both the Nagas and the Kukis were at one time head hunters (taking of enemies' head as trophies of war). It was a sad truth that the Nagas themselves raided each other and the Kukis also did the same things. Even the weaker Nagas used to hire the neighbouring Kukis to protect themselves against the attacks of the stronger Nagas.
   (iii) That all three communities classified as Tibeto-Burma stock of Mongoloid race.
   (iv) That peace can come to land only when the Naga waging against the Kukis stop their war of the so called ethnic cleansing.

(c) Indian Government should Change its Policy towards the Kukis

That there has been some misconception of the Government of India towards the Kukis and in view of this it has become necessary to clarify certain points under:

1. Kukis are not secessionists nor are they waging war against the Government of India.
2. It is on record that the Kukis were in the forefront of the freedom movement against the British as manifested in the Kuki War of Independence, 1917-1919. Further, Kukis took active part in the INA/Azad Hind Fauz War effort against British imperialism. Till today, the Kukis have never waged war against the Indian Government.
3. It is, therefore, incorrect to treat the Kukis and the secessionist Nagas on equal footing. This approach of the Government of India towards the Kukis stands condemned by the Kuki people.
4. If the Government of India does not revise its approach towards the Kukis, the Kukis will have no alternative but to review their own standpoint *vis-a'-vis* the Indian Government.

Sd/-

(Holkhomang Haokip)
Inpipu (President) Kuki-Inpi,
Manipur

ANNEXURE – B

Second Kuki-Inpi General Assembly Political Resolutions

The second Kuki-Inpi General Assembly held at Kuki-Inn, Imphal, with full delegates adopted the following political resolutions:

Present and Future Policies

1. Kuki State

The Government of India and Burma (Myanmar) have allocated a State each to other neighbouring tribes and communities, whereas the demand of the Kukis for a separate State launched well thirty years back, have not been heeded till date. For restoration of peace and normalcy in the region, the KIM resolved to appeal the two Governments to hold talks with the people concerned with immediate effect.

2. On the Proposed Talk between Government of India NSCN (I-M)

The Government of India be asked to clarify and solve the following Kuki problems before holding talk with the NSCN (I-M) who have brought 'about innumerable crisis' with the intention to annihilate the Kukis:

(a) Who will compensate for more than 750 Kukis killed, 320 villages destroyed that led to 50.000 displaced on account of the NSCN (I-M) led atrocities?

(b) Since the Government of India has termed the crisis as a "Conflict between Nagas Kukis" how could a peace talk be held without the participation of the Kukis?

(c) Whether the NSCN (I-M) killed the Kukis as Kukis or as citizens of India?

3. On Sadar Hills District

The Chief Minister of Manipur Shri Rishang Keishing, who time and again, failed his promise to inaugurate Sadar Hills as a 'full-fledged district' be asked to inaugurate the same within January, 1997.

4. Demand of High Power Delegation of India

The General Assembly of KIM took strong note of the ineptitude of the Government of India on the demand of KIM for sending High Power Body to assess the damage done by the NSCN (I-M) led atrocities and condemned in strongest terms the attitude of the Government of India and resolved further that the Government be asked to reply before February 10, 1997 failing which KIM will take its own course of action for Peace in the region.

Sd/-	*Sd/-*
(Holkhomang Haokip)	(Holkholet Khongsai)
Inpipu (President) KIM	(Speaker), KIM

REFERENCES

1. Jean L. Cohen and Andrew Arato, *Civil Society and Political Theory*, MIT Press, Cambridge, 1992, p. 17.
2. Ernest Gellner, *Conditions of Liberty: Civil Society and Its Rivals*, Allen Lane/Penguin Press, New York, 1994, p. 20.
3. Francis Fukuyama, *Trust: The Social Virtues and the Creation of Prosperity*, Free Press, New York, 1995 p.15 ; Robert Putnam, *The Prosperous Community: Social Capital and Public Life*. The American Prospect 13 (Sring):35-42. Available on line at http://epn.org/prospect/13/13putn.html.
4. Interview with late Thangkhopao Kipgen, IAS retired, Imphal, 3 March, 2005.
5. Lal Dena, *British Policy towards Manipur*, 1762-1947, Imphal, 2008, pp. 93-100.
6. The structural composition of the Kuki-Inpi is derived from the interaction and discussion with Kuki village chiefs and local scholars.
7. Kuki Inpi Manipur (Souvenir), 1995-1997, Imphal, p.1.
8. Kuki Inpi Manipur (Souvenir), 1994, Imphal, p.1.
9. Interview with Nehkhothang Haokip, Chief of Molphei Village, Chandel District, Manipur, 25 January, 2009.
10. *Ibid.*
11. *Ibid.*
12. *Ibid.*
13. The Telegraph, 8 December 1996.
14. See Annexure- B.
15. Kuki Inpi Manipur(Souvenir), 2001, Imphal, p. 19.
16. *Ibid.*, pp. 3-4.

16

PROBLEM OF THE DISPLACED PERSONS AND VICTIMS OF ETHNIC CLASHES OF 1990s

MANIPUR EXPERIENCE

S. Mangi Singh & Ningombam Akbar Singh

More than anything else, the 1990s in the history of Manipur shall be remembered for the ethnic clashes in the hills of the State. Starting around the middle of 1992, the clashes continued for most of the remaining period of the decade with strayed cases of ethnic violence being reported in the local dailies till the closing months of 1999. Once started, the clashes spread like wildfire, and within no time the entire State was under the grip of the clashes. Though initially the clashes were mainly between the Nagas and Thadou speaking tribes of the Kuki-Chin-Mizo group of tribes, a number of other tribes were also in one way or the other drawn into the whirlwind of the clashes which led to further catastrophic consequences, most notoriously in the form of the Kuki-Paite clashes in 1997. Overall, the violent clashes have claimed about 2000 lives and many more injured. Many were maimed for the rest of their lives. More than 500 villages were attacked and about 7,000 houses were burnt down to ashes. Altogether, it also led to the displacement of around 15,000 families and more than one lakh people. The clashes brought untold sufferings of extreme magnitude to the displaced persons in so many different ways and for so many long days, nights, weeks, months and years, and it will be utterly preposterous to assume that one can put into record all the miseries and sufferings, the entire gamut of losses of life and property, etc. that followed in the wake of the clashes. This chapter is only a very humble attempt to highlight some aspects of the soul wrenching sufferings which the victims of the clashes have experienced

The immediate problem was that of fear and hunger. While fleeing, they faced all sorts of problems, as safe refuges were far and distant. Apart from hunger, they were haunted by an ever present sense of fear. In a situation where even MLAs with all their escorts found it insecure for them to travel, it can easily be imagined how difficult it will be for the affected people to venture out in search for food, work or go on looking for their loved ones who were found missing. Relief assistance from the government was regularly irregular and very late coming. Often the victims were in places which were not accessible by motor. On many occasions, it was difficult for the administration to deliver the relief materials because of this. So the people had to walk miles in the sun and rain along the muddy hill tracks to collect the materials. But even then there was more to their problem, the problem of their security while going to collect the badly needed relief materials by themselves. Sometimes the farthest that a vehicle could reach will be 15 miles away from the place where the victims lived and they had to walk on foot to come and collect them. In addition to that there were security problems for them to go that far to pick up the supplies.[1] Yet, ironically enough, they often needed ammunitions more than food for their own survival. With essential supplies already depleted then, thanks to the blockades of the two national highways, the living conditions of these people were gradually nearing the sub-human level and the approaching monsoons only made matter worst.[2]

There were often instances of food materials movement restricted due to checking by militants. For instance, there were three grouping centres at Chakpikarong Circle. These were at (1) Aigezang, having 50 households located near Sajitampak Zou village; (2) Haiker (L), having 90 households located near Poldai village (Jou); and (3) Longja, having 50 households located near Poldai village (Jou). Movement of food material to these group centres often got restricted because there was a gate at Sunlup (Anal village) controlled by Naga militants. Every material supplied to these camps had to pass through Sunlup gate. Apart from these group centres, there were other Zou villages beyond this gate and they also suffered the same.[3] (It may be noted here that the Zous there usually have sufficient food from December to May. From June to November they have to depend on rice coming from outside. When food materials are brought, these were thoroughly checked at Sunlup gate by Naga militants so that no food material could pass to the Kuki camps. This method of restriction on the movement of food materials created serious problems to the people living there.[4]

Often people had to provide for their own security in the grouping centres. During day time, they had to work for their livelihood and during night time they looked after their safety. The campers needed warm clothes to protect themselves from cold weather. When some donors supplied what was needed, these articles were sold out to meet their immediate food requirements. The State government sometimes issued G.I. sheets for roofing of the grouping centres. The campers, however, were often compelled to sell these in order to get their food and other urgent requirements.[5]

The people also lived in a very panicky condition. They could not meet their fellow people in other villages. Those who have their close and dear ones in other vulnerable areas were helpless to do anything and they lived under constant fear and anxiety for them in addition to their own safety concerns.[6] Venturing out to look for their close ones who were found missing and have not returned were extremely risky because militant groups loomed at large. For instance, the members of one study team of the Manipur Cultural Integration Conference (MCIC) which toured many of the affected sites in Chandel District said that they were always perturbed with the possibility of coming face to face with a hostile militant group of any of the two clashing communities. The people themselves were often harassed by militant outfits of both Nagas and Kukis. Out of fear they paid taxes to the militants. Even then, the militants will come often and take away their livestock, fire woods, and other foodgrains if they so desire.

Many of the villages continued to be exposed to attacks due to failure of the government and security forces to provide security post around the area. This was in spite of repeated requests from the concerned people themselves. In fact, many of them were ruthlessly attacked. For instance, the KSO, Chandel District blamed the State Government for giving no attention to the demand of Security Posts for the Grouping Centres of communal prone zone like Tollen, Gomi, Chelep, etc. It also accused the Security Forces for failure to undergo combing Operations in the nearby Tangkhul/Maring villages to search out the culprits as they had done in other Kuki villages of the State. Such partial and one sided attitude of the Government towards its citizens created more problems.[7]

Some of the villages were attacked three times within a period of one year alone. For instance, Bongbal Khullen, a Kuki village was attacked by the NSCN (IM) three times in one year. The first incident took place on June 8, 1993. Following the incident, the Naga militants also burnt down many other Kuki villages nearby the area which is dominated by the Tankhul Naga villages. "The land should not be allowed to be settled by other people if they are not Tankhuls", the NSCN(IM) reportedly told the villagers.[8] The villagers sought the advice of the people of Manipur specially the Government of Manipur on whether they should pay taxes to the NSCN(IM) agreeing to the idea of South Nagaland or not.[9]

Sometimes, *jhooms* and fields abandoned by original villagers were cultivated by displaced persons coming to the site from other areas. However, once the situation calmed down, problems started as to the question who will harvest the crops. For instance, after the Sunlup villagers had deserted their village, the vacant paddy fields were cultivated by the Kukis. When the paddy matured, problems arose regarding the question as to who shall have the right to the harvest.[10] Some other serious problems acutely felt by the IDPs were in the form of insufficient land, *jhoom* sites or fields for cultivation, inadequate drinking water, etc.[11] Often venturing out to collect paddy from the *jhooms* or to cultivate there were extremely dangerous as many died on such ventures. Indeed, in many *jhoom* sites lots of paddy remained uncollected because of fear to go there.

Relief materials provided in the Grouping Centres were far from satisfactory. At times it even became a total failure. [12] Soon they were lost sight of from the government and the public's memory, and they remained uncertain when their next meal will be available. Some of the relief camps did not receive any relief material from the government at all.[13] Sometimes, relief materials will be air dropped once in a while and the people will be almost starved to death before the next supply comes. For instance, a memorandum of the KIM submitted to the Chief Minister of Manipur said: "Maokot village, being important place has a Detachment of Assam Rifles and they got their supply either by airdrop and/or ponies. About 700 souls now at Maokot face starvation and the Deputy Chief Minister is well aware of the situation. The time is running out. Any death due to starvation will cause great unrest and disappointment amongst the Kukis..."[14] There were also many villages which did not receive any relief assistance from the government. For instance, the Majuron Kuki Village did not receive any relief material as yet (9-10-2003). They urgently needed water supply, housing amenities, electricity, improved roads, school, dispensary, etc. The majority of the victims of Kuki Aimol Village of Churachandpur District also have not received the rehabilitation assistance the government is supposed to provide in the form of some bundles of GI sheets though a few of them have received. This was a village which was attacked twice, the first in November 1993 in which 43 houses were burnt down to ashes, and the second in March 1994.

The people also needed not only help for immediate relief. They needed much more than that. For instance, for the victims affected by the clashes in 1993, assistance for the next year was also needed because they missed cultivation and harvesting in 1993 and will need food till 1994 harvest.[15] The displaced people did not have livestock like bullocks or buffaloes required for cultivation. There were people who were skilled and inclined to carry out weaving, carpentry, etc. But they had neither the tools nor the raw materials for carrying out them.[16] In their desperate situation, coming to Imphal from their very far flung areas and apply for government assistance was an uphill task. Besides they were already disheartened and were often driven to further desperation by insensitive officials. Even after more than ten years after the clashes, many people do not have a place for cultivation and the struggle for survival remains very hard with no source of income.

Their prospects of a secure means of livelihood also continued to be a distant dream as long as they didn't have a permanent place to settle or return to their original villages. The prospects were somewhat better when they settled more or less permanently in a particular site. For instance, Champhai and Chansang are in Saikul area of Senapati District. The former was newly established by displaced Kukis coming mainly from Ukhrul District and other parts of Senapati District affected by the clashes. On the other hand the latter was vacated by Tangkhul Nagas when the clashes started and displaced Kukis coming from Ukhrul district and other areas settled there. Earlier the name of the village was Mapao while it was inhabited by the Tangkhuls. The Kukis, after their settlement there, renamed it as Changsang which was the name of the village they left in Ukhrul. The new arrivals there carried out *ganja* plantation works along the river bed of Iril river. In fact, most of the *ganja* plantation works are performed by the Kukis with Nepalis in the Saikul Circle.[17] The Meiteis purchased the product. All these result to some sort of an economic integration leading to socio-economic interdependence among the participating partners. In fact, at present also, in Saikul Circle, Meiteis, Nepalis and Kukis live peacefully carry out economic and social activities jointly or separately.[18]

Usually their livelihood options became much limited once they got displaced. Most of them started earning their livelihood as daily unskilled labourers. Many skilled workers could not get suitable works and had to work as daily wage earners doing unskilled and intensive labour as most of the others also did. They also had extreme difficulties in sending their children to schools. While in the midst of their kith and kin they did not suffer from any stigma. However, even then they did not get any financial assistance, as their neighbours were very poor.

There were also many cases when the displaced persons found themselves in the midst of ethnic clashes all over again after they have come to take shelter in another place. The case of Thingkangphai of Churachandpur District may be cited as an example here. The village came under attack during the Kuki Paite clashes on 20 July, 1997. The attackers were both civilians and militants. Women also took part in the attack. All the male attackers wore in uniform and head band. They were equipped with sophisticated weapons. During the Naga Kuki clashes, 40 households had migrated into the village from Lambung Village of Bishnupur District and Zoupi. All these migrants were caught all over again in the Kuki Paite clashes after their arrival to Churachandpur where they came to take shelter. All of them again left the village following the Kuki Paite clashes.

In their search for secure places after fleeing from their original villages due to clashes, the displaced people usually looked towards the places where there kindred people are in majority and lived safely. The host villagers usually helped the displaced persons with utensils, clothes and some rations at the initial stage. The villagers also helped the displaced persons in constructing houses and finding them some work so that they may earn something. But in most of the cases, such helps dried up within no time at all. Many worked as daily wage earners in their new places if they were fortunate enough to get such an opportunity. Many also needed financial assistance to start some business so that they could earn some money on a regular basis. These moves sometimes led to the emergence of new villages in new areas or expansion of already existing villages. A suitable example will be that H. Champhai Village in Saikul Circle of Senapati District. The word Champhai means "peace land". This village was established in 1992 itself by displaced people coming from areas in Ukhrul District and other parts of Senapati District.

Altogether, 37 families settled in the newly established village. The surrounding area is a Kuki dominated area and there was no danger of being attacked by the Nagas. Hence, the site was selected for their new settlement.[19] However, there were also times when the arrival of the IDPs in a village led to some problems. Because their arrival made additional demands to the land the village had as the new arrivals had to be provided with land for both household purposes and cultivation. Finding a solution to such problems was not always easy.

During the clashes, both the Nagas and Kukis felt their freedom to move freely restricted even in the district headquarters. The Kukis in particular could not enter Tamenglong and Senapati District Headquarters.[20] One complaint from the KIM said that of the five districts in the hills of Manipur, only in Churachandpur District, the Kukis had free access to the District and sub divisional district headquarters.[21] After the clashes broke out, many people in vulnerable areas waited for State protection in vain. For instance, the KIM had urged the State and the Central Government to give protection to Kukis at vulnerable, strategic and isolated grouping centres such as Jangnoi, Thingphou, Chonjang (Gallam), Kamu Saichang and Bongpal Khullen villages in Sadar Hills; Tollent, Gomi, Mombi (Lonpi), Teiyang villages in Chandel District and Buning, Lasan and Talaolong villages in Tamenglong District where the Kukis are in minority and lived in isolated Grouping Centres. But none was provided in spite of repeated requests.[22] On the contrary, the KIM alleged all the Naga villages were provided Army, Para-military and Manipur Rifles, and hence, they were quite safe and secured.[23]

There were also numerous blockades during the clashes. This further led to price rise in the hills thereby making things all the more difficult for the affected people. These blockades were put up on many occasions by the conflicting groups in areas where they were in control on the State and National Highways. Yet, in spite of all the financial hardships, the people had to spend at times a considerable amount of their earnings for buying ammunitions to protect their village.

On many occasions, the people had to suffer extreme

harassment in the hands of the security personnel as well. There were many instances when villagers, in view of the failure of the government's failure to provide security to the village, organized their own village guards. They armed their village guards with licensed guns local made barrel guns and pistols, and other traditional weapons. However, they were sometimes mistaken as militants and they suffered heavily in the hands of the security personnel. Besides, many villages were accused of harbouring militants and they also suffered a lot in the hands of the security personnel. But the fact was that it was the villagers who were not protected by the security people and they could not stand up against the militants who were armed with sophisticated weapons.

There were deaths while in displacement due to hunger, disease, sickness, etc. This accounted for another grave misery heaped upon the displaced persons. Their problems got worsened due to the lack of medical facilities in the hills. The health centres were not properly manned and equipped. They lacked doctors, x-ray machines, technicians, surgery equipments and adequate supply of medicines. Many lived in malaria prone regions and epidemic diseases like cholera often frequented the unfortunate victims.[24] Fever and cold were the most common problems and the victims, lacking proper medical attention, suffered heavily from these ailments. This further resulted in many deaths while in displacement. For instance, four males and one child of Ngarian Rongmei Village died while in displacement. Eight of the villagers of Kha Aimol Village of Churachandpur District also died while in displacement. Two daughters of the chief of Toljang Village of Churachandpur also died because of lack of medical facilities while in displacement. Sometimes, while in displacement, finding burial sites for their death was a problem. Many were maimed for the rest of their lives. Many also faced the stigma of being "refugees" to some extent.

Many villagers also left their villages without actual attacks taking place but for fear of attacks. For instance many households left Zalengbung village, another Kuki village under Litan Police Station in Ukhrul District, for fear of possible attacks thereby reducing the number of households in the village from 65 to 45 at one time.[25] This village did not receive any quit notice but always took caution since the clashes started. During the height of the clashes, i.e., from 1993 to 1995, the educated members of the village took the responsibility of teaching the students, as all the teachers of the Zalengbung UJB School did not attend the school during the period. Electricity was there in the village from 1986 but it was discontinued after the clashes.[26]

Many Kuki villages in Ukhrul were abandoned not because they were actually attacked but for fear of attacks. One more such example will be that of the Lamlai Chingphei Village, again under the Litan Police Station of Ukhrul District. The village was not burnt down during the clashes. Nonetheless all the villagers left the village in October 1993 and stayed at the Sangkai Group Centre up to October 1994. In 1994, while at the Sangkai Grouping Centre, a malaria epidemic took place and claimed the lives of 26 persons of the Group Centre. Out of these 10 were from Lamlai Chingphei.[27]

Instances of displaced persons who have given up any hopes for returning to their earlier places were also many. And it was not always because they did not want to return. It was mainly because they feel insecure to return there. Sometimes their villages have already been occupied by other communities while they were in displacement. Even when they knew that their village remains unoccupied since the time they fled from there, many decided not to go back because of insecure future prospects. For instance, the villagers of Toljang have come to Kholmun Village of Churachandpur. While in Toljang, there was a dispute between the Thadou Kukis of the village and Tangkhuls who were not from the village over the question of ownership of land. The Tankhuls, as a last resort, tried to kill the chief of the village. Out of fear, the chief fled to Churachandpur along with his family and took shelter in Kholmun Village. This was later followed by his villagers leaving their village as well. Now the village remains deserted and unoccupied. There is no turning back for them, no hope for them to return.

When a village got abandoned, it was usually one of the nearby villages which will occupy the village. For instance, Khonglo (Vaiphei) Village, Phunjong (Thadou Kuki) Village and Kulbung (Thadou Kukii) Village were abandoned during the clashes. They are all in Ukhrul District. The villagers left them when the clashes started gaining momentum. In Khonglo Vaiphei Village's case, it went to a nearby village of the Nagas called Bolyang and the Nagas have given the village a new name Manthouram. In case of Phungjang Thadou Kuki Village, it is now inhabited by the Tangkhul Nagas and is now called Punouram. About Kulbung, it has gone into the hands of the Tangkhuls living nearby though they have not yet started residing there.[28] Some villages remain still uninhabited. For instance, Thomyang Thadou Kuki village still remains deserted. It has not been occupied by the Tangkhuls so far.[29]

For many, it took more than 10 years to return to their villages. There were also many others who did not or could not return to their village at all. They left their place for all times to come. They wondered from place to place in a state of abject poverty without security of food or shelter or security, getting them exposed to all sorts of discriminations. At one time many Kukis were wondering about in the capital city without any shelter.[30] Even when the villagers returned, most of the time not all returned. Many of those who returned to their earlier sites also felt unsafe for a long time. In fact many were attacked again after they returned from the places where they fled after their village was attacked the first time. For instance the people of Laimanai Kabui Village, Churachandpur District were attacked again after they returned to their village.

Even when the danger is gone and majority of the villagers have returned, many decided not to return. Security reasons and better prospects elsewhere to earn a living in the difficult times were the main considerations that made them stay away. They had extreme difficulties paying rent while in displacement. Their MLAs and MP did not care much for them. Many still continue to live in displacement. For instance, many villagers of villages like Laimanai Kuki Village, Geljang, Langjingmanbi, Syjang, etc., are still in displacement. Some of those displaced from these villages are presently residing at Ningthiching.

When some villages had to be abandoned due to the mounting tension, the villagers who were leaving sometimes said farewell to the villagers of nearby villages and requested them not to harm them or to do whatever they can so that no harm comes to them while they are on the way moving to another place. This is what the villagers of Molen and Natzang requested to the villagers of other villages living nearby. Prior to 1992/93 there was no tension or conflict between them and other Naga villages nearby them.[31] There were cases when those villagers who had abandoned their villages during the clashes returned to their village and do not face any problem with other villages nearby inhabited by people with whom they were in conflict during the clashes. For instance, the people of Molen and Natzang have returned to their village and they faced no objection from the nearby Naga villages. Yet there are also many cases when the villagers found their village occupied by other people. For instance, the Aimols Louchilbung Village, Churachandpur, returned to their village after about three years of displacement. But they found their village occupied by the Kabuis. So they took temporary settlement at a nearby area. The area they are settling now is too small and they have no land for doing plantation work. (DPV-8) In connection with that they have applied an application to the DC and SDC quite earlier for regaining the village. But so far no response has come from either side. Afterwards they put forward the matter to the Zeliangrong Union, the apex body of the Zeliangrong people in Manipur for intervention. The Zeliangrong Union then in their judgment told the villagers of Aimol Louchilbung that the land will not be returned but, if they so desire, they can collect the monetary value of land from the Kabuis. But the Anals are not ready to accept it as they have no alternative site to live. In the words of the village chief: "Kabuis confiscated our land, we cannot chase them away as we belong to micro-population groups".

The internally displaced persons had no capital to start something so that they could earn a steady income. Their access to forest resources was also restricted by the dangers of someone attacking them and also by militants. For example, the Kuki villagers of Sekong Village of Churachandpur were not allowed to use forest resources by the NSCN(IM) Friends, family members and their loved ones got scattered far and wide with no knowledge of their whereabouts in many cases. Many also suffered the killing suspense of not knowing whether a dear one found missing is death or alive. Life in the villages where they resided earlier was much better and secure with rich harvests. Now memories of their loved one whose lives were so brutally cut short visit them time and again to haunt them, thereby adding grief, loneliness and anguish to the hardships they faced while trying to survive themselves. Many survived by collecting wood from the jungle and selling them. They also made charcoal by burning wood and sold them by coming all the way to the State capital with extreme difficulties. There were also so many times when their conditions worsened day by day. The surrounding villagers, after the initial sympathy, were indifferent. They were also looked down upon in many places and they suffered a certain stigma to some extent unless they were in the midst of their kith and kin.

The displaced persons also suffered from all sorts of insecurities. They suffered from inferiority complex and their dignity and self esteem hit rock bottom. Earlier they were the proud owners of their land and they reaped rich harvest in the fields. But after the clashes, they had to shift to an altogether new location and their source of subsistence came from working on the fields of other people. In other words, the owners became tenants.

There were also many instances when the government/ security forces failed to provide preventive measures even after they were informed about potential attacks well in advance. Laimanai (Tingpui) Village received information from Loktak Police Post on September 3, 1993 that Kuki militants will attack the village sooner or later. The villagers also informed the Police Outpost nearby about the measures they have taken up for their own self defence in view of possible attacks from the Kuki on 4-9-93. Yet the Army in collision with the Kukis came and attacked the villagers killing innocent village volunteers and wounded 4 persons and arrested several others.

It may also be noted here how the involvement of the militants harmed the innocent villagers. For instance, on 14th April, 1993, a Special Task Force of the Kuki Defence Force raided and destroyed one NSCN(IM) base camp at Lamlongkhunou in Chandel District. The KDF said that the NSCN(IM) was using the village as their base for 14 months and the KDF was forced to destroy the village. The KDF also said that they attacked Leisi village and Paraolon Village in Chandel District for the same reason. The retreating NSCN(IM) personnel from Paraolon were pursued upto Lamkang Kotal Khuntak Village which was also burnt down in the process. While regretting the loss of life and civilian properties, the KDF said that the villagers should have thought earlier before harbouring NSCN(IM) personnel in their midst. It also warned, "Any villages harbouring NSCN personnel will suffer the same fate in future encounters. So as to avoid such unfortunate incident they are advised not to harbour and help the NSCN in any way". The KDF also said that "The Kuki Defenes Force fight only to defend our home and hearth from NSCN (Muivah) depredation. We have no ill-will against any of our other Naga brothers."[32]

The efforts of the people to draw the attention of the Central Government also did not result in any significant uplift of the victims. For instance, The Kukis also tried to present their plight to the Government of India time and again. However, their efforts have so far not yielded any substantial positive results. On 21 July, 2001, the KIM met the then Prime Minister Atal Behari Vajpayee and the Union Minister of State (Home) and Mr. Padmanabhaiah, the then NSCN(IM) negotiator. They also submitted a memorandum where they gave details for settlement of the issues pertaining to the rehabilitation of the Kukis amicably. But nothing concrete materialized.[33] An assurance given by Padmanavaiah on August 14, 2002 to arrange an exclusive meeting of the Kuki-Inpi and the Prime Minister also did not happen even after a lapse of three and half years. All these also show that the Central Government did not give the necessary attention they ought to give to the plight of the affected people.

About the problems concerning children, youths and women, the clashes had a pauperizing effect on them. Poverty, coupled with human insecurities and limitations on their physical movement while trying to venture out from their safe territory, made them greatly demoralized. Even after the clashes, the parents could not send their children to schools due to extreme financial hardships. In many villages, except for little kids, all the other school going children discontinued their education permanently. In Misao Lhouvom Village of Churachandpur District, all those children above class VII have permanently given up their education. In Misao Simoul Village of the same district, many students suffered three years academic break because of the clashes and many more gave up their education forever. In Cheihjang Village of the district again, the children had three years academic break. Prior to the attack to their village, there were about 30 students who were at the pre-Matric level. Out of these, almost 19 of them gave up their study permanently because of the clashes. In Louchilbung Village in the same district again, the drop out rate at the pre-Matric level was as high as 80 per cent. (DPV-8) In Kungpi Nungsen Village of the Thadous in Churachandpur District also, most of the children had an academic break of one or two years. Repairing works or new construction of many of the schools and dispensaries destroyed during the clashes still remained neglected thereby depriving the children the services which are so essential for their overall well-being and growth. When schools were burnt down and children were made to abandon their studies and engage in hard and intensive labour in order to support themselves as well as supplement their family income, all the pathways to development are blocked for them and they are pulled down towards the abyss of deprivation.

Lack of healthcare services was another problem which seriously affected the children. Most of the water supply arrangements, community halls and electricity connections which were destroyed during the clashes. Many children died because of the lack of proper medical treatment. For example, two daughters of even the chief of Toljang Village died while in displacement as they could not be given adequate medical treatment. The village was a newly established one by Chongloi (recognized as Thadou Kukis) villagers who got displaced from Ukhrul District during the clashes. Because of the vagabond type of life style the youths were compelled to lead, the youths including girls became mischievous and involved in viscous activities as elders roles as agents of social control were not available to them.

The children were also compelled to contribute in earning money for the maintenance of the family. Thus, instead of attending school, they started engaging themselves in hard, intensive and tiring labour. They also became extremely vulnerable to all sorts of temptations. Both the youths and women were greatly demoralized by the hardships they had to endure. Many boys became militants and many more lost their direction in life. Pauperized by the clashes, cases of drug addiction, theft and burglary were on the rise among the youths.

At present there is an orphanage of the child victims of the ethnic clashes in Churachandpur run by one Kuki Women's Union. Kuki Women's Union is a non-profit voluntary organization. This organization was also very active in campaigning for peace and normalcy, both during the Kuki Naga and Kuki Paite clashes. In case of Kuki Paite clashes they used to meet very frequently with Zomi Mother's Association for mutually exchanging their views. In 1993, members of the Union decided to bring up those orphans whose parents were killed during the clashes. From that year onwards they observed fasting and prayer on the 15th of every month. Rice meant for that day was contributed for generating funds for realizing their goal. On 1998, 15 October, Sanga Mounnin Inn was formally started with eight children (five boys and three girls). All of them were from Churachandpur District. Because of financial limitations, only those children whose both parents were killed in the clashes were allowed admission. Land for setting up this orphanage was donated by Mr. and Mrs.

Zangam Haokip. Mr Haokip was a local church elder at that time. Afterwards some portion of the adjoining lands was also acquired for expansion. Doors were and are open to all the ethnic groups. But no applicants came forward from among the Paite community. At present there are 24 boys and 11 girls in the orphanage. Other than the Kuki children, there are also children from Simte, Meitei, etc.

The plight of the displaced women was also extremely pitiable and vulnerable. Traditionally women are equal contributors in earning the bread of the family. They shared the hardships in the difficult times along with their men folk, perhaps sometimes more. After the clashes, their problems in earning became multiplied by manifolds. They ventured out for fetching water and firewood despite fear, with possible dangers lurking behind every bush, corner, etc., they had to lead a life of going from door to door seeking work so that they can earn something. In the process many got exposed to extreme indignities. Left without any men folk to protect and provide for the surviving families many married and even unmarried women were compelled by the circumstances to sell their bodies in the grim struggle to fight hunger, poverty and survival. The situation was worse for women in families without male earning members. This was true for all the families of Joupi Village whose male population including infants was brutally butchered on 13 September, 1993 while they were fleeing in the jungle. They also suffered from acute mental traumas.

Regarding the rehabilitation efforts taken up by the State Government much were left to be desired. The government at most provided temporary relief. The initial *ex gratia* amount was only Rs 20,000. The amount was too little and the many criticized it in view of the fact that the Bombay blast victims were given an *ex gratia* payment of Rs. 2,00,000 per victim. The payments were also too belated a payment. On 31st May, 1993, the State government sanctioned a sum of Rs. 8,60,000 only for paying *ex gratia* grant to the bereaved families of the deceased persons of ethnic violence.[34] Later the amount was increased up to Rs 1,00,000 per victim. However, many of the families of the victims are still not getting *ex gratia* as the bodies of the victims were not found. The government also failed to provide relief materials in many relief camps. For instance, many of the displaced persons took shelter in Etham Meitei Village. However, though the camp was opened on 11 December, 1997, the government did not provide any relief material to the camp.[35] In fact, one of the local dailies remarked that giving relief material to the grouping centres were far from satisfactory and at times it had become a total failure.[36] The government also made, at times, arrangements for those people who were affected, and could not go back to their respective villages immediately, to directly apply to the Relief Commissioner at government Secretariat at Imphal.[37] The government also tried to provide immediate arrangements to be made in community halls, school buildings, churches, etc., wherever there was a concentration of displaced families due to the clashes. The people were to be provided with Rs. 100 per head subject to a maximum of Rs. 500 per family for giving immediate relief in the form of rice, etc. But there were complaints of the relief assistance not reaching the camps even when concentrations have already taken place long back.

There were also many obstacles which hindered whatever efforts the State government made to provide relief and rehabilitation to the affected people. The government entrusted the task of strengthening the administration of relief works on the officers at the district levels. Yet these officials were often not available in the places of their postings. They were completely demoralized by the NSCN(IM) and they lacked support from the top.[38] There was no proper organization for relief works. Villagers who have no MLAs were without any help. Almost all the time they had no office to approach and in many places it was not safe for them to visit the areas where the offices were located. One Commissioner at the State secretariat was not enough.

About the relief and rehabilitation work taken up by the NGOs, mention can be made of the Volunteers for Village Development (VVD) and the Fraternal Green Cross (FGC). The VVD, along with the Committee for the Restoration of Normalcy (CRN), was involved in distributing Rs. 35 lakhs worth of relief materials in the form rice, blankets, utensils, tarpaulins, mosquito nets and petromax. The exercise covered 395 families including 189 Naga, 199 Kukis, four Meetei and three Muslim villages comprising a total of 107,41 families including 5,026 Naga, 5,578 Kuki, 53 Meetei and 84 Muslim families and a total population of 63,379 including 29,773 Nagas, 33,132 Kukis, 302 Meeteis and 172 Muslims.[39] Even then their efforts were thwarted because of conflicts between the VVD and the CRN. There were also differences between the KIM and The UNC which led to the dismantling of the CRN. The KIM and the UNC were also not happy with the manner in which the Project for the relief and rehabilitation of the affected people was carried out by the VVD.[40] (DP-50) They often indulged in allegations, counter allegations and clarifications thereby jeopardizing their own reputation at times. The CRN alleged embezzlement of funds by the VVD. It alleged that Ashok Tipnis of the VVD began flaunting the rules included in the Memorandum of Understanding while spending money and that he unilaterally converted the VVD/ CRN Relief/rehabilitation programme into a Fraternal Green Cross (FGC)/VVD programme and tried to project FGC as partner of the project. Ashok Tipnis was also charged of having given away in loan a sum of Rs. 2,40,000 to 26 schools without sanction from the Finance Committee and without any term of repayment of the loans. He was also charged with turning the vehicles brought for the use in the programme as property of VVD.[41]

While the tension has eased significantly over the last few years, it is unfortunate that the people are being left to their own to build up their lives all by themselves. The government has failed to take up a systematic and long standing rehabilitation programme apart from providing some immediate reliefs or organizing group centres and providing some materials of day to day use. The question was to provide them adequate assistance on a sustained basis till they are able to stand on their own. It was a question of enabling them to find a means of livelihood, to find them a secure shelter and make them free from the fear of hunger and starvation.

REFERENCES

1. Memo. No. KIM/GEN/5/93 submitted to the Chief Minister and the Deputy Chief Minister of Manipur by the President, KIM, 20-7-93 in DP 61.
2. Yambem Laba, Can't See Guitars for Guns, A Brief Look at the Recent Kuki-Paite Clashes in Manipur, presented in the Three-day Seminar on Ethnic Values and Ideals of Emerging Egalitarian Society, Department of Philosophy, Manipur University, sponsored by the Indian Institute of Advanced Studies Shimla,7-9 March, 2006, p. 1.
3. Protest against Divisive Policy of India on 14 June, 2002 and Forging a Bigger and Stronger Unity on 18th June, 2002, a leaflet issued by The All Manipur United Clubs' Organization (AMUCO), Imphal, 25 May, 2002.
4. Manipur Cultural Integration Conference and Ethnic Community in Manipur (A report of the MCIC visiting team), 1996, p. 2.
5. *Ibid.*
6. *Ibid.*
7. *The Freedom*, 26-10-94.
8. *The Freedom*, 6-1-98.
9. *The Freedom*, 6-1-98.
10. Manipur Cultural Integration Conference and Ethnic Community in Manipur (A report of the MCIC visiting team), *op. cit.*, p. 1.
11. *Ibid.*, p. 4.
12. *The Freedom*, 21-11-94.
13. *The Freedom*, 6-1-98.
14. Memo. No, KIM/GEN 5/93 submitted to the Chief Minister and the Deputy Chief Minister of Manipur by the President, KIM, 20.7.93 in DP 61.
15. Memorandum submitted to His Excellency, the Governor of Manipur by the Kuki-inpi in DP 61.
16. Manipur Cultural Integration Conference and Ethnic Community in Manipur (A report of the MCIC visiting team), *op. cit.*, p. 4.
17. *Ibid.*
18. *Ibid.*
19. *Ibid.*, p. 3.
20. No. KIM-18/Court/95, Memorandum submitted to the CM, Manipur from the President, KIM, 18/10/95.
21. No. KIM-10/ASSEM/95, Memorandum submitted to Sri I.K. Gujral, Hon'ble Prime Minister of India, camp : Imphal by President & General Secretary, KIM. 22/5/97.
22. No KIM-18/Cor/95. Memorandum submitted to the Chief Minister of Manipur by the KIM, 18/10/95.

23. No. KIM-10/ASSEM/95, Memorandum submitted to Sri, I.K. Gujral. Hon'ble Prime Minister of India, camp; Imphal by President & General Secretary, KIM, 22-5-97.
24. *The Freedom,* 16-7-95.
25. Report from the field work.
26. *Ibid.*
27. *Ibid.*
28. Intterview with S. Jonah, 50, Lairam Khullen, BPO Kasom Khullen, Ukhrul South Sub-division, 1/11/04.
29. *Ibid.*
30. Souvenir of Kuki-lnpi Manipur, 1995-97, published by Souvenir Committee on behalf of the Kuki-lnpi Manipur, 1997.
31. *Ibid.*
32. Press release by the Commander, KDF, 16-4-93, highlighting their counter attack against the NSCN (IM) offensive, appeared in *The Freedom,* 19-4-93.
33. Memorandum submitted to the Prime Minister of India by the President, KIM, and the Vice-Chairman, Kuki Movement for Human Rights and the President, Kuki Students' Organization (GHQ).
34. No. 4/14(2)/9H. Government of Manipur. Home Department Order, *The Freedom,* 27 June, 1993.
35. *The Freedom,* 6-1-98.
36. *The Freedom,* 10-8-1993.
37. *The Freedom,* 22-11-1994.
38. Memorandum submitted to His Excellency, the Governor of Manipur by the Kuki-Inpi in DP 61.
39. Financial involvement under the relief measure (FGC/CRN) 26 December to 31 December 1995 dated 6-4-96.
40. Letter to the Director, The Healing Mission Resources, the EZE and the ICCO from Holkhomang Haokip, President, KIM (not dated).
41. *The Freedom,* 31-12-1996.

17

DEVELOPMENT OF ADULT EDUCATION IN MIZORAM, 1963-2011

A SYNOPTIC VIEW

Lalnithar Joute

Introduction

During the colonial period, Mizoram was known as Lushai Hills District forming a part of Assam. After India's independence, 1952 it was made as an autonomous district of Assam by the Government of India in 1952. In 1954 by an Act of Parliament, the name was changed to Mizo Hills District of Assam. In the year 1972 the Mizo Hills District was separated from Assam and was given the status of Union Territory and it was named as Mizoram. On 20th February, 1987 Mizoram became the 23rd State of the Indian Union and for proper administrative set up the State was divided into eight districts at present, namely, 1. Aizawl District, 2. Champhai District, 3. Serchhip District, 4. Kolasib District, 5. Mamit District, 6. Lunglei District, 7. Lawngtlai District, and 8. Saiha District.

Education in Mizoram

In Mizoram there was no organized educational institution in the area till 1893 and no written language; all the instructions

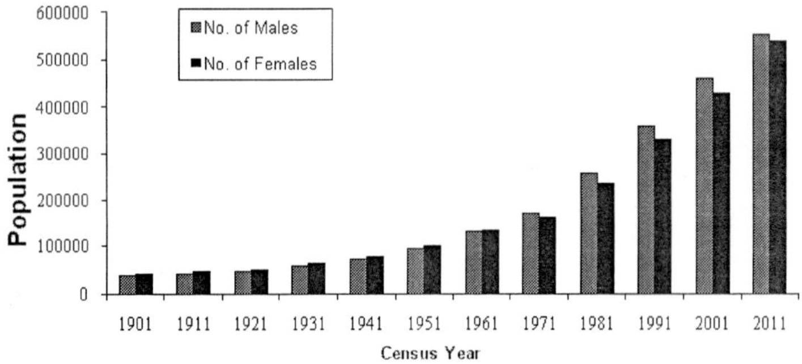

Fig. 17.1 : Population of Mizoram 1901-2011

were verbal in nature. With the coming of the Christian missionaries in the year 1894, there were remarkable changes in the State. It was these missionaries who transformed the language to writing and developed Mizo alphabets by adopting Roman script with a phonetic form of spelling. After this the missionaries started opening the schools. There were some experimental schools opened in a few villages. In 1909, the first Middle English School was opened at Aizawl. The first high school was started at Aizawl in 1944 through public donations and collaborations, the opening of high school marked a new epoch of event in the educational progress in this part of the country. The Christian missionaries were the teachers and led the people of Mizoram from darkness to light, from unknown to known. They were the torch bearer for Mizoram in every field of development through education.

During this period education was still in insignificant stage among the Mizos. In March 1894, J.H. Lawrence and F.W. Savage (*Pu Buanga leh Pu Sapupa*) the two pioneer missionaries developed alphabet *A, AW, B,* of Mizo in Roman script. The pioneer missionaries built a cottage as a school on this very place (where the present high school is located) then they started teaching. Before the establishment of this kind of institution, Mizos began to learn how to read and write at the verandah's of the missionaries. The first literate persons among the Mizos were *Thangphunga, Suaka, Lalchhinga and*

Khamliana. So, eradication of illiteracy from the soil of Mizoram was started by the Christian missionaries.

The opening of these educational institutions in the State marked a new important era in the field of education for the people of Mizoram. The government's attention to education increased significantly after independence. Earlier the efforts were mainly to increase primary education. Quite a number of primary schools were gradually upgraded to middle and high school level. The number of educational institutions is keeping pace with the thirst of the Mizos for formal education in the area.

Adult Education in Mizoram

Its beginning and development : The first five decades of the twentieth century saw the expansion and steady consolidation of the first level of education and beginning of second level of education for Mizoram. The Christian missionaries supervised the educational administration till 1952 in Mizoram. As time passed by, some Social Education Organizers were posted from Government of Assam in Mizoram under the Block Development Project. In 1963 a separate Social Education Wing came into existence with the appointment of District Social Officers under the umbrella of DPI/ Education Department. Table 17.1 shows literacy rate of Mizoram.

Table 17. 1 : Literate Population and Literacy Rate of Mizoram — 1951-2011

Year	*Male Literate*	*Female Literate*	*Total no. of Literates*	*Literacy rate (%)*
1951	44,375	16,718	61,093	30.57
1961	70,743	46,354	1,17,097	44.01
1971	1,03,324	75,469	1,78,793	53.79
1981	1,65,812	1,29,873	2,95,685	74.26
1991	2,51,551	2,10,379	4,61,930	82.27
2001	3,50,105	3,11,340	6,61,445	88.80
2011	4,38,949	4,08,643	8,47,592	91.85

Source: Directorate of Census Operation Aizawl, Mizoram.

With the attainment of Union Territory status by Mizoram in 1972 the Social Education Wing had been expanded and upgraded to a State level status and in 1973 strengthening of the administrative structure had been accorded by the Central Government. The term "Social Education" had been substituted with "Adult Education" since 2nd October, 1978 as such the District Social Education Officer was redesignated as District Adult Education Officer and also the Social Education Organizer was redesignated as Circle Adult Education Officer. Not much could be done in the field of adult education (social education) prior to the Fifth Plan Period. Because Mizoram suffered a great setback in almost all fields of developmental activities due to political disturbances which broke out in 1966.

When the National Adult Education Programme was inaugurated in 1978, adult education in Mizoram received a new impetus. The administrative structure was strengthened by the Central Government and thereby sanctioned a post of Deputy Director, Adult Education, which was again upgraded to the status of Joint Director, Adult Education since 12th February, 1985. Simultaneously a centrally sponsored scheme, three Rural Functional Literacy Projects, each comprising of 100 Adult Education Centres had been implemented.

Adult Education Wing exists as one of the wings under the Directorate of School Education headed by the Joint Director assisted by a Deputy Director and one Assistant Director (Monitoring), one Assistant Publication Officer and other ministerial staff with the guidance and control of the Director of School Education. Though Mizoram has eight district headquarters, but for proper administrative set up in the field of adult education it is headed by three district Adult Education Officers for the entire State one in each district. (1) District Adult Education Officer Aizawl East. (2) District Adult Education Officer Aizawl West, and (3) District Adult Education Officer Lunglei. Besides these there are two Project Officers to look after the Rural Functional Literacy Projects (RFLP) who are assisted by Supervisors and supporting ministerial staff. This Project has been run in Mamit District under Aizawl West District Adult Education Officer.

Social Education

In Mizoram Social Education Wing (Adult Education Wing at present) came into existence as a separate wing since 1963 with the appointment of District Social Officers under Education Department. Before the inception of Union Territory in Mizoram, all Adult Education (Social Education) programme was taken up by the Social Education Wing. Due to various reasons, there was less progress in the field of Social Education during the Fifth Plan Period (1974-1979) as Mizoram suffered a great setback in every field of development because of political disturbances which broke out in 1966. In order to promote literacy in the area the wing took various steps.

With a view to implement Social Education (Adult Education) Programme better and more effectively in Mizoram, 20 Social Education Circles with 20 main centres were established in 1974. Each main centre had 3 sub-centres (60 sub- centres) they were called as social education main centres or main centres and sub-centres. Altogether there were 80 centres in Mizoram. The aim of establishing these centres was to disseminate and inculcate the need and importance of literacy in the mind of the people of Mizoram. The main centres were looked after by Social Education Organizers (Circle Adult Education Officers at present). These centres had a separate building of their own. In each main centres and sub-centres, a library was established and books were supplied from the department. In each sub-centre, one 'helper' was engaged among the villagers with fix remuneration of Rs. 200 per month. The duties of the helper was to provide assistance to Social Education Organisers as and when required, to maintain Library in the sub-centres, identify the illiterates and animators with the co-ordination of local NGOs. Classes were held at night to the adult learners teaching how to read and write with a simple arithmetic and among the public also disseminate the importance of having a latrine, immunization, etc.

In case of social education sub-centres, responsibility and

authority were given to helper and non-government organisations such as Young Mizo Association (YMA), Young Lai Association (YLA), Young Chakma Association (YCA), Mara Theoplali (MTP) and certain church organisations. Survey and identification of illiterates were done by them. On top of this, the Social Education Organisers of the circle concerned actively supervised their activities.

In the year 1978, when social education was renamed as adult education these social education centres were later converted into circle adult education main centres and social education sub-centres into adult education sub-centres by the State government of Mizoram. The concern department provides the following materials to the centres such as petromax, lanterns, kerosene oil, candles, teaching/learning materials like exercise books, pencils, blackboards, chalks, etc. Reading materials published by the department '*Thiamna Kailawn* (Ladder of Education), *Hmasawnna Kailawn* (Ladder of Progress), and *Ziak Zirna* (Learning of Writing)' were provided. Sport materials for Adult learners football, volleyball, carom boards, draught board, etc., were also provided. For the better benefit of the neo-literates in the area, the department provided duplicating machine, typewriter and other necessary materials for publishing a weekly bulletin to all the 20 main centres to publish their own but the name remain the same for all called as *Khawtlang Entu* and each centre send a copy to the headquarters Adult Education Wing Aizawl.

The establishment of 20 main centres with 3 sub-centres in each only was considered inadequate as more needs was felt for the rural remote and interior villages in the areas to reach by the adult education programme. For this purpose, adult education centres were established in the nearby villages for a period of one year temporarily which were solely rely upon the non-government organisations of the locality.

As per Central Government norms a minimum number of 30 learners must be available but the minimum numbers were relaxed where magnitude of illiteracy is small. Being temporary, the centres were closed down after one year and opened from time to time to other villages depending upon availability of illiterates. In these centres, illiterate adults were taught reading, writing and simple numeric. There was no library book for these centres, and the purpose of adult education Centre was only the place of teaching and learning. The teachers so called Instructors identified by the non-government organisations were given Rs. 10 as remuneration for making one illiterate person literate and the new literate person was given Rs. 5 as a token of appreciation.

All these activities were mostly performed with the active involvement of non-government organisations such as Young Mizo Association (YMA), the Church activists and political organisations. Cultural activities and social works were performed with the locality like cleaning of the village roadside; cemetery, water fountain and construction of play ground were also performed with the locality and had been carried out by the State with a limited fund.

Rural Functional Literacy Project (RFLP)

In the year 1978, the Farmers Functional Literacy Project (FFLP) and the ongoing scheme of Non-Formal Education (NFE) Programme for youth between the age group of 15 to 25 were merged together on a new programme called 'Rural Functional Literacy Project (RFLP)' was started. This scheme was a mass programme intended to mobilize and involve all sections of the society to promote and implement an effective scheme of adult education. The project was a Centrally Sponsored Scheme (CSS) and all field cost and other training expenses were borne by the Central Government.

Rural Functional Literacy Project (RFLP) was introduced by Government of India in the year 1978 under Centrally Sponsored Scheme (CSS). The project was meant for a period of 5 years. After a lapse of 5 years, in the year 1984, the project was taken over by the State government and the incumbents were absorbed in the department.

In order to eradicate illiteracy from the soil of Mizoram, two identical adult education programmes had been implemented from the year 1979 till 1997, one under Centrally Sponsored Scheme (CSS) this is known as Rural Functional Literacy Project (RFLP) and another one, State Adult Education Programmes. Under these programmes, adult education centres have been run where the adult illiterates are taught reading writing and simple arithmetic mean.

Under Rural Functional Literacy Project different activities had taken up in the field of adult education in Mizoram during these eighteen years (1979-1997). Table 17. 2 shows number of centres, enrolment and achievement under RFLP.

Table 17. 2 : RFLP in Mizoram (1979-1997)

Year	*No. of Centres*	*No. of enrolment*	*Achievement*
1979 -1980	277	8363	4898
1980-1981	285	6795	3152
1981-1982	267	7775	4871
1982-1983	290	7388	3258
1983-1984	300	10397	3049
1984-1985	400	12030	3684
1985-1986	500	10807	5492
1986-1987	500	11127	6077
1987-1988	500	10738	5909
1988-1989	500	10977	5436
1989-1990	500	11102	6411
1990-1991	300	12843	6166
1991-1992	300	8735	5714
1992-1993	300	30167	15000
1993-1994	300	31211	18000
1994-1995	300	32136	14584
1995-1996	300	30183	10021
1996-1997	300	22320	4966

Source: Adult Education Wing, Aizawl.

Experimental Adult School

Two adult schools had been started in Mizoram since 1980 under adult education programme on experimental basis, one at *Phullen* village in Aizawl district and the other one at

Bunghmun village in Lunglei district, to enable the neo-literates to prosecute their studies and enhance their literacy competence. Two adult teachers have been engaged to look after these schools. In the year 1987 on 28th April the school at *Bunghmun* was closed down due to lack of enrolment and shifted to Tuikawi village in the same district. The schools were closed down due to fund constraints in the year 2000. The teachers were absorbed as primary school teachers by the State government.

Vocational School for Adults

In order to facilitate vocational training for adult learners, one vocational school had been started in Aizawl since August 2nd 1984 where adult learners had a chance to undergo vocational training during their leisure time and thereby developed their occupational skills and enhanced their daily earnings. At the initial stage two trades namely, carpentry and hollow block making had been started, but after one year the school faced serious difficulty in procuring, stocking, etc., of cement and due to lack of sufficient water the second trade, i.e., hollow block making could not be continued. The school continued to function only with one trade, carpentry. The instructors engaged in this school were the local carpenters with remuneration of Rs. 700 per month and the successful learners were given a certificate of appreciation. The number of enrolment may be less but the establishment of the school under Adult Education Programme was very useful for the area and success in producing skilful learners for earning their daily bread. Because most of the successful learners got job in the State government as craft teachers while some established private furniture workshop. The school was closed down in the year 2000, due to lack of enrolment and fund constraint on the side of the department concern.

Each-One-Teach-One Scheme

The Government of Mizoram has been running adult education centres in the interior villages, but the literacy drives still failed to reach many illiterates even in their own village. This is due to the fact that many illiterates, in spite of residing in the same village where the centre was located, could not attend the literacy classes which were held in the centre to receive education. As many of the adult learners have to work in the field to earn their living from dawn to dusk and due to distance factors. Also many illiterates are house wives who need to look after their children; busy with domestic chores and could not find chance to leave their houses to attend the centre. Therefore, in order to achieve a higher literacy rate in the area, mere setting up of adult education was considered inadequate.

The National Literacy Mission (NLM) has been trying to make 80 million persons literate by 1995 and thereby bringing total literacy in the country, but the Mizoram government as a part of observance of the International Literacy Year has been trying to achieve hundred percent literacy by 1990-1991. In the mean time Mizoram Government had been trying to achieve 100 per cent literacy during 1990-1991 but it was obvious that the normal programme of centre-base approach would never extend total coverage of illiterate adult population since there were many villages where only a few number of illiterate adults were there which did not qualify for opening a centre. For opening a centre there must be a minimum number of 30 illiterate adult in the locality. But Central Government permitted Mizoram to open centres where there were 20 to 25 illiterates. Therefore, it was found imperative to evolve a new scheme which may cover all illiterate adults. That scheme was called Each-One Teach-One that means any literate person may teach and make literate at least one illiterate adult. The scheme, therefore, envisaged that no illiterate adult should be left uncovered by the adult education programme.

To run the scheme successfully a Village Adult Education Committee was formed in each and every village. It consists of the following members — Village Council President (V.C.P.) as chairman of the committee and one each representative from voluntary organisations in the locality, Teachers Association, Women Organisations, Service Association, any prominent person interested in the programme of adult education as members of the committee. Functions and responsibilities of the committee are — conducting adult illiterate survey in their area from the age group of 15 to 35 and 35 years above, maintaining records/registers of the illiterates, identifying volunteers for animators who would undertake teaching responsibility of the illiterates, arranging suitable place where teaching learning programme may be carried out, supervising the animators teaching learning process and how to utilize materials, evaluate the learners progress and literacy competence, submit achievement reports of the animators and learners also make recommendations for award of honorarium to deserving animators and conduct a review of the centre overall performance and make suggestion for improvement in the subsequent session.

The person who involved in the implementation of the literacy programme under this scheme was given remuneration of Rs. 100 in making one illiterate adult literate. But an animator was allowed to teach five maximum illiterates at a time and he/she may teach another batch after imparting literacy to the former ones successfully. The prescribed duration of the course was 200 hours. But this was relaxed for those learners who had acquired some knowledge of literacy/ numeracy and in case of semi-literates.

During the current year literacy campaigns have been conducted all over Mizoram as the government has been trying to achieve total literacy in the State and almost all the villages are visited by adult education officers and field staff. In driving literacy various agencies like Young Mizo Association (YMA), Mizo Hmeichhe Inchhuikhawm Pawl (MHIP), local church organisations, and school teachers are engaged. The efforts and contributions made by them are quite commendable and very fruitful in the State about 548 villages have been achieved total literacy as on 1st October, 1996. Due to the great contribution and full co-operation by the non-governmental organisations and educated persons especially in rural remote areas, the programme of Each-One-Teach-One was successful in the State. So, the programme was run till the year 1999 successfully. The then Education Minister considered it so important that all the government officials were instructed to involve in this literacy drive. The fruitful result of this launch can be clearly seen as there was a rapid rise in literacy percentage during this period. The support provided by the State government in promoting literacy is worth mentioning. Table 17. 3 shows enrolment and achievement under the programme of Each-One-Teach-One.

Table 17. 3 : Each-One-Teach-One Programme Year-wise Enrolment and Achievement

Year	*Enrolment*	*Achievement*
1990-1991	30112	21112
1991-1992	8738	5714
1992-1993	30147	15000
1993-1994	31211	18000
1994-1995	32136	14584
1995-1996	30183	10021
1996-1997	5711	4966
1997-1998	2260	2120
1998-1999	1992	1901
Total	172490	93418

Source: Adult Education Wing, Aizawl.

Continuing Education

Mizoram State by its own way took various steps in respect of literacy drive. With the active guidance and participation, encouragement of the then Education Minister Dr. R. Lalthangliana, a total literacy campaign was launched in the year 1990-1991. Prior to this campaign as a sort of post-literacy campaign, a series of activities such as establishment of 38 Jana Shikshan Nilayam (JSN) for cluster villages, organization of Mass Programme for Functional Literacy Project (MPFL) were conducted. The then Rural Functional Literacy Project (RFLP) also took active part in the movement. As a result, when the assessment was done the State achieved a high literacy percentage. Therefore the State did not implement the post-literacy campaign programme. Understanding that tremendous achievement made by the department and in appreciation of the high literacy percentage attained, the Central Government directly introduced a new scheme called Continuing Education in the year 1997-98 under Centrally Sponsored Scheme (CSS) for 40 Nodal Continuing Education Centres (NCEC) and 360 Continuing Education Centres (CEC). Consequently the existing 20 Circle Adult Education Main Centres and 60 adult education sub-centres were merged into NCEC and CEC respectively. The rest 20 NCEC and 300 CECs were established by the department. It includes post-literacy for neo-literates and school drop outs for retention of their literacy competences, continuation of learning beyond elementary literacy, and application of this learning for improving their living conditions, etc. The State Government of Mizoram started implementing all the adult education programmes in the centres under this new scheme called Continuing Education since 1999.

The Central Government sanctioned funds through National Literacy Mission to Mizoram State government for the implementation of Adult Continuing Education Programme for the past five years (1999 April to 2004 March) to manage this programme properly in the State. From the year 2004 April, the concerned department started depending on State liability in managing the programme till this day and faced many financial problems which hindered to run the programme successfully as the State government could not sanctioned the required amount of funds to run the programme since 2004. Comparing to the other programmes which were already implemented in Mizoram there is less progress in this continuing education programme. Table 17.4 below shows the achievement of adult continuing education programme in Mizoram.

In Mizoram till 2012 April, there are 40 Nodal Continuing Education Centres (NCEC) and 360 Continuing Education Centres (CEC), altogether there are 400 adult education centres throughout the entire State. Out of these 400 centres 366 centres are in rural areas and 34 centres are in urban areas. Each and every centres had one Prerak and one assistant Prerak known as instructors and there are 800 instructors in

Table 17.4 : Achievement of Continuing Education in Mizoram — 2001-2009

Year	*Learners Enrolled*			*Made Literate*			*Drop-Outs*		
April -March	*Male*	*Female*	*Total*	*Male*	*Female*	*Total*	*Male*	*Female*	*Total*
2001-2002	985	857	1842	833	602	1435	152	255	407
2002-2003	1201	1078	2279	1023	811	1834	178	267	445
2003-2004	1218	1040	2258	1073	780	1853	145	260	405
2004-2005	1089	837	1926	899	486	1385	190	351	541
2005-2006	915	759	1674	717	445	1162	198	314	512
2006-2007	1191	1310	2501	1009	922	1931	182	388	570
2007-2008	1033	1229	2262	881	955	1836	152	274	426
2008-2009	981	1155	2136	871	925	1796	110	230	340
Total	8613	8265	16878	7306	5926	13232	1307	2339	3646

Source: Adult Education Wing, Aizawl.

adult education centres throughout the entire State. At present, among these 800 instructors 201 are female and 599 are male. The instructors were given monthly honorariums, but the honorariums given to them were not the same. Preraks from NCEC were given Rs. 1200 per head per month and Assistant Preraks were given Rs. 700 per head per month, whereas Preraks from CEC were given Rs. 700 per head per month and Assistant Preraks were given Rs. 500 per head per month. The department used to organise short course training for the instructors, special literacy drives at some selected villages, celebration of international literacy day every year at some selected villages under three district adult education officers and the centres were also provided learning materials according to the fund received from the State government. The on-going programme of adult continuing education scheme is planned for till the year 2015. Table 17.5 shows number of centres in rural areas and urban areas with Preraks and Assistant Preraks.

Conclusion

All the above discussions show that how adult education in Mizoram has been progressing for the last several decades. The adult education is one of the most important factors that lead the Mizos into an educated society. Educating the adult people is one of the stepping stones for building a developed strong nation. Realising this, the Government of Mizoram has taken a large number of initiatives for providing adult education to her people and this has brought radical changes both in urban and rural life of Mizo society.

REFERENCES

1. *Adult Education* and Its *Implementation in Mizoram*, Directorate of School Education, Adult Education Wing, Mizoram, 2000.
2. *Adult Education in Mizoram* (Status and Functioning), Directorate of School Education, Adult Education Wing, Mizoram, 2007.
3. J.C. Aggarwal, *Adult Education*. Doaba House, Delhi, 2008.
4. S.C. Dutta, *History of Adult Education in India*, Indian Adult Education Association, New Delhi, 1986.

Table 17.5 : Adult Continuing Education Centres in Mizoram from 2001- 2008

Year	*No. of Centres*			*No. of Preraks and Assistant Preraks*						*Total number of Preraks & Assistant Preraks*		
				Rural			*Urban*					
	Rural	*Urban*	*Total*	*Male*	*Female*	*Total*	*Male*	*Female*	*Total*	*Male*	*Female*	*Total*
2001	366	34	400	412	320	732	48	20	68	460	340	800
2002	366	34	400	404	328	732	36	32	68	460	340	800
2003	366	34	400	421	311	732	44	24	68	460	340	800
2004	366	34	400	501	231	732	38	30	68	460	340	800
2005	366	34	400	551	181	732	48	20	68	460	340	800
2006	366	34	400	549	183	732	50	18	68	460	340	800
2007	366	34	400	549	183	732	50	18	68	460	340	800
2008	366	34	400	549	183	732	50	18	68	460	340	800

Source: Adult Education Wing Aizawl.

5. Government of Mizoram, Census of India 2011, Mizoram Provisional Population Totals, Paper-I, Directorate of Census Operation, Chaltlang.
6. H.G. Joshi, *Mizoram Past and Present,* Mittal Publications, New Delhi, 2005.
7. C. Lianzawna, *History of Education in Mizoram* (Mizoram Education Chanchin), Aizawl, 2005.
8. Mizoram Literacy Souvenir 1999, Directorate of School Education, Government of Mizoram, Aizawl, 1999.
9. N.C.E.R.T. *Education and National Development: Report of the Education Commission, 1964-66,* New Delhi, 1970.
10. Soti Shivendra Chandra. *Adult and Non-Formal Education,* Surjeet Publications, Delhi, 2003.

BIBLIOGRAPHY

Primary Sources

Administration Report, Manipur, MSA, Imphal, 1913-14.

Financial Involvement under the Relief Measure (FGC/CRN) 26 December to 31 December 1995, dated 6-4-96.

Foreign Department-A, May 1898, Nos. 13-14, Assam Secretariat.

Foreign Department: Political A.1870, Relation between Looshais and Munipurees, Calcutta, 1979.

Letter to the Director, The Healing Mission Resources, the EZE and the ICCO from Holkhomang Haokip, President, KIM (not dated).

Memo. No. KIM/GEN/5/93 submitted to the Chief Minister and Deputy Chief Minister of Manipur by the President, KIM, dated 20-7-93 in DP 61.

Memorandum submitted to His Excellency, the Governor of Manipur by the Kuki Inpi in DP 61.

Memorandum submitted to the Prime Minister of India by President, KIM, Vice-Chairman Kuki Movement for Human Rights and President Kuki Students' Organization (GHQ).

No. KIM-10/ASSEM/95, Memorandum submitted to Sri I. K. Gujral, Prime Minister of India, by the President and General Secretary, KIM dated 22-5-97 .

No. KIM-18/Court/95, Memorandum submitted to the CM, Manipur from the President, KIM dated 18-10-95 .

Political Agent-Tour Diary, 10 February, 1986, MSA, Imphal.

Report on the Administration of Assam for the Year 1921-22, Mittal Publications, Delhi, 1984.

Gazetteers

E.W. Dun, *A Bridged Gazetteer of Manipur*, Vivek Publishing House, Delhi, 1975.

_____ *Gazetteer of Manipur*, Manas Publications, Delhi, 1992.

M. Bhattacharjee, *Gazetteer of India: Manipur*, Calcutta, 1963.

Souvenirs

Espirit de Corps, 1917-1919, Patriotic Souvenir, Imphal, 27 February, 2010.

Kuki Inpi Manipur, Souvenir, 1994, Imphal.

Kuki Inpi Manipur, Souvenir, 1995-1997, Imphal.

Kuki Inpi Manipur, Souvenir, 2001, Imphal.

Mizoram Literacy Souvenir 1999, Directorate of School Education, Government of Mizoram, Aizawl, 1999.

Interviews

Ating Haokip,Chief, Saivom Village, Chandel District, Manipur.

Awei Haokip, founder member of Kuki Women Union, 47, Motbung Village, 2012.

Bandana Sehgal, 43, Mohalla, Chawgan, Chamba, Himachal Pradesh, 16 May, 2010.

Bulshi Touthang, 75, New Lambuland, 1 March, 2009.

D. Letkhojam Haokip, a close cousin of Chief of Chassad, 19 July, 2005.

Dr. Seikho Singsit, 58, Tuibong, Churachandpur, 18 July, 2006.

Holkhomang, Haokip Veng, Imphal, July, 2012.

Lhingjaneng Gangte, Member, Manipur State Commission for Women.

Lhkhothang Haokip, Chief, Molphei Village , Chandel District, Imphal, 25 January, 2009.

Reverend Kaikhosie, 60, Old Lambulane, Imphal, 7 April, 2005.

S. Jonah, 50, Lairam Khullen, Ukhrul, 1 November, 2004.

S.L. Singson, 70, Old Lambulane, Imphal, 3 May, 2004.

Seijkhojang Singson, 75, Canaan Veng,1 November, 2008.

Thangkhopao Kipgen (Late) Imphal, 3 March, 2005.

Thonglhun Haokip, 75, New Lambuland, 15 July, 2011.

Thonglhun Haokip, 75, New Lambuland, 15 July, 2011.

Veikhoneng Haokip, 76, Game Village, 3 August, 2008

Newspapers

The Freedom

The Telegraph

Encyclopedia

Encyclopedia Britannica, Vol. 13, 1962.

The New Encyclopedia Britannica, Vol.VII, William Benton, Chicago, London. 1980.

Reports/Documents/Census/Surveys

13th MZP Assembly 2005, General Headquarters Report.

A Media Report from Department of Information & Public Relations, Government of Mizoram, entitled *ZOFEST – 2006 TANANITA*, 13 December, 2006.

Adult Education in Mizoram (Status and Functioning) Directorate of School Education, Adult Education Wing, Mizoram, 2007.

Adult Education its Implementation in Mizoram, Directorate of School Education Mizoram, Adult Education Wing, 2000.

Government of Mizoram, *Census of India 2011*, Mizoram Provisional Population Total, Paper-I, Directorate of Census Operation, Chaltlang.

Kuki Research Forum Cave Expedition Report, 2012.

Manipur Cultural Integration Conference and Ethnic Community in Manipur (A Report of the MCIC visiting team), 1996.

NCERT Education and National Development: Report of the Education Commission, 1964-66, New Delhi, 1970.

Leaflets

Protest against Divisive Policy of India on 14th June, 2002 and Forging a Bigger and Stronger Unity on 18th June, 2002 (The All Manipur United Clubs' Organization (AMUCO), 25 May, 2002, Imphal.

Books in English

A. Mackenzie, *The North-East Frontier of India* (Originally A History of the Relations of the Government with the Hill Tribes, Calcutta, 1884), Mittal Publications, New Delhi, 1995.

A.G. McCall, *Lushai Chrysalis*, Tribal Research Institute, Aizawl, 2003.

A.R. Radcliff Brown and Daryll Forde, *African System of Kinship and Marriage*, OUP, London, New York, Toronto, 1950.

Anthony D. Smith, *The Ethnic Revival*, Cambridge University Press, London, 1981.

Arnold Green, *Sociology*, McGrow-Hill Book Co. Inc., New York, 1956.

B. Lalthangliana, *India, Burma & Bangladesh:A Mizo Chanchin*, Aizawl, 2001.

B. Lalthangliana, *India, Burma Leh Bangladesh: A Mizo Chanchin*, Aizawl, 2001.

B. Shivaramayya, *Inequality and Women*, Eastern Book Company, Lucknow, 1984,

B.C. Chakravartee, *British Relation with Hill Tribes*, Calcutta, 1964.

B.N. Bordoloi & G.C. Sharmach Thakur, *Tribes of Assam*, Part XI, Tribal Research Institute, Guwahati, 1988.

Benedict Anderson, *Imagined Communities: Reflections on the Origin and Spread of Nationalism*, Verso, London, New York, 1991.

Bertram S. Carey & H.N. Tuck, *The Chin Hills*, Vol. I, Delhi, 1983.

____ *The Chin Hills: A History of the People, Our Dealings with their Customs and Manners and a Gazetteer of their Country*, Tribal Research Institute, Aizawl, 2008.

Bimal J. Deb and Dilip Kumar Lahiri, *Lushai Customs and Ceremonies*, Mittal Publication, Delhi, 1983.

C. Chawngkunga (ed.), *Important Documents of Mizoram*, Aizawl, 1998.

C. Chawngkunga, *Genealogical Tree of the Mizo*, Aizawl 1996.

C. G. Crawford, *Hand Book of Kuki Custom*, Directorate of Printing & Stationery, Manipur, 1984.

C.A. Soppit, *A Short Account of the Kuki-Lushai Tribe*, Firma KLM Pvt. Ltd., 1979.

Cynthoe Enloe, *The Morning after Sexual Politics after End of Cold War*, UK, 1993.

D. Letkhojam Haokip, *Thempu Ho Thu*, Churachandpur, 2000.

Debiprassad Chattopadhyaya (ed.), *Taranatha's History of Buddhism in India*, Simla, 1970.

Dena Lal, *Christian Missions and Colonialism : A Study of Missionary Movement in North-East India with particular reference to Manipur and Lushai Hills 1894-1947*, Vendrame Institute House, Shillong, 1995.

E.B. Elly, *Military Report on the Chin-Lushai Country*, Firma KLM (P) Ltd., Calcutta, 1978.

E.T. Dalton, *Tribal History of Eastern India*, Cosmo Publication, Delhi, 1973.

Ernest Gellner, *Conditions of Liberty: Civil Society and Its Rivals*, Allen Lane/Penguin Press, New York, 1994.

Ester Boserup, *Women's Role in Economic Development*, St. Martin's Press, New York, 1986.

F.K. Lehman, *The Structure of Chin Society*, University of Illinois Press, Urbana, 1963.

Francis Fukuyama, *Trust: The Social Virtues and the Creation of Prosperity*, Free Press, New York, 1995.

G. A. Grierson, *Languages of North-Eastern India* , Vol. 11, Gyan Publishing House, New Delhi, 2006.

G. Barkataki, *Tribes of Assam*, NBT, 1969.

G.A. Grierson, *Linguistic Survey of India*, Vol. III, Part III, Motilal Banarsidas, Delhi, 1967.

G. Herzog, *Jabo Proverbs from Liberia*, London, 1936.

Gangmumei Kabui, *History of Manipur—Pre Colonial Period*, Vol. 1, National Publishing House, New Delhi, 1991.

Gangmumei Kamei, *Ethnicity and Social Change: An Anthology of Essays*, Imphal, 2002.

Gillen and Gillen, *Cultural Sociology*, MacMillan Co., New York, 1950.

Ginjathang, *Zomi Inkuan Laibu*, 1973.

H. Khamkhenthang, S. Prim Vaiphei, Romoeo Serto, Hawlngam Haokip, Songkhopao Gangte (eds), *In Search of Identity*, Kuki-Chin Baptist Union, Imphal, 1986.

H.G. Joshi, *Mizoram Past and Present*, Mittal Publications, New Delhi, 2005.

H.R. Trivedi, *Scheduled Caste Women*, Concept Publishing Co. Delhi, 1974.

Horton and Hunt, *Sociology*, McGraw-Hill, New York, 1968.

J. Shakespear, *Lushei-Kuki Clans*, Cultural Publishing House, Delhi, 1912.

J.C. Aggarwal, *Adult Education*. Doaba House, Delhi, 2008.

James George Scott, *Gazetteer of Upper Burma and the Shan State*, Govt. Press, Rangoon, 1990.

James Johnstone, *Manipur and the Naga Hills*, Delhi, 1983.

Jamini, *Education in Manipur*, Imphal, 1980.

Jean L. Cohen and Andrew Arato, *Civil Society and Political Theory*, Cambridge, 1992.

John H. Bodley, *Cultural Anthropology: Tribes, Status and Global System*, USA, 2011.

John R. Mackenzie, *The Uncivilized Races of Men*, Vol. I, Daya Publishing House, Delhi-6, 1986.

Joseph Suantak, *Chin+Kuki+Zo Genesis and Exodus*, Akansha Publishing House, New Delhi, 2012.

____ *Khulmi? Chhinlung, Hurpi, Khol, Khul, Khur, Sinlung-Beyond Identity and Political Crises.*

____ *The Vaiphei: Their History and Culture*, Akansha Publishing House, Delhi, 2010.

Joytimoy Roy, *History of Manipur*, East Light Book House, Calcutta, 1973.

K. Robin (ed.), *Chin: History, Culture and Identity*, Dominant Publishers and Distributors, New Delhi, 2009.

K. S. Singh, *The Scheduled Tribe People of India*, Vol. I, Delhi, 1994.

K.R. Palit, *My Adventure with INA Movement*, Lion Press House, New Delhi, 1946.

Kaihau Vaiphei, *Maite Vangkhua*, Imphal, 2001.

Kamkhenthang, *The Paite – A Transborder Tribe of India and Burma*, Mittal Publications, Delhi, 1988.

Kenneth Scott Latourette, *The Chinese — Their History and Culture*, Macmillan Company, New York, 1964.

Khaikhotinthang Kipgen,*The Thadou Kukis*, Motbung, 1982.

Kuki-Chin Baptist Union, *In Search of Identity*, Kuki Baptist Convention Press, Imphal, 1986.

L. Jayaseelan, *Impact of Missionary Movement in Manipur*, Scholar Publishing House, New Delhi, 1990.

L. Songate, A Historical Study of the Changes in the Hmar Society of Manipur Resulting from the Introduction of Christianity, 1910-1935, Mississippi, 1999.

Lal Dena, *British Policy towards Manipur*, 1762-1947, Imphal, 2008.

____ *In Search of Identity: Hmars of North-East India*, Akansha Publishing House, New Delhi, 2008.

Lalkhawlien Pulamte, *An Examination of Factors that led to the Conversion of the Hmar People: A Historical Consideration, 1910-1950*, Bangalore, 1985.

Lian H. Sakhong, *In Search of Chin Identity*, Thailand, 2003.

Liankhawthang, *Bedrock of the Suantak: Vaiphei Society*, Imphal 2000.

Lois Tyson, *Critical Theory Today*, Routledge, 2006.

McCulloch, *Account of the Valley of Manipur and the Hill Tribes*, Mittal Publications, New Delhi, 1980.

Morris Ginsberg, *Psychology of Society*, Methuen, London, 1949.

National Identity, Penguin Books, London, 1991.

N. Sanajaoba, *Manipur Past and Present*, Vol. II, New Delhi, 1991.

N. Chatterji, *Status of Women in the Mizo Society*, Tribal Research Centre, Aizawl, 1975.

P.S Haokip, *Zalengam: The Kuki Nation*, Kuki National Organisation Publication, 1988.

Paramesh Choudhury, *The Mystery of the Chinese Dragon*, Kolkata, 2005.

Prim Vaiphei, *The Vaiphei Tribe*, MBC, Imphal, 1975.

Pudaite Rochunga, *The Education of the Hmar People*, Calcutta, 1963.

R. Lalsim, *Tribes of N.C. Hills*, Assam, 2005.

R. Pakhuongte, *The Power of the Gospel among the Hmar Tribe*, Shillong, 1983.

R.M. MacIver, *Society: A Textbook of Sociology*, Farrar and Rinehart, New York, 1945.

R.S. Peters, *Social Principles and Demographic State*, London, 1959.

Rajat Kanti Das, *Manipur Tribal Scene*, Delhi, 1985.

RC Majumdar, H.C. Raychaudhuri, and Kalikinkar Datta, *An Advanced Hstory of India*, Macmillan, 1970.

Robert Reid, *History of Frontier Areas Bordering on Assam* , Spectrum Publications, Guwahati, 1942.

Robert Reid, *The Lushai Hills*, Firma KLM Private Ltd., Calcutta, 1978.

S.H.M Razvi and Shibani Roy, *Kuki-Chin Tribes of Manipur and Mizoram*, Delhi, 2006.

S. Thangkhangin Ngaihte, *History of the Zomi of Mizoram and the Surrounding Area: Aspects of Pre-colonial Society*, Aizawl, 1979.

S.C. Dutta, *History of Adult Education in India*, Indian Adult Education Association, New Delhi, 1986.

Sajal Nag, *Contesting Marginality Ethnicity, Insurgency and Sub-nationalism in North-East India*, Manohar Publications, New Delhi, 2002.

Satinder Kumar, *Encyclopedia of South Asian Tribes*, Vol. VI. Anmol Publications Pvt. Ltd., New Delhi, 2000, Sipra Sen, *Tribes and Castes of Manipur*, Mittal; Publications, Delhi, 1992.

Soti Shivendra Chandra, *Adult and Non-Formal Education*. Surjeet Publications Delhi, 2003.

Susheela Kaushik (ed.), *Women's Oppressions: Patterns and Perspectives*, Shakti Books, Delhi, 1985.

T.S. Gangte, *The Kukis of Manipur: A Historical Analysis*, Gyan Publishing House, New-Delhi, 1993.

T. Gougin, *History of Zomi*, Churachandpur, 1984.

T.C. Hodson, *The Naga Tribes of Manipur*, B.R. Publishing Corporation, New Delhi, 1974.

T.H. Lewin, *Wild Races of South-Eastern India*, Mittal Publications, Delhi, 1978.

T.H. Lewin, *The Hill Tracks of Chittagong and the Dwellers Therein*, Tribal Research Institute, Aizawl, 2004.

Tingneichong G. Kipgen, *Women's Role in the Twentieth Century: A Historical Study*, Kalpaz Publication, Delhi, 2010.

Tsepon W.D. Shakabpa, *Tibet: A Political History*, Yale University Press, 1967.

Tylor, E.B., *Primitive Culture* , New York, 1871.

Vumkhohau, *Profile of a Burma Frontier Man*, Kilatmadju Press, Bandung, Indonesia, 1963.

Vumson, *Zo History*, Aizawl, 1986.

William Shaw, *Notes on the Thadou Kukis*, Delhi: Spectrum Publications, Guwahati, 1997.

Woodward Sutherland and Maxwell, *Introductory Sociology*, Oxford and IBH, Publishing Co., Bombay, 1961.

Books in Manipuri

Laikhuram Ibobi Singh, *Manipur Praja Sanmelani Amasung Anisuba Nupi Lan* , Imphal, 2003.

Books in Dialects

Challiana, *Pi Pu Nun*, Aizawl, 1971.

Darliensung, *The Hmars*, Churachandpur, 1988.

H. Thuomte, *Hmar Nunhlui*, Churachandpur, 1997.

H. Vara, *Hmar Nunphung*, Churachandpur, 2000.

H.H, Hrangchhuana, *Hmar Chanchin*, Aizawl, 1987.

L. Keivom, *Hla Suina*, Churachandpur, 1980.

_____ *Hmar Pi Le Pu Dan*, Imphal : Goodwill Press, 1982.

_____ *Hmar Tolung*, Imphal, 1990.

Articles

Aheibam Koireng Singh, 'Growth of Sub-nationalism and Displacement in Northeast India with special reference to Manipur, *The Orient Vision*, Vol. 2, Issue 3, 2005.

Dr. H. Kamkhenthang, 'Identity Crisis among the Tribes of Manipur', B. Pakem (ed.), *Nationality, Ethnicity and Cultural Identity in North-East India*, Omsons, New Delhi, 1993.

G. Amarjit Sharma (2011), 'Inside and Outside of Ethnic Enclosure: Khoibu as a Separate Tribe', cadmanipur.org/ 2011/06/29.

Gangmumei Kabui, 'Defining the Indigenous Tribal Religion', in S. Shyamkishore Singh (ed.), *History of Science, Philosophy and Culture in Indian Civilization*, Vol. VII. Part VII, 2012.

____ 'Genesis of the Ethnoses of Manipur', N. Sanajaoba (ed.), *Manipur: Past and Present,* Vol. III, Mittal Publications, New Delhi: Mittal, 1995.

Gautam Bhadra, 'The Kuki Uprising (1917-1919)', *Man In India,* Vol. 55 (1), 1975.

H. Kamkhenthang, 'Groping for Identity', in H. Kamkhenthang(ed.), *In Search of Identity,* Imphal,1986.

—., 'Groping for Identity', in H. Kamkhenthang (ed.), *In Search of Identity,* Imphal, 1986.

H. Kamkhenthang & T. Chingzaman, 'Traditional Paite Society: With Special Reference to Women', in B. Datta Ray & Ashok Kumar Ray (eds), *Dynamics of Power Relations in Tribal Societies of Northeast India*, Om Publications, New Delhi, 2006.

Lal Dena, 'The Kuki-Naga Conflict: Juxtaposed in the Colonial Context', in K Agarwal (ed.), *Dynamics of Identity and Inter-Group Relation in Northeast India,* IIAS, Shimla, 1999.

M.M. Agarwal, 'Nationality and Secularism' in P.C. Chatterji (ed.), *Self Images, Identity and Nationality,* IIAS, Shimla, 1989.

Malini Bhattacharya, *'Woman and Education'* in P. Krishnaprasad (ed), *Women and Society in India,* Student Struggle, Vol. 31, Issue No. 2, 2002.

Pakem, 'The Biates', in Daya Sreema Mudra (ed.), *The Tribes of North East India,* Vendram Institute, Shillong,1984.

R.K. Ranjit Singh, 'Emergent Ethnic Processes in Manipur', B. Pakem (ed.), *Nationality, Ethnicity and Cultural Identity in Northeast India,* Omsons, New Delhi, 1990.

Rodney Needham, 'Vaiphei Social Structure', *Southern-Western Journal of Anthropology,* Vol. 15, 1959.

S Prim Vaiphei, 'The Kukis' in N. Sanajaoba (ed.), *Manipur: Past and Present*, Vol. 3, Mittal Publications, New Delhi, 1995.

____ 'Who are We', in H. Kamkhenthang (ed.), *In Search of Identity*, Imphal,1986.

S. Thankhangin, 'Why should We be called Zomis?', in H. Kamkhenthang (ed.), *In Search of Identity*, Imphal, 1986.

S.K. Acharya, 'Ethnic Processes in North-Eastern India' in B. Pakem (ed.), *Nationality, Ethnicity and Cultural Identity in North East India*, Omsons Publications, New Delhi & Guwahati, 1990.

Sao Saimong Mangrai, *The Shan States and the British Annexation* : Data Paper Number 57, Southeast Asia Program, Dept., of Asian Studies, Cornwell University, Ithaca, New York, July 1965.

T.S. Gangte, 'Who are the Kukis? Where are They?' Souvenir of the Kuki Rebellion, 1985, p. 36.

___ 'Whither Kuki Ethnicity: Is this a Centrifugal Force', *Tri-Millennium Souvenir Kuki Students Organisation*, Manipur: KSO Souvenir Sub-Committee, 2000.

W. Nabakumar, 'The Inter Ethnic Relationship of the Different Communities of Manipur: A Critical Appraisal', *The Orient Vision* Vol. 2, Issue 1, 2004.

____'The Inter Ethnic Relationship of the Different Communities of Manipur: A Critical Appraisal', *The Orient Vision*, Vol. 2, Issue 1, 2004.

William Bascom, 'Folklore' in Sills (ed.),The Encyclopedia of Social Sciences, Vol.V, MacMillan, 1968.

Yulian V. Bromley, 'Ethnic Processes', *Social Science Today*, USSR Academy of Sciences, Moscow, 1983.

Theses/Dissertations

D.L Haokip, Historical Traditions and Customary Laws of the Chassad, Unpublished PhD Thesis, MU, 2006.

J. Pulamte, Development of Education in Churachandpur District, Unpublished PhD Thesis, MU, 2002.

Paul B. Chonzik, Nationality Question of North East India: A Case Study of Mizo, unpublished PhD Thesis, MU, 2009.

R. Simon, Social Structure and Rise of Middle Class among the Manipur Tankhul Naga Tribe, Unpublished PhD Thesis, MU, 2010.

Ruolkhumzo, Traditional Administrative System and Customary Laws of the Hmars in Manipur, Unpublished PhD Thesis, MU, 2004.

S.L. Alun Vaiphei, The Vaiphei: An Ethno Historical Study, Unpublished PhD Thesis, MU, 2008.

S. Kipgen, Political and Economic History of the Kukis of Manipur, unpublished PhD Thesis, MU, 2005.

Senjam Mangi Singh, A Study of Some Selected Socio-Political Problems in Manipur, unpublished PhD Thesis, MU, 1996.

Journals/Magazines/Periodicals

HSA Annual Magazine, Shillong, 1995.

Journal of the 69th Anniversary of the Kuki Rebellion, 1917-19, 1985.

The Evening Post, Aizawl, 4 May, 2007.

The North East Sun, 17-23 December, 1994.

Onlines/Websites

J. Guite, Memories of Origin and Migration, JNES, ISSN 2277-6869(online).

J. Shakespeare and T.C. Hodson, Folktales of the Lushais and their Neighbours, Taylor and Francis Ltd publication on behalf of Folklore enterprise Ltd. able URL: http://www.jstor.org/stable/1254435 .Accessed: 01/03/2012 06:32.

J. Shakespeare and T.C. Hodson, Folktales of the Lushais and their Neighbours, Review Works, Folklore, Vol. 20, No. 4, 1909) L: http://www.jstor.org/stable/1254435 Accessed: 01/03/2012 06:32.

James S. Aber (2008), "*Brief History of Maps and Cartography*", academic.emporia.com.

R. W. Bernard, The Hollow Earth, Chapter II: Agharta, Subterranean World, New York, 1964 (access from Hollow Earth Website on the 3 October 2012).

Robert Putnam, The Prosperous Community: Social Capital and Public Life, The American Prospect 13 (Spring):35-42.Available on line at *http://epn.org/prospect/13/13putn.html.*

Wikipedia search on Ring fire, accessed on 1 October 2012.

Unpublished Papers

K. Saratchandra Singh, 'An Anthropology Profile of North-East India with special reference to Manipur', Presented in the *98th Session of Indian Science Congress*, January 3-7, 2011, Chennai, India.

Lal Dena, 'The Christian Religion and the Hmar Culture', presented to Hmar Assembly, Churachandpur, 1982.

P.M. Gangte, 'Institution of 'Neilah' and 'Kong-Lo' Marriage for Maintenance of Social Order and Cultural Identity among the Chin-Kuki-Mizo Society', presented at a National Seminar on *Indigenous Knowledge Tradition in North East India*, Guwahati, 27-29 March, 2006.

S. Vaiphei, 'Historical Background of the Vaiphei Tribes' (unpublished seminar paper).

Sina Khayi, 'Cultural Significance of Tribal Costumes in Modern Times', unpublished seminar paper, MUTSU, March, 1996.

T.S. Gangte, Chin-Kuki-Mizo Nationalism' presented at the General Assembly of Kuki Students' Organization, Tuibong, Churachandpur, 29 January, 2002.

W. Nabakumar, 'Communalism and Ethnic Divide: Anathema to Secular Society, presented at the National Seminar on *Indigenous Tribal Religions of Manipur of the North East India,* Imphal, 21-23 March, 2005.

Yambem Laba, "Can't See Guitars for Guns — A Brief Look at the Recent Kukipaite Clashes in Manipur", presented in the 3-day Seminar on *Ethnic Values and Ideals of Emerging Egalitarian Society,* Department of Philosophy, Manipur University sponsored by the Indian Institute of Advanced Study, Shimla, 7-9 March, 2006.

INDEX